TEL DAN IN ITS NORTHERN CULTIC CONTEXT

Society of Biblical Literature

Archaeology and Biblical Studies

Tammi J. Schneider, Editor

Number 20

TEL DAN IN ITS NORTHERN CULTIC CONTEXT

Andrew R. Davis

Society of Biblical Literature
Atlanta

Library of Congress Cataloging-in-Publication Data

Davis, Andrew R., 1978—
    Tel Dan in its northern cultic context / Andrew R. Davis.
        p. cm. — (Society of Biblical Literature archaeology and biblical studies ; number 20)
    Includes bibliographical references.
    ISBN 978-1-58983-928-1 (paper binding : alk. paper) — ISBN 978-1-58983-929-8 (electronic format) — ISBN 978-1-58983-930-4 (hardcover binding : alk. paper)
    1. Dan (Extinct city) 2. Excavations (Archaeology)—Israel—Dan (Extinct city) 3. Cults—Israel—Dan (Extinct city) 4. Bible. Old Testament—Antiquities. 5. Bible. Old Testament—Criticism, interpretation, etc. 6. Israel—Antiquities. I. Society of Biblical Literature. II. Title.
    DS110.D33D38 2013
    933'.45—dc23   2013035353

Printed on acid-free, recycled paper conforming to
ANSI/NISO Z39.48-1992 (R1997) and ISO 9706:1994
standards for paper permanence.

For Emily

Contents

ACKNOWLEDGMENTS

It is a pleasure to thank here the colleagues, teachers, institutions, and family who have supported my work on this book, which is a revision of the dissertation I completed at Johns Hopkins University in 2010. Let me begin by thanking Billie Jean Collins and Tammi Schneider for accepting this study for publication in the SBL Archaeology and Biblical Studies series. At Johns Hopkins I had the privilege to work with exceptional professors and classmates, and I am especially grateful for the mentorship of my advisor Theodore Lewis. At every stage of my graduate studies, I have benefited from his wisdom, insight, and encouragement. P. Kyle McCarter and Glenn Schwartz also counseled me on various aspects of my research, and in every instance their advice improved my approach and sharpened my focus. Together these mentors have saved me from numerous errors and lapses in judgment. Needless to say, those that remain are my responsibility alone. I also want to thank Barry Gittlen and Matthew Roller for their thoughtful questions and comments during my oral examination. Finally, I would like to recognize Richard Clifford, S.J., and John Kselman, S.S., who introduced me to biblical studies at the Weston Jesuit School of Theology and who remain treasured mentors.

I am grateful to the institutions that have sponsored my graduate work. First, the present project would not have been possible without the generous support of David Ilan, who, as director of the Nelson Glueck School of Biblical Archaeology at the Hebrew Union College in Jerusalem, invited me to work with the material from Area T at Tel Dan. The academic year I spent working in Jerusalem became the foundation of this study, and I would like to thank Gila Cook, Rachel Ben-Dov, Dalia Pakman, Levana Tsfania, Yifat Thareani, and Malka Hershkovitz for their support and instruction. I am especially indebted to Ross Voss, the longtime supervisor of Area T, who generously shared his vast knowledge of the temple complex with me. I would also like to acknowledge the significant support of the W. F. Albright Institute of Archaeological

Research, where I was the recipient of a Samuel H. Kress Fellowship. The hospitality and collegiality of the Albright Institute and its director, Seymour Gitin, provided a first-rate environment for research. At Johns Hopkins I received financial support from several sponsors. In addition to a generous fellowship from the Department of Near Eastern Studies, I am grateful to have received the department's Iwry Fellowship and the Schaefer Research Award in Near Eastern Studies. My research was also sponsored by the Leonard and Helen R. Stulman Jewish Studies Research Grant and the J. Brien Key Graduate Student Assistance Fund, and I was honored to have received the Catholic Biblical Association Memorial Stipend for multiple years. Finally, I am grateful for the support of my colleagues at the Seattle University School of Theology and Ministry.

Throughout my life I have been blessed to have the love and support of a wonderful family. My parents, Peter and Mary Davis, were my first teachers and remain models of hard work and learning. The value they placed on education was formative in shaping my career goals, and their love and encouragement have made those goals seem achievable. I was also blessed to grow up with Catherine, Brendan, and Nicholas, whose care and humor continue to remind me that family is first. Throughout all of this process my wife, Emily, has been a constant source of love and friendship. Our life together with our sons Michael and Peter is my greatest joy and gives meaning to all other endeavors, including the present work. With immense love and gratitude I dedicate this book to her.

Abbreviations

AASOR	Annual of the American Schools of Oriental Research
AB	Anchor Bible
ABD	*Anchor Bible Dictionary.* 6 vols. Edited by D. N. Freedman. New York: Doubleday, 1992.
ABSA	*The Annual of the British School at Athens*
ÄgAbh	Ägyptologische Abhandlungen
AJA	*American Journal of Archaeology*
AJBA	*Australian Journal of Biblical Archaeology*
AJSL	*American Journal of Semitic Languages and Literatures*
ANEP	*The Ancient Near East in Pictures Relating to the Old Testament.* Edited by J. B. Pritchard. Princeton: Princeton University Press, 1954.
ANESS	Ancient Near Eastern Studies Supplement
AOAT	Alter Orient und Altes Testament
AS	Assyriological Studies
ATANT	Abhandlungen zur Theologie des Alten und Neuen Testaments
ATD	Das Alte Testament Deutsch
BA	*Biblical Archaeologist*
BAR	*Biblical Archaeology Review*
BASOR	*Bulletin of the American Schools of Oriental Research*
BBRSup	Bulletin for Biblical Research Supplements
Bib	*Biblica*
BibOr	Biblica et orientalia
BJS	Brown Judaic Studies
BKAT	Biblischer Kommentar, Altes Testament
BN	*Biblische Notizen*
BZAW	Beihefte zur Zeitschrift für die alttestamentliche Wissenschaft

CANE	*Civilizations of the Ancient Near East.* Edited by J. Sasson. 4 vols. Peabody, Mass.: Hendrickson, 2004.
CBQ	*Catholic Biblical Quarterly*
CBQMS	Catholic Biblical Quarterly Monograph Series
ConBOT	Coniectanea biblica: Old Testament Series
COS	*The Context of Scripture.* Edited by W. W. Hallo. 3 vols. Leiden: Brill, 1997–2002.
CSR	Contributions to the Study of Religion
EAEHL	*Encyclopedia of Archaeological Excavations in the Holy Land.* Edited by M. Avi-Yonah. 4 vols. Englewood Cliffs, N.J., Prentice-Hall, 1975–1978.
EI	*Eretz-Israel*
EncJud	*Encyclopaedia Judaica.* 16 vols. Jerusalem: Encyclopaedia Judaica, 1972.
EncRel	*The Encyclopaedia of Religion.* Edited by Mircea Eliade. 16 vols. New York: Macmillan, 1987.
ESI	*Excavations and Surveys in Israel*
ExAud	*Ex auditu*
FAT	Forschungen zum Alten Testament
FO	*Folia orientalia*
FRLANT	Forschungen zur Religion und Literatur des Alten und Neuen Testaments
GKC	*Gesenius' Hebrew Grammar.* Edited by E. Kautzsch. Translated by A. E. Cowley. 2nd. ed. Oxford: Oxford University Press, 1910.
HACL	History, Archaeology, and Culture of the Levant
HALOT	Koehler, L., W. Baumgartner, and J. J. Stamm. *The Hebrew and Aramaic Lexicon of the Old Testament.* Translated and edited under the supervision of M. E. J. Richardson. 4 vols. Leiden: Brill, 1994–1999.
HS	*Hebrew Studies*
HSM	Harvard Semitic Monographs
HTR	*Harvard Theological Review*
HUCA	*Hebrew Union College Annual*
IBHS	*An Introduction to Biblical Hebrew Syntax.* B. K. Waltke and M. O'Connor. Winona Lake, Ind.: Eisenbrauns, 1990.
ICC	International Critical Commentary
IEJ	*Israel Exploration Journal*
Int	*Interpretation*

JANESCU	*Journal of the Ancient Near Eastern Society of Columbia University*
JAOS	*Journal of the American Oriental Society*
JBL	*Journal of Biblical Literature*
JCS	*Journal of Cuneiform Studies*
JEA	*Journal of Egyptian Archaeology*
JNES	*Journal of Near Eastern Studies*
JNSL	*Journal of Northwest Semitic Languages*
Joüon	Joüon, P. *A Grammar of Biblical Hebrew.* Translated and revised by T. Muraoka. 2 vols. Subsidia biblica 14/1–2. Rome: Pontifical Biblical Institute, 1991.
JQR	*Jewish Quarterly Review*
JSOT	*Journal for the Study of the Old Testament*
JSOTSup	Journal for the Study of the Old Testament Supplement Series
JSS	*Journal of Semitic Studies*
KAANT	Kleine Arbeiten zum Alten und Neuen Testament
KAT	Kommentar zum Alten Testament
KTU	*Die keilalphabetischen Texte aus Ugarit.* Edited by M. Dietrich, O. Loretz, and J. Sanmartín. AOAT 24/1. Neukirchen-Vluyn: Neukirchener, 1976. 2nd enlarged ed. of *KTU: The Cuneiform Alphabetic Texts from Ugarit, Ras Ibn Hani, and Other Places.* Edited by M. Dietrich, O. Loretz, and J. Sanmartín. Münster: Ugarit-Verlag, 1995 (= *CTU*).
LHB/OTS	Library of Hebrew Bible/Old Testament Studies
LSAWS	Linguistic Studies in Ancient West Semitic
OBO	Orbis biblicus et orientalis
OIP	Oriental Institute Publications
OLA	Orientalia lovaniensia analecta
OLP	Orientalia lovaniensia periodica
OTL	Old Testament Library
OtSt	*Oudtestamentische Studiën*
PEQ	*Palestine Exploration Quarterly*
RB	*Revue biblique*
RDAC	*Report of the Department of Antiquities, Cyprus*
RIMA	The Royal Inscriptions of Mesopotamia, Assyrian Periods
SAOC	Studies in Ancient Oriental Civilizations
SBAB	Stuttgarter biblische Aufsatzbände

SBLAIL	Society of Biblical Literature Ancient Israel and Its Literature
SBLDS	Society of Biblical Literature Dissertation Series
SBLMS	Society of Biblical Literature Monograph Series
SBLWAW	Society of Biblical Literature Writings from the Ancient World
SHANE	Studies in the History (and Culture) of the Ancient Near East
SJLA	Studies in Judaism in Late Antiquity
SOTSMS	Society for Old Testament Studies Monograph Series
SR	*Studies in Religion*
TA	*Tel Aviv*
TDOT	*Theological Dictionary of the Old Testament.* Edited by G. J. Botterweck, H. Ringgren, and H.-J. Fabry. Translated by J. T. Willis, G. W. Bromiley, and D. E. Green. 8 vols. Grand Rapids: Eerdmans, 1974–2006.
TTZ	*Trierer theologische Zeitschrift*
UF	*Ugarit-Forschungen*
Ugaritica V	J. Nougayrol et al. *Ugaritica V.* Mission de Ras Shamra 16. Paris: Imprimerie Nationale/Librairie Orientaliste Paul Geuthner, 1968.
VT	*Vetus Testamentum*
VTSup	Vetus Testamentum Supplements
WBC	Word Biblical Commentary
WMANT	Wissenschaftliche Monographien zum Alten und Neuen Testament
WO	*Die Welt des Orients*
WVDOG	Wissenschaftliche Veröffentlichungen der deutschen Orientgesellschaft
ZAW	*Zeitschrift für die alttestamentliche Wissenschaft*
ZDPV	*Zeitschrift des deutschen Palästina-Vereins*

List of Figures

1
INTRODUCTION: CULT PLACES AND SACRED SPACES

In his review article of R. Albertz's important history of Israelite religion, W. Dever applauds the overall scope and depth of the work, especially its attention to "unofficial cults," but at one point he expresses surprise that Albertz makes no mention of the cultic precinct at Tel Dan, not even in his discussion of northern cult.[1] Unfortunately, Albertz's omission is not exceptional, for although Tel Dan has been excavated for over thirty seasons and has yielded an impressive array of cultic artifacts and monumental architecture, in most studies of ancient Israelite religion the site remains marginal at best. Part of this neglect is due to the limited publication of the site's Iron Age strata, though numerous articles and essays have been published over the years by the site's excavators, Avraham Biran and later David Ilan, and by others. Taken together, these works constitute a sturdy base for further study, and with the final reports of these strata forthcoming, Tel Dan will hopefully take its rightful place at the center of discussions of Israelite religion.[2]

This monograph addresses this lacuna by offering an interpretation of the cultic remains that were excavated in Area T at the site of Tel Dan in northern Israel. Its approach is twofold: first, I will study the remains of the site's Iron II strata. This part of the book will present archaeological portraits of Strata III and II, which will describe each stratum's defining architecture and artifacts. These portraits are based on published articles and also on unpublished season reports, field notes, and diaries that were made available to me at the Hebrew Union College in Jerusalem, which

---

1. W. Dever, review of R. Albertz, *A History of Israelite Religion in the Old Testament Period, BASOR* 301 (1996): 86; see also T. Lewis, review of R. Albertz, *A History of Israelite Religion in the Old Testament Period, Int* 51 (1997): 77.
2. See p. 21 below.

has conducted excavations at the site for over four decades.[3] Then, using the spatial theory of Henri Lefebvre—namely, his conceptual triad of spatial practice, representation of space, and spaces of representation—I will discuss what these remains might tell us about the construction of sacred space at Area T. The archaeological portraits themselves will detail the spatial practices of each stratum, and Lefebvre's representation of space will provide an opportunity to consider the conceptual significance of these spatial practices.

In the second part of this study, I will again use Lefebvre's conceptual triad, this time to analyze literary representations of space in the Hebrew Bible. The biblical texts under examination in these chapters are the story of Elijah on Mt. Carmel (1 Kgs 18:20–40) and selected passages from the book of Amos (e.g., 3:14; 4:4–5; 5:21–27; 7:10–17; 8:14; 9:1), which were chosen because their depictions of sacred space correspond most closely to the time and place of Strata III and II at Tel Dan. Alternatively, I could have chosen all texts that mention Dan in some way, but this approach seemed less promising. Besides the fact that three recent studies have already collected and analyzed such references,[4] these works highlight the methodological problems that make biblical references to Dan ill-suited for illuminating the site's archaeology. The principal obstacle is that so many of these biblical references date well after Strata III–II, and even those texts that depict earlier periods come to us only after substantial editing. Thus even though Judg 17–18 and 1 Kgs 12:25–33 seem like indispensable witnesses to cultic life at Dan, their Deuteronomistic editing takes us further from the archaeological realia of Strata III–II than texts that show less redaction. This is not to say that 1 Kgs 18 and the book of Amos are themselves free of later editing, which complicates attempts to connect their depictions of sacred space to particular strata at Tel Dan, but as I will discuss more fully in the introduction to the textual part of this

---

3. In particular, I would like to thank Ross Voss, the longtime supervisor of Area T, and Gila Cook, the chief surveyor of Tel Dan. Both were exceedingly generous in sharing their vast knowledge of Area T.

4. See M. Bartusch, *Understanding Dan: An Exegetical Study of a Biblical City, Tribe and Ancestor* (JSOTSup 379; Sheffield: Sheffield Academic Press, 2003); J. Bray, *Sacred Dan: Religious Tradition and Cultic Practice in Judges 17–18* (LHB/OTS 449; New York: T&T Clark, 2006); and H. Niemann, *Die Daniten: Studien zur Geschichte eines altisraelitischen Stammes* (FRLANT 135; Göttingen: Vandenhoeck & Ruprecht, 1985).

monograph, these texts do offer a better opportunity for comparison with the sacred precinct at Tel Dan in Strata III–II.

A final goal of this study is to contribute to the growing body of literature dedicated to the integration of textual and archaeological data. Although I have been trained primarily in textual studies and cannot claim expertise in the field of archaeology, I agree with those scholars who have argued that both fields are necessary to investigate Israelite religion.[5] This work represents my attempt at combining these two sets of data. However, before turning to these data, it will be worthwhile to expand on the theoretical framework within which this study will proceed, especially the concept of sacred space and Lefebvre's spatial theory.

1.1. SACRED SPACES AND CULTIC PLACES

1.1.1. SACRED SPACE

In recent years the concept of "sacred space" has enjoyed a wide-ranging currency in the study of ancient Israelite religion,[6] but Tel Dan has been

---

5. See T. Lewis, "How Far Can Texts Take Us? Evaluating Textual Sources for Reconstructing Ancient Israelite Beliefs about the Dead," in *Sacred Time, Sacred Place: Archaeology and the Religion of Israel* (ed. B. Gittlen; Winona Lake, Ind.: Eisenbrauns, 2002), 169–217; idem, "Family, Household, and Local Religion at Late Bronze Age Ugarit," in *Household and Family Religion in Antiquity* (ed. J. Bodel and S. Olyan; Malden, Mass.: Blackwell, 2008), 62–63.

6. This interest has resulted in edited volumes and journal issues dedicated to the topic (e.g., P. Dorman and B. Bryan, eds., *Sacred Space and Sacred Function in Ancient Thebes* [SAOC 61; Chicago: Oriental Institute of the University of Chicago, 2007]; B. Gittlen, ed., *Sacred Time, Sacred Place*; vol. 14.2 of *Journal for Semitics* [2005]; and vol. 67.1 of *Near Eastern Archaeology* [2004]) as well as many individual studies, such as S. Kang, "Creation, Eden, Temple and Mountain: Textual Presentations of Sacred Space in the Hebrew Bible" (Ph.D. diss., Johns Hopkins University, 2008); W. Kort, "Sacred/Profane and Adequate Theory of Human Place-Relations," in *Constructions of Space I: Theory, Geography, and Narrative* (ed. J. Berquist and C. Camp; New York: T&T Clark, 2007), 32–50; S. Kunin, *God's Place in the World: Sacred Space and Sacred Place in Judaism* (London: Cassell, 1998); S. Japhet, "Some Biblical Concepts of Sacred Space," in *Sacred Space: Shrine, City, Land: Proceedings of the International Conference in Memory of Joshua Prawer* (ed. B. Kedar and R. Werblowsky; Jerusalem: Israel Academy of Sciences and Humanities, 1998), 55–72; B. Levine, "Mythic and Ritual Projections of Sacred Space in Biblical Literature," *Journal of Jewish Thought and Philosophy* 6 (1997): 59–70; J. Branham, "Sacred Space in Ancient Jewish and Early

largely absent from this scholarly trend.[7] Although the site's excavator Avraham Biran has invoked the phrase in some publications,[8] he does not in these works articulate a precise definition of "sacred space"; it seems that for Biran Area T at Tel Dan was self-evidently such a space, and the best definition of sacred space was found in a presentation of the site's cultic artifacts. Modern visitors to Tel Dan and anyone who has studied its cultic assemblages will have a hard time arguing against Biran on this point, but it is also true that Tel Dan's contribution to the study of ancient religion can be greatly enhanced by engaging the concept of "sacred space" from a theoretical perspective. For embedded in this short phrase are two fundamental questions—namely, What is meant by "sacred," and, What is meant by "space"?—that have received considerable attention from historians of religion. A survey of this literature will not only present potential avenues of interpretation but also, hopefully, reveal opportunities for Tel Dan to contribute to the state of these theoretical questions.

The first question—What is meant by "sacred"?—brings us to an enduring division in the study of religion that has been summarized by D. Pals:

> some theorists strongly prefer *substantive* definitions, which closely resemble the commonsense approach. They define religion in terms of the beliefs or the ideas that religious people commit to and find important. Other theorists think this approach just too restrictive and offer instead a more *functional* definition. They leave the content or the ideas of religion off to the side and define it solely in terms of how it operates in human life. They want to know what a religion does for an individual person psychologically or for a group socially. Less concerned with the actual substance of people's beliefs or practices, they are inclined to describe religion, *whatever its specific content*, as that which provides support for a group or brings a sense of comfort or well-being to an individual.[9]

Medieval Christian Architecture" (Ph.D. diss., Emory University, 1993); B. Bokser, "Approaching Sacred Space," *HTR* 78 (1985): 279–99. For an introduction to the topic, one should consult J. Brereton, "Sacred Space," *EncRel* 12:7978–86.

7. See, however, B. Nakhai, "What's a 'Bamah'? How Sacred Space Functioned in Ancient Israel," *BAR* 20.3 (1994): 18–29, 77–79.

8. E.g., A. Biran, "Sacred Spaces: Of Standing Stones, High Places and Cult Objects at Tel Dan," *BAR* 24.5 (1998): 38–45, 70.

9. D. Pals, *Eight Theories of Religion* (2nd ed.; New York: Oxford University Press, 2006), 13 (italics original). Alternatively, these two modes of inquiry have been termed "substantial" and "situational" (see D. Chidester and E. Linenthal, "Introduction," in

The locus classicus for a substantive explanation of sacred space is M. Eliade's essay titled "Sacred Places: Temple, Palace, 'Centre of the World,'" in which he defines sacred space as the result of a hierophany that "transforms the place where it occurs; hitherto profane, it is thenceforward a sacred area."[10] For Eliade, human agency is involved in this process only insofar as "the sacred place in some way or another reveals itself to [a person]."[11] Such revelations were "hierophanies," which he defines as "an irruption of the sacred that results in detaching a territory from the surrounding cosmic milieu and making it qualitatively different."[12] As these statements show, Eliade's approach emphasizes "the autonomy of hierophanies" and tends to disregard the social and political aspects of sacred space.

American Sacred Space [ed. D. Chidester and E. Linenthal; Bloomington: Indiana University Press, 1995], 5–6). A classic exhibition of these contrasting modes may be found in R. Otto's reaction against the functional approach of É. Durkheim. The latter in his important 1912 book examined the experience of believers and concluded that "this reality, which mythologies have represented under so many different forms, but which is the universal and eternal objective cause of these sensations sui generis out of which religious experience is made, is society. … Then it is action which dominates religious life, because of the mere fact that it is society which is its source" (*The Elementary Forms of the Religious Life* [trans. J. Swain; Mineola, N.Y.: Dover, 2008], 418). By contrast, Otto's own seminal work just five years later focused in the "numinous," which he defined as the irreducible *mysterium* that evokes awe and fascination in a person. For Otto, the substance of religion consists of principles that "must be *a priori* ones, not to be derived from 'experience' or 'history'" (*The Idea of the Holy: An Inquiry into the Non-Rational Factor in the Idea of the Divine and Its Relation to the Rational* [trans. J. Harvey; London: Oxford University Press, 1958], 175).

10. M. Eliade, *Patterns in Comparative Religion* (trans. R. Sheed; London: Sheed & Ward, 1958), 367.

11. Ibid., 369. Similarly, G. van der Leeuw wrote: "The place thus selected, because it has shown itself to be sacred, is at first merely a position: man adds nothing at all to Nature; the mysterious situation of a locality, its awe-inspiring character, suffice" (*Religion in Essence and Manifestation: A Study in Phenomenology* [trans. J. Turner; London: George Allen & Unwin, 1938], 394). As this statement suggests, van der Leeuw anticipated Eliade's substantive approach, but D. Chidester has recently shown that a close reading of the van der Leeuw shows that he was more attuned to "the politics of sacred space" than is often recognized ("The Poetics and Politics of Sacred Space: Towards a Critical Phenomenology of Religion," *Analecta Husserliana* 43 [1994]: 211–31).

12. M. Eliade, *The Sacred and the Profane: The Nature of Religion* (trans. W. Trask; San Diego: Harcourt, 1987), 26.

As I will show below, this inattention has been the basis for subsequent criticism of Eliade's theories, but first I would note that his concept of sacred space remains a useful heuristic model for the study of Area T at Tel Dan.[13] Indeed, several of his points are applicable to the cultic situation at the site, and it will be worthwhile to mention them here. First, Eliade's emphasis on springs as a "manifestation of a sacred presence" is certainly consistent with Tel Dan, whose springs are a source of the Jordan River.[14] Although we cannot be certain, the site's cultic foundations are probably related to these springs: Area T itself was built less than a hundred meters from them, and the sound of their output is unmistakable as one stands on the mound.[15] The springs' importance at Tel Dan is confirmed

---

13. Several important studies of Israelite religion have taken Eliade as their starting point; see Kang, "Creation, Eden, Temple and Mountain: Textual Presentations of Sacred Space in the Hebrew Bible"; D. Clines, "Sacred Space, Holy Places and Suchlike," in *On the Way to the Postmodern: Old Testament Essays, 1967–1998* (JSOTSup 293; 2 vols.; Sheffield: Sheffield Academic Press, 1998), 2:542–54; repr. from *Trinity Occasional Papers* 12/2 (1993); J. Levenson, *Sinai and Zion: An Entry into the Jewish Bible* (San Francisco: Harper & Row, 1985), 102–42; and R. Cohn, *The Shape of Sacred Space: Four Biblical Studies* (SR 23; Chico. Calif.: Scholars Press, 1981), 63–79.

14. Eliade, *Patterns in Comparative Religion*, 199. Cf. W. F. Albright, "The Mouth of the Rivers" (*AJSL* 35 [1919]: 161–95), in which he investigates the Akkadian phrase *pî nārāti* in the Gilgamesh Epic and, in doing so, demonstrates the religious significance of rivers' sources throughout the ancient Near East. This significance is consistent with the recognition of P. Taçon that "junctions or points of change between geology, hydrology, and vegetation" tend to be regarded as sacred places ("Identifying Ancient Sacred Landscapes in Australia: From Physical to Social," in *Archaeologies of Landscape: Contemporary Perspectives* [ed. W. Ashmore and A. Knapp; Malden, Mass.: Blackwell, 1999], 36–42).

15. See A. Biran, D. Ilan, and R. Greenberg, *Dan I: A Chronicle of the Excavations, the Pottery Neolithic, the Early Bronze Age and the Middle Bronze Age Tombs* (Jerusalem: Nelson Glueck School of Biblical Archaeology, Hebrew Union College–Jewish Institute of Religion, 1996), Plan 1. The uncertain correlation between the springs and the sanctuary is due to the fact that Tel Dan was not just a cult site but also a city, where we might expect to find religious architecture whether there are springs nearby or not. On the one hand, the discovery of a large (3–4 m thick) stone wall from the Early Bronze Age indicate that Area T was part of Tel Dan's earliest building activity (see ibid., 51–53; A. Biran and R. Ben-Dov, *Dan II: A Chronicle of the Excavations and the Late Bronze Age "Mycenaean" Tomb* [Jerusalem: Hebrew Union College–Jewish Institute of Religion, 2002], 30–32), and the constructions of the Middle Bronze and Iron Age gates precisely opposite the spring suggest a design that insulated Area T and the springs from the rest of the city. On the other hand, most large communities tend

by certain artifacts and architecture that attest to the ritual use of water.[16] Moreover, this abundant water has resulted in lush vegetation all over the mound, which lends the site an Edenic quality. Indeed, the region around Mt. Hermon was regarded in antiquity as a veritable utopia, according to the Hebrew Bible (e.g., Judg 18:7–10) as well as numerous ancient Near Eastern mythological texts.[17] In light of this depiction, it would be tempting to connect Tel Dan's utopian qualities to Eliade's theory that humans' attraction to sacred space is rooted in their "nostalgia for Paradise" and that their actions are attempts to realize the archetypes represented by this "paradise."[18] However, this theory has little to contribute to our study of Tel Dan. While the site's natural features probably played no small role in its foundation as a cult center, Eliade's emphasis on nostalgia overlooks the important political and social realities that attend every sacred space, as will be discussed below.[19] In fact, one of the central questions I hope to answer in this work is how these realities played out at Tel Dan.

---

to have religious architecture, and the buildings in Area T during the Iron II period may simply reflect the religious needs of the local population.

16. The most significant in this regard is the so-called Pool Room in the southern part of Area T, which featured a thick layer of plaster that sealed a flagstone pavement and evidence of a channel through one of the walls. Its identification as a "pool room" was bolstered when the high-water level prevented further excavation of the room; here the spring was most likely incorporated in the room itself. Outside the entrance to the room was a large terracotta tub. Both the room and the tub belong to Stratum IVA (see A. Biran, *Biblical Dan* [Jerusalem: Israel Exploration Society/Hebrew Union College–Jewish Institute of Religion, 1994], 174–75).

17. See E. Lipiński, "El's Abode: Mythological Traditions Related to Mount Hermon and to the Mountains of Armenia," *OLP* 2 (1971): 13–69; M. Smith, *Introduction with Text, Translation and Commentary of KTU 1.1–1.2* (vol. 1 of *The Ugaritic Baal Narrative*; VTSup 55; Leiden: Brill, 1994), 225–35. P. K. McCarter has even suggested that this long-standing religious tradition underlies the creation account in Genesis 2–3 ("The Garden of Eden: Geographical and Etymological Ruminations on the Garden of God in the Bible and the Ancient Near East" [paper presented at the Colloquium for Biblical Research, Duke University, 19 August 2001]; I am grateful to Professor McCarter for sharing this unpublished paper with me).

18. According to Eliade rituals are "meaningless" unless they involve "the abolition of time through the imitation of archetypes and the repetition of paradigmatic gestures" (*The Myth of the Eternal Return or, Cosmos and History* (trans. W. Trask; Princeton: Princeton University Press, 1971), 34–35). This repetition also applied to cultic structures that were "indefinitely copied and copied again" based on a primeval archetype (idem, *Patterns in Comparative Religion*, 371–72).

19. Cf. the remark by J.-C. Margueron that "car si l'on pense avec Mircéa Eliade

Before discussing these social dimensions of sacred space, however, I must mention another point stressed by Eliade, namely, his argument that once a sacred space has been established, it remains so permanently. Moreover, he argues that this continuity of sacred space is especially true at springs, which "have a certain autonomy, and their worship persists in spite of other epiphanies and other religious revolutions."[20] Tel Dan undoubtedly bears out this point; as I will show in the next chapter, the site served as a cult center from at least the Middle Bronze Age through the Hellenistic period.[21] Over these centuries, as the site was inhabited by various peoples worshiping various deities, Tel Dan remained a cult center, and this longevity shows that its status as sacred space persisted irrespective of which cult was practiced there. However much we emphasize the social and political processes at Tel Dan, we must also acknowledge that its sanctity was not merely a function of these processes but, to some extent, transcended them. Thus Eliade's study remains a valid starting point for exploring the concept of sacred space. In particular, his attention to natural phenomena as manifestations of the sacred and to the continuity of sacred space has provided some valuable perspective for understanding the cultic area at Tel Dan.

1.1.2. CULTIC PLACE

In the decades since Eliade's seminal work, his theories of religion have been subjected to considerable criticism, much of it from those who take a more "functional" view of religion (as defined in the quotation above).[22]

---

qu'une hiérophanie est à l'origine de la sacralisation d'un espace, il faut encore comprehendre comment on a pu donner une dimension en superficie (territoire), voire en volume (édifice construit) à ce qui, au départ, n'était qu'une manifestation purement ponctuelle. Ce transfert ne me paraît nullement évident a priori" ("Prolégomènes a une étude portant sur l'organisation de l'espace sacré en Orient," in Temples et sanctuaires: séminaire de recherche 1981–1983 [ed. G. Roux; Travaux de la Maison de l'Orient 7; Lyon: GIS/Maison de l'Orient; Paris: Diffusion de Boccard, 1984], 24).

20. Eliade, Patterns in Comparative Religion, 200.
21. See below, pp. 22–28.
22. See R. Brown, "Eliade on Archaic Religions: Some Old and New Criticisms," SR 10 (1981): 429–49; Pals, Eight Theories of Religion, 222–26. Indeed, some archaeologists have questioned whether Eliade's basic dichotomy of the "sacred" and the "profane" is meaningful for ancient societies; see T. Insoll, Archaeology, Ritual, Religion (London: Routledge, 2004), 1–32, 88–90; J. Brück, "Ritual and Rationality: Some

With regard to his theory of sacred space, one of Eliade's most thorough critics has been J. Z. Smith, who introduces a new dichotomy of "locative" and "utopian" visions of the world.[23] The difference between these two orientations has been summarized by D. Chidester and E. Linenthal, who write that "locative space is a fixed, bounded, sacred cosmos, reinforced by the imperative of maintaining one's place, and the place of others, in a larger scheme of things. By contrast, utopian space is unbounded, unfixed to any particular location, a place that can only be reached by breaking out of, or liberated from, the bonds of the prevailing social order."[24] Whereas Eliade's theory of sacred space tended to neglect its social dimensions, Smith's locative vision recognizes that the way a society perceives the cosmos (and humans' place in it) is strictly ordered and that this order reflects the social structures of that society.[25] Furthermore, in his theory of "emplacement" Smith has argued that it is precisely this social orientation that distinguishes a space from a place; whereas the former refers to the undifferentiated "out there," the latter denotes "a social position within a hierarchical system."[26] This distinction is relevant to the present study

---

Problems of Interpretation in European Archaeology," *European Journal of Archaeology* 2 (1999): 313–44.

23. J. Z. Smith, *Map Is Not Territory: Studies in the History of Religions* (Chicago: University of Chicago Press, 1993), 101.

24. Chidester and Linenthal, "Introduction," 15.

25. Smith, *Map Is Not Territory*, 137–38.

26. J. Z. Smith, *To Take Place: Toward Theory in Ritual* (Chicago: University of Chicago Press, 1987), 45; see also 26–28, 110. See also K. Knott, *The Location of Religion: A Spatial Analysis* (London: Equinox, 2005), 29–34; Y. Tuan, *Space and Place: The Perspective of Experience* (Minneapolis: University of Minnesota Press, 1977), 6; M. Parker Pearson and C. Richards, "Ordering the World: Perceptions of Architecture, Space and Time," in *Architecture and Order: Approaches to Social Space* (London: Routledge, 1996), 4.

The distinction between space and place has also been addressed within the field of archaeology (e.g., C. Orser Jr., *A Historical Archaeology of the Modern World* [New York: Plenum, 1996], 131–58; R. Preucel and L. Meskell, "Places," in *A Companion to Social Archaeology* [ed. L. Meskell and R. Preucel; Malden, Mass.: Blackwell, 2007], 215–29; and E. Blake, "Space, Spatiality, and Archaeology," in *A Companion to Social Archaeology*, 233–36). The subject has been part of a larger discussion of landscape archaeology, i.e., how human societies transform and are transformed by their physical environment. See A. Smith, *The Political Landscape: Constellations of Authority in Early Complex Polities* (Berkeley and Los Angeles: University of California Press, 2003); W. Ashmore, "Social Archaeologies of Landscape," in *A Companion to Social*

because Smith goes on to state that the sacrality of a *space* depends on the rituals that take *place* there. Eliade had defined sacred space as an autonomous reality found in nature, but Smith emphasizes that the sacred and the profane "are not substantive categories, but rather situational ones. Sacrality is, above all, a category of emplacement."[27] A space is sacralized by the rituals that are performed there,[28] and in this sense we cannot talk about sacred space without talking about the cultic activity that is practiced in that space. Or to put it another way, every sacred space implies a cult place.

This emphasis on the role of ritual in sacralizing space gives the concept of sacred space a distinctly social orientation. As Smith himself notes, "ritual is systemic hierarchy par excellence."[29] Moreover, it introduces the possibility that a cult place (i.e., sacred-space-in-action) can become the site of competing interests. Chidester and Linenthal, recognizing the theme of cult places as contested space, write that "sacred spaces are always highly charged sites for contested negotiations over the ownership of the symbolic capital (or symbolic real estate) that signifies power relations."[30] On this same theme, Chidester has elsewhere emphasized the role that "the politics of exclusion" play in the demarcation of a sacred space; unlike Eliade, for whom the line between the sacred and the profane was fixed and ontological,[31] Chidester focuses on the social context in which religious boundaries are constructed and maintained.[32] This approach reso-

---

Archaeology (ed. L. Meskell and R. Preucel; Malden, Mass.: Blackwell, 2007), 255–71; A. Knapp and W. Ashmore, "Archaeological Landscapes: Constructed, Conceptualized, Ideational," in *Archaeologies of Landscape: Contemporary Perspectives* (ed. W. Ashmore and A. Knapp; Malden, Mass.: Blackwell, 1999), 1–30; S. Steadman, "Reliquaries on the Landscape: Mounds as Matrices of Human Cognition," in *Archaeologies of the Middle East: Critical Perspectives* (ed. S. Pollock and R. Bernbeck; Malden, Mass.: Blackwell, 2005), 286–307; A. Mack, "One Landscape, Many Experiences: Differing Perspectives of the Temple Districts of Vijayanagara," *Journal of Archaeological Method and Theory* 11 (2004): 59–81; and J. Moore, "The Social Basis of Sacred Spaces in the Prehispanic Andes: Ritual Landscapes of the Dead in Chimú and Inka Societies," *Journal of Archaeological Method and Theory* 11 (2004): 83-124.

27. Smith, *To Take Place*, 104.

28. Smith notes that this is the etymology of the Latin *sacrificium*, from the combination of *sacer*, "sacred," and *facio*, "to make" (ibid., 105).

29. Ibid., 110.

30. Chidester and Linenthal, "Introduction," 16.

31. See Eliade, *The Sacred and the Profane*, 23, 63.

32. Chidester, "The Poetics and Politics of Sacred Space," 217–22; cf. Durkheim, *Elementary Forms of the Religious Life*, 11–12.

nates with the religious situation in ancient—and modern—Israel. Indeed, numerous texts from the Hebrew Bible depict cult sites as places where competition and disagreement abound,[33] and in modern times the Temple Mount/*al-haram al-sharif* in Jerusalem remains a classic example of contested sacred space.[34] Moreover, the prevalence of this theme throughout the Hebrew Bible invites us to consider how this aspect of sacred space may have been operative at Israelite cult places in general, and at Tel Dan in particular.

1.2. THE SPATIAL THEORY OF HENRI LEFEBVRE

For a spatial theory that addresses the issue of contested space I turn to Henri Lefebvre, who also emphasized this theme in his work *The Production of Space*.[35] At the center of Lefebvre's theory is his understanding of space as a conceptual triad consisting of (1) *spatial practice*, which is the lived space that "structures all aspects of daily life and ... is experienced through practical perception, through commonsense, and is taken for granted"; (2) *representation of space*, or "conceptual space," which refers to "those dominant, theoretical, often technical, representations of lived space that are conceived and constructed by planners, architects, engineers, and scientists of all kinds"; and (3) *spaces of representation*, or "symbolic space," which are lived spaces that are "imbued with distinctively local knowledge [and] often run counter to spaces generated by formal technical knowledge."[36] In this way these spaces of representation may

---

33. Some examples include Gen 4:3–8; 32:24–32; Exod 32:1–35; Lev 10:1–20; Josh 22:10–34; Judg 6:28–35; 9:46–49; 18:14–25; 1 Sam 5:1–5; 13:8–14; 1 Kgs 13:1–10; 18:20–40; 2 Kgs 10:18–27; 23:4–15; Ezra 4–6; Jer 36:1–19; Ezek 8:3–18; Amos 7:10–17; Hag 1–2.

34. See R. Friedland and R. Hecht, "The Politics of Sacred Place: Jerusalem's Temple Mount/*al-haram al-sharif*," in *Sacred Places and Profane Spaces: Essays in the Geographics of Judaism, Christianity, and Islam* (ed. J. Scott and P. Simpson-Housley; CSR 30; New York: Greenwood, 1991), 21–61.

35. H. Lefebvre, *The Production of Space* (trans. D. Nicholson-Smith; Cambridge: Blackwell, 1991). As the title may suggest, Lefebvre himself was working out of a Marxist background, but subsequent developments of his theory have shown that its application does not require engagement with dialectical materialism (see Knott, *The Location of Religion*, 11–58; J. Flanagan, "Ancient Perceptions of Space/Perceptions of Ancient Space," *Semeia* 87 [1999]: 15–43).

36. See Lefebvre, *Production of Space*, 33, 38–40; however, the definitions quoted

constitute a resistance to the ideologies that constitute the second aspect. According to Lefebvre, all three aspects are dialectically connected and are present in every space, though not always equally. Because this conceptual triad will be the theoretical basis for the present study, it is important to look more closely as each of its parts.

1.2.1. SPATIAL PRACTICE

Spatial practice refers to the physical realities of a space. Such realities include the dimensions of the space, the architectural features that divide the space into its constituent parts, and the material objects that are found in the space. At an archaeological site, spatial practice consists of all the data one is likely to find in a site report: its size and topography; its architectural features, such as walls, floors, thresholds, passageways, stairs, benches, altars, podiums, columns, and so on; its building materials, such as travertine blocks, fieldstones, plaster, bronze, iron; artifacts, such as pottery, metals, small finds, seal impressions, bowls, and so on. Thus Lefebvre's spatial practice attends to the material realities of a particular space, which, in the case of Area T at Tel Dan, means the archaeological remains that have been excavated and recorded over the last few decades.[37]

However, spatial practice is not simply a catalog of these material realities but also questions how these realities create a coherent and distinctive space. As we will see, many of the remains found at Area T have parallels elsewhere, but at no other site will one find the particular assemblage of artifacts that has been discovered at Tel Dan. Assessing the spatial practice of Area T, then, is a question of understanding the unique space that is cre-

---

here have been taken from Knott, *Location of Religion*, 36–39. See also R. Shields, *Lefebvre, Love and Struggle: Spatial Dialectics* (London: Routledge, 1999), 160–70; M. George, *Israel's Tabernacle as Social Space* (SBL Ancient Israel and Its Literature 2; Atlanta: Society of Biblical Literature, 2009), 20–44. Following George's example, I will refer to "representation of space" and "spaces of representation" as "conceptual space" and "symbolic space," respectively (ibid., 22).

37. One problem in trying to apply Lefebvre's theory to an archaeological site is that, unlike the modern spaces that interested Lefebvre, ancient cities are observable only in the results of archaeological excavation, which represents a small fraction of the spatial practices that existed at the site. At Tel Dan this limitation pertains to Area T in particular, since certain parts of the temple complex remain unexcavated. Despite this limitation, however, I hope to show that his theory is still a valuable tool for understanding (sacred) space in antiquity.

ated by its unique assemblage of material remains. Moreover, spatial practice also refers to the social practices that are suggested by the remains. Pathways, doors, walls, and stairs are all indications of how people moved through the site. In a sacred precinct like Area T, an altar may mark the locus of cultic activity and give clues about the kind of rituals that took place. In this way, spatial practice at Area T is a question of how the sacred space reflects the cultic practices that took place there and determined the organization of the space. But beyond simply reflecting such practices, it is also a question of how the organization of space in turn shaped the worship that took place at the temple. Thus spatial practice is a consideration of the ways in which the physical realities of a space and its social practices are mutually transformative.[38]

1.2.2. Conceptual Space

Unlike spatial practice, which attends to physical realities, conceptual space is abstract, referring to the mental blueprint that maps out how a particular space is to be organized. This blueprint is the mental product of architects and others who have the power to determine the purpose of the space and the spatial practices that will achieve that purpose. The impact of such a blueprint is considerable: because spatial practices shape social practices and relations, the conceptual space that orders those spatial practices also effectively orders social relations. As such, the space comes to reflect the values and ideologies of those empowered to conceptualize the space. For example, Mark George has argued that the biblical description of the tabernacle reflects the Priestly writers' concerns over genealogy, heredity succession, and the importance of the "congregation" (Heb. 'ēdâ),[39] while others have regarded holiness as the primary concern that organizes the tabernacle space.[40] These analyses demonstrate how one space can express multiple concerns or ideologies. Conceptual space is not

---

38. See George, *Israel's Tabernacle as Social Space*, 47–48.

39. Ibid., 89–135.

40. See P. Jenson, *Graded Holiness: A Key to the Priestly Conception of the World* (JSOTSup 106; Sheffield: Sheffield Academic Press, 1992); M. Haran, *Temples and Temple-Service in Ancient Israel: An Inquiry into the Character of Cultic Phenomena and the Historical Setting of the Priestly School* (Oxford: Clarendon, 1978); F. Gorman, *The Ideology of Ritual: Space, Time and Status in the Priestly Theology* (JSOTSup 91; Sheffield: JSOT Press, 1990).

produced in a vacuum but in the midst of different, perhaps competing, interests, such that one space may reflect more than one set of social and political values.

Textual sources are often the best opportunity to discern the conceptual space that has determined the order and organization of a physical space,[41] but I hope to show that a close reading of Area T's architecture and material culture does permit some tentative remarks on the priorities and concerns that produced the cultic space we find in Strata III–II. Furthermore, the textual analysis of part 2 of this monograph is intended fill out the conceptual space that emerges from the archaeological data. Besides the "House of David" inscription, our best written sources for assessing the cultic space at Tel Dan come from the Hebrew Bible, which for all its editorial layers may still shed important light on how sacred space was conceived in the northern kingdom during the Iron Age. These literary representations of sacred space, which correspond most closely to Strata III–II at Tel Dan, will expand our perspective on the conceptual space that underlies the spatial organization of Area T.

1.2.3. SYMBOLIC SPACE

If it is difficult to determine the conceptual space of Area T at Tel Dan, it is virtually impossible to discern its symbolic space. This is because symbolic space refers to the various social meanings that a space represents for a particular society. George contrasts it with conceptual space in this way: "Conceptual space ... is mental space, those logical, conceptual systems a society develops to organize, arrange, and classify space. Conceptual space is rational space, rather than symbolic, emotional space. By contrast, symbolic space is the space of emotion, affectation, and aesthetics, which gives such space social meaning."[42] Thus symbolic space concerns how people actually experience a space and the meaning that they ascribe to that space, and because such meaning can be as various as the people themselves, symbolic space is a kind of spatial palimpsest. Often the symbolic meanings of a space are rooted in the history and mythology, as in the description of the biblical tabernacle, which, according to George's analysis, drew

---

41. Lefebvre, *Production of Space*, 39; George, *Israel's Tabernacle as Social Space*, 90.
42. Ibid., 141–42.

on the social significance of ancient Near Eastern building deposits, royal building projects, and the Priestly cosmology presented in Gen 1.[43]

The obstacles involved in trying to assess the symbolic space of an archaeological site like Tel Dan should be obvious. First, we have no access to the emotional and aesthetic responses of those who worshiped at Tel Dan. Here our limited written sources, such as the "House of David" inscription and the Hebrew Bible, offer no help, since they represent the perspective of authority and power. It is this perspective that makes them important for understanding conceptual space, but less capable of conveying the numerous symbolic meanings that are produced in a sacred precinct like Area T. In fact, Lefebvre thought that symbolic space offered the best opportunity for people to resist the ideologies that are embedded in conceptual space.[44] Second, the symbolic meanings of a space are fluid and often hidden from the very people who use the space, so that access to the experience of worshipers at Tel Dan would not necessarily bring us any closer to understanding its symbolic space. For these reasons, I will not speculate on the symbolic space of the sacred precinct at Tel Dan but will restrict my discussion to its spatial practice and conceptual space and how those two spatial fields resonate with the sacred space that is depicted in 1 Kgs 18 and the book of Amos.

I would like to conclude this introduction with a quote from K. Knott, whose work demonstrates what Lefebvre's theory might contribute to the field of religious studies.

> Religion, then, which is inherently social, must also exist and express itself in and through space, and must play its part in the constitution of spaces. The spatial underpinnings of religion is witnessed at all levels, from the expression of hierarchical relations ... to the local, national and global extension of religious structures and institutions. ... That spaces themselves may be constituted by socio-religious relations is illustrated not only in the development of places of worship and other sacralised sites, but also by such things as ritual transformations of the human body and the religious production of distinctive narrative and doctrinal spaces (capable of winning the support of individuals and communities and thus engaging in ideological struggles in the public arena).[45]

---

43. Ibid., 137–90.
44. Lefebvre, *Production of Space*, 230–33.
45. Knott, *Location of Religion*, 21.

In line with this statement, my study of Area T proposes to show how the arrangement of its cultic space reflects some of the socioreligious relations that existed at Tel Dan, including how the development of its physical space represents certain hierarchical relations that were operative at the site. The second step of my analysis concerns what Knott calls "the religious production of distinctive narrative spaces." The biblical texts that constitute the second part of this study are examined as "narrative spaces," which offer another perspective on how sacred space functioned in ancient Israel, especially in the northern kingdom. As literary representations of social space, they expand our knowledge of the religious ideologies that may have been prevalent at a site like Tel Dan.

These are some of the issues I will address in our study of Area T at Tel Dan, but this emphasis on the social processes that constituted the cultic life at Tel Dan does not mean to discount the substantive aspects of the site's religious tradition. I purposely began this chapter with Eliade's theory of sacred space because parts of it remain viable and applicable to Tel Dan. Yet even as we acknowledge that the site's verdant natural setting and longevity constitute a sacred space in the Eliadian sense,[46] the primary interest of this work concerns how sacred space at Tel Dan was socially constructed, with special attention given to the spatial practice and conceptual space of Area T.

---

46. Even Lefebvre, in his discussion of "absolute space," acknowledges the "intrinsic qualities" of certain natural settings, such as caves, mountaintops, springs, and rivers, which are recognized as sacred sites (*Production of Space*, 48). For a recent treatment and critique of "absolute space"—a term apparently coined by Isaac Newton—see A. Smith, *Political Landscape*, 30–57.

PART 1
THE SITE OF TEL DAN AND ITS SACRED PRECINCT

The site of Tel Dan (Arab. *Tell el-Qāḍi*) is a 20-hectare site located in the northeastern Huleh Valley (fig. 1).[1] Its mound is set against the karstic springs of 'Ain Leddan (Arab. *al-Liddān*),[2] which constitute one of the site's defining topographical features.

These springs feed the Dan River, which is one of the three major tributaries of the Jordan River.[3] Although the Dan River has the smallest catchment area of the three (8 km^2)—upon seeing the river, Mark Twain laconically reported, "This puddle is an important source of the Jordan"[4]—it is the most abundant tributary, discharging 250 million m^3 per year.[5] Because this discharge displays relatively little seasonal fluctuation, the

---

1. Cf. Judg 18:28, which locates Dan/Laish "in the valley belonging to Beth-rehob."

2. E. Scott related the Arabic name of the springs "el-Leddân" to the toponym "Dan" by reconstructing a series of definite articles thus: *dân* > *ed-Dân > *el-Eddân > *el-Leddân (cited in E. Robinson et al., *Later Biblical Researches in Palestine, and in the Adjacent Regions: A Journal of Travels in the Year 1852* [Boston: Crocker & Brewster, 1856], 392 n. 2).

3. The other two are the Hermon River, which is fed in part by the springs at Baniyas, and the Snir River (see D. Gil'ad and J. Bonne, "The Snowmelt of Mt. Hermon and Its Contribution to the Sources of the Jordan River," *Journal of Hydrology* 114 [1990]: 2–3).

4. M. Twain, *The Innocents Abroad, or The New Pilgrims' Progress* (2 vols.; New York: Harper & Row, 1869), 2:205.

5. See F. Por et al., "River Dan, Headwater of the Jordan, an Aquatic Oasis of the Middle East," *Hydrobiologia* 134 (1986): 123–24, esp. table 1. By comparison, the Hermon River from the Baniyas springs has a catchment area of 145 km^2 but a mean annual discharge of only 120 million m^3. This difference in catchment area probably accounts for Josephus's calling the Dan River "the so-called little Jordan" (Gr. *ton mikron kaloumenon Iordanon* [*J.W.* 4.3; cf. *Ant.* 8.226]) as well as "the lesser Jordan" (*elassonos Iordanou* [*Ant.* 5.178]).

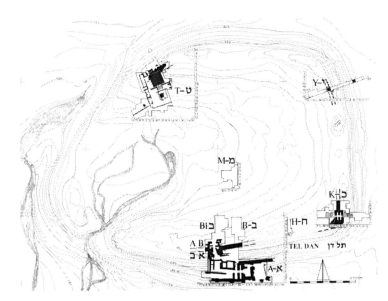

Figure 1. The site of Tel Dan (site plan courtesy of the Nelson Glueck School of Biblical Archaeology, Hebrew Union College/Jewish Institute of Religion).

Dan springs also constitute the Jordan River's most stable source.[6] The site of Tel Dan has been identified with *Tell el-Qāḍi* since it was proposed by E. Robinson in 1838,[7] and this identification was confirmed in 1976, when excavators discovered at the site a second-century-B.C.E. bilingual inscription describing a votive offering made "to the god who is in Dan" (fig. 2).[8]

The etymology of "Dan" has proved an interesting puzzle over the centuries. The current consensus holds that the name most likely derives from

---

6. Por et al., "River Dan, Headwater of the Jordan," 123.

7. E. Robinson, *Biblical Researches in Palestine, Mount Sinai and Arabia Petræa: A Journal of Travels in the Year 1838* (3 vols.; Boston: Crocker & Brewster, 1841), 3:350–52; see also W. F. Albright, "The Jordan Valley in the Bronze Age," *AASOR* 6 (1924–25): 16–18. For a recent treatment of the evidence for this identification, see Y. Elitzur, *Ancient Place Names in the Holy Land: Preservation and History* (Jerusalem: Magnes; Winona Lake, Ind.: Eisenbrauns, 2004), 201–9.

8. The full inscription reads, "To the god / [w]ho is in Dan / [Z]oilos made a vow," and is based primarily on the Greek text: *theō / [t]ō en Danois / [Z]ōilos euchēn*; only part of the Aramaic text survives: [] *ndr zyls l'* [] (see A. Biran, "To the God Who Is in Dan," in *Temples and High Places in Biblical Times: Proceedings of the Colloquium in Honor of the Centennial of Hebrew Union College–Jewish Institute of Religion, Jerusalem, 14–16 March 1977* [ed. A. Biran; Jerusalem: Nelson Glueck School of Biblical Archaeology of Hebrew Union College–Jewish Institute of Religion, 1981], 142–51).

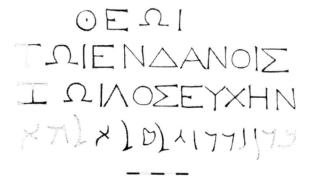

Figure 2. The bilingual votive inscription from Tel Dan (drawing courtesy of the Nelson Glueck School of Biblical Archaeology, Hebrew Union College/Jewish Institute of Religion).

the root *dyn, "to judge," which is well-attested in the Hebrew Bible,[9] most notably in Gen 30:6 and 49:16, where the verb is linked to the tribe of Dan.[10] Interestingly, if we take this root as the source of the city and tribe called "Dan" in the Hebrew Bible, Y. Elitzur has noted that it would be "*the only case in the nomenclature of the Holy Land* in which there is a positive identification of a biblical site with a place whose *Arabic* name seems to be a translation."[11] Here he is referring to the fact that Arabic qāḍi also means "judge," a coincidence that brings us no closer to the ancient etymology of Dan but that is noteworthy all the same. Alternatively, Y. Yadin has proposed that the tribe name Dan should be related to the sea people known

---

9. See *HALOT*, 220.

10. In the latter reference, the tribe Dan seems to be the subject of *dyn. The Hebrew reads *dān yādîn ʿammô,* which many translate "Dan will judge his people" (see C. Westermann, *Genesis 37–50: A Commentary* [trans. J. Scullion; Minneapolis: Augsburg, 1986], 234). The derivation of *yādîn* from *dyn is not certain, however, as several recent interpreters have taken the verb from the root *dnn "to be strong" (cf. Akk. *danānu*), which is only attested in the Hebrew Bible in the toponym *dannâ* (Josh 15:49). Arguments for this derivation may be found in J. Emerton, "Some Difficult Words in Genesis 49," in *Words and Meanings: Essays Presented to David Winston Thomas on His Retirement from the Regius Professorship of Hebrew in the University of Cambridge, 1968* (ed. P. Ackroyd and B. Lindars; Cambridge: Cambridge University Press, 1968), 88–91; and R. de Hoop, *Genesis 49 in Its Literary and Historical Context* (OtSt 39; Leiden: Brill, 1999), 163–69.

11. Elitzur, *Ancient Place Names in the Holy Land*, 208 (italics original).

as *denyen* (Gr. "Danai").[12] Beyond these two proposals there is little worth considering, and that includes unconvincing attempts to relate "Dan" to Hebrew *yardēn*, "Jordan." The association of the two words, which is cited in several ancient sources and even some modern,[13] is understandable considering Tel Dan's location by the headwaters of the river, but nowhere in the Hebrew Bible are the two linked. Moreover, E. Smick has argued that the use of the definite article with *yardēn* (e.g., Gen 32:11) and expressions like *yardēn yĕrî/ēḥô* (Num 34:15; Josh 20:8; 1 Chr 6:63) suggest that the term was originally a common noun for "river."[14]

The site of Tel Dan was first dug in 1966 by Avraham Biran, who excavated the site more or less continuously until his retirement in 2003. The chronicles of the 1966–1992 seasons were published in *Dan I*, a final report that dealt principally with the Neolithic, Early Bronze, and Middle Bronze strata.[15] The *Dan II* volume updated the chronicle of excavations with a summary of the 1993–1999 seasons and features R. Ben-Dov's analysis of the Late Bronze Age "Mycenaean" Tomb.[16] Most recently, Ben-Dov has

---

12. Yadin (Heb. ידין), "'And Dan, Why Did He Remain in Ships' (Judges, V, 17)," *AJBA* 1 (1968): 9–23; cf. M. Astour, *Hellenosemitica: An Ethnic and Cultural Study in the West Semitic Impact of Mycenaean Greece* (Leiden: Brill, 1965), 45–53. In his dissertation on the Iron Age I period at Tel Dan, D. Ilan is sympathetic to this thesis, especially in light of the sea people material culture found at the site ("Northeastern Israel in the Iron Age I: Cultural, Socioeconomic and Political Perspectives" [2 vols.; Ph.D. diss., Tel Aviv University, 1999], 1:134–35, 147–49; cf. 93–96).

13. Josephus (*Ant.* 1.177) and Jerome (*Qu. heb. Gen.* 14:14) both contend that Yor (< Heb. *yĕʾōr*, "brook") and Dan are the two sources of "Jordan"—the river and the name. For its part, the Talmud asserts that the river is called Jordan "because it descends from Dan" (*šeyyôrēd middān*; see *b. Bek.* 55a). For a modern example of this erroneous linkage, see Z. Maʿoz, *Dan Is Bāniyās, Teldan Is Abel-Beth-Maʿacha* (Aechaeostyle Scientific Research Series 2; Qazrin: Archaestyle, 2006), 13.

14. Smick, "The Jordan of Jericho," in *Orient and Occident: Essays Presented to Cyrus H. Gordon on the Occasion of his Sixty-Fifth Birthday* (ed. H. Hoffner; AOAT 22; Kevelaer: Butzon & Bercker; Neukirchen-Vluyn: Neukirchener, 1973), 177–79.

15. A. Biran, D. Ilan, and R. Greenberg, *Dan I: A Chronicle of the Excavations, the Pottery Neolithic, the Early Bronze Age and the Middle Bronze Age Tombs* (Jerusalem: Nelson Glueck School of Biblical Archaeology, Hebrew Union College–Jewish Institute of Religion, 1996). For Area T, see 32–49.

16. A. Biran and R. Ben-Dov, *Dan II: A Chronicle of the Excavations and the Late Bronze Age "Mycenaean" Tomb* (Jerusalem: Hebrew Union College–Jewish Institute of Religion, 2002). Excavations were conducted at Area T in only four of these seasons—1993, 1994, 1998, and 1999—and were restricted to the Hellenistic and Roman levels (pp. 28–30).

published the *Dan III* volume, which covers the Late Bronze Age at the site.[17] Since 2003, excavations have continued at Tel Dan under the direction of David Ilan, whose analysis of Tel Dan in the Iron I period will be published in a forthcoming site report.

In the course of excavations, Tel Dan has been divided into seven main areas (see fig. 1): Area A, on the south of the mound, which includes the ninth-century-B.C.E. gate complex and paved area; Area B, which began as a northward continuation of Area A; Area AB, which lies between the two and includes the eighth-century-B.C.E. gate complex; Area M, north of Area B and near the center of the mound, which includes an eighth-century-B.C.E. pavement; Area T, in the northwestern corner of the mound, which includes the temple complex; Area Y, in the northeastern corner of the site, which consists of Middle Bronze Age rampart; and Area K, on the eastern side of the mound, which includes the Middle Bronze Age triple-arched gate.[18]

The focus of the present work is Area T, which the excavators at Tel Dan divided into five sections (see fig. 3): T-North, which includes a large podium (the so-called "bamah" platform[19]); T-Center, which includes the

---

17. Ben-Dov, *Dan III: Avraham Biran Excavations 1966–1999. The Late Bronze Age* (Jerusalem: Nelson Glueck School of Biblical Archaeology, Hebrew Union College–Jewish Institute of Religion, 2011).

18. See A. Biran et al., *Dan I*, Plan 1. Another area (Area H) located 80 m east of Area B was excavated for one season in 1968 and revealed Iron I–II occupation levels (ibid., 29). It also yielded a Phoenician ostracon that reads *lb'l plt* "Belonging to Ba'l-palt" (see Biran, *Biblical Dan*, 264, ill. 218; cf. the name *pltb'l* in a fourth-century-B.C.E. Phoenician text [KAI 11]).

19. This is the term that A. Biran used to describe the large square platform in Area T, and his preference for this appellation has made "bamah" quite prevalent in his publications and excavation notes and in just about every other scholarly treatment of the cultic complex at Tel Dan. But Biran's use of this term, based it seems on the work of P. Vaughan (*The Meaning of "bāmâ" in the Old Testament: A Study of Etymological, Textual and Archaeological Evidence* [SOTSMS 3; London: Cambridge University Press, 1974]), no longer reflects current opinion on this word's meaning. Contrary to Vaughan, who thought the use of *bāmâ* to denote a sanctuary in general was a late development (ibid., 25), more recent studies of the term have shown that *bāmâ* and temple were originally more synonymous than is commonly recognized (see W. Barrick, "What Do We Really Know about 'High-Places'?" *Svensk Exegetisk Årsbok* 45 [1980]: 50–57; idem, review of M. Gleis, *Die Bamah* in *JBL* 118 [1999]: 532–34; see also B. Nakhai, *Archaeology and the Religions of Canaan and Israel* [ASOR Books 7; Boston: American Schools of Oriental Research, 2001], 193). For this reason I will

altar platform; the rooms of T-West, which provided some of the area's clearest phasing; T-South, which includes the olive press installation; and finally T-East, which was the least exposed section of Area T.

In addition to these sections, two subareas were opened in Area T: first, in the southwestern corner of Area T and adjacent to the spring was Area T1, which consists primarily of the Roman fountain house but also includes some Iron Age phases; and second, in the northeastern part of Area T excavators opened Area T3, which was intended to expose more of the Middle Bronze rampart.

Before delving into the data from specific strata of Area T, however, it is necessary first to establish the area as a cultic precinct. After all, in this study I am primarily interested in what Tel Dan contributes to our understanding of Israelite religion during the Iron Age, and for this reason it will be worthwhile to review some of the data that indicate its status as a cultic center. For this task I will compare artifacts from the various sections of Area T to C. Renfrew's sixteen archaeological indicators of ritual (see table 1 below), citing parenthetically the indicator(s) to which each artifact corresponds.[20]

Many of these indicators correspond to the architecture and artifacts of Area T and support its identification as a sacred precinct. In terms of attention-focusing, we should first reiterate the importance of Tel Dan's natural features; as noted above (pp. 6–7), the site's status as a cult center is closely linked to the springs that surround the site (1). Also the monumentality of the platform in T-Center, which in Stratum II supported a large altar with stairs, marks it as a "special building set apart for sacred functions," and this separation is underscored by the temenos wall that eventually surrounds the platform (2). Besides these architectural remains, numerous artifacts suggest the performance of rituals in Area T and mark it as a site of cultic activity. For example, T-Center yielded a four-horned incense altar (3, 13); fragments of two different incense stands (3, 4, 13); and some figurine/mask fragments (14).[21] Similarly, T-West featured two

---

use the more neutral term *podium* to describe this large platform and to distinguish it from the altar platform in T-Center.

20. These definitions were taken almost verbatim from C. Renfrew and P. Bahn, *Archaeology: Theories, Methods and Practice* (3rd ed.; London: Thames & Hudson, 2000), 408–9.

21. The altar from T-Center will be discussed below (see section 2.1.2), but the incense stand and figurine fragment belong to Stratum IVA, which lies outside the

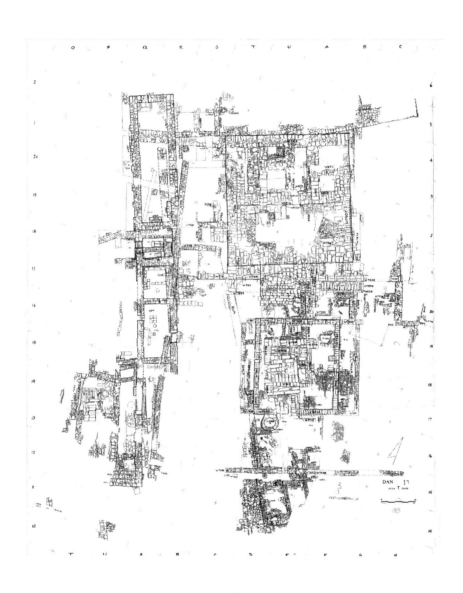

Figure 3. Plan of Area T at Tel Dan (illustration by G. Cook courtesy of the Nelson Glueck School of Biblical Archaeology, Hebrew Union College/Jewish Institute of Religion).

TABLE 1. RENFREW'S ARCHAEOLOGICAL INDICATORS OF RITUAL

Focusing of Attention	Boundary Zone between This World and the Next	Presence of the Deity	Participation and Offering
1—Ritual may take place in a spot with special, natural associations (e.g., a cave, a grove of trees, a spring, or a mountaintop).	5—Ritual may involve both conspicuous public display (and expenditure), and hidden exclusive mysteries, whose practice will be reflected in the architecture.	7—The association with a deity or deities may be reflected in the use of a cult image, or a representation of the deity in abstract form (e.g., the Christian Chi-Rho symbol).	10—Worship will involve prayer and special movements—gestures of adoration—and these may be reflected in the art or iconography of decorations or images.
2—Alternatively, ritual may take place in a special building set apart for sacred functions (e.g., a temple or church).	6—Concepts of cleanliness and pollution may be reflected in the facilities (e.g., pools or basins of water) and maintenance of sacred area.	8—The ritualistic symbols will often relate iconographically to the deities worshiped and to their associated myth. Animal symbolism (of real or mythical animals) may often be used, with particular animals relating to specific deities or powers.	11—The ritual may employ various devices for inducing religious experience (e.g., dance, music, drugs, and the infliction of pain).
3—The structure and equipment use for the ritual may employ attention-focusing devices, reflected in the architecture, special fixtures (e.g., altars, benches, hearths), and		9—The ritualistic symbols may relate to those seen also in funerary ritual and in other rites of passage.	12—The sacrifice of animals or humans may be practiced.

movable equipment (e.g., lamps, gongs and bells, ritual vessels, censers, altar cloths, and all the paraphernalia of ritual).

4—The sacred area is likely to be rich in repeated symbols (this is known as "redundancy").

13—Food and drink may be brought and possibly consumed as offerings or burned/poured away.

14—Other material objects may be brought and offered (votives). The act of offering may entail breakage and hiding or discarding.

15—Great investment of wealth may be reflected both in the equipment used and in the offerings made.

16—Great investment of wealth and resources may be reflected in the structure itself and its facilities.

incense altars (3, 4, 13), a sacrificial altar (3, 12) surrounded by iron shovels/censers (3), and a deposit of animal bones (12).[22] Finally, in T-South excavators discovered another incense stand (3), the olive press installation (3) with its related figurines (14), and a large terracotta tub (3, 6).[23] This evidence from the Iron Age, combined with the possibility that Tel Dan served as a cult site in earlier periods[24] and certainly did in later

---

scope of the present study. Both have been studied recently by D. Pakman, who shows that the figurine fragments—one with a beard and the other without—are masks, comparable to Phoenician votive masks, and that they would have been fixed to one of the incense stands ("'Mask-like' Face Reliefs on a Painted Stand from the Sacred Precinct at Tel Dan," EI 27 [2003]: 196–203 [Hebrew]). Pakman's analysis of these artifacts has effectively ruled out C. Uehlinger's unlikely proposal that the bearded fragment belonged to a statue (see "Eine anthropomorphe Kultstatue des Gottes von Dan?" BN 72 [1994]: 89–91; idem, "Anthropomorphic Cult Statuary in Iron Age Palestine and the Search for Yahweh's Cult Images," in The Image and the Book: Iconic Cults, Aniconism, and the Rise of Book Religion in Israel and the Ancient Near East [ed. K. van der Toorn; Leuven: Peeters, 1997], 116–18).

22. The faunal remains from Area T have been extensively analyzed by J. Greer, whose "Dinner at Dan: A Biblical and Archaeological Exploration of Sacred Feasting at Iron II Tel Dan" (Ph.D. diss., Pennsylvania State University, 2011) is forthcoming in Brill's Culture and History of the Ancient Near East series. His analysis and the other artifacts from T-West are discussed below, pp. 81–82.

23. These artifacts also fall outside the parameters of this study. The incense stand was found in secondary use as a drainage pipe (see Biran, Biblical Dan, 174, ills. 134–35). The olive press and tub are from Stratum IVA and therefore date before the period under examination in the present study (see Biran, Biblical Dan, 174–83). The press is especially noteworthy because of the figurine fragments found inside its receptacles (see Biran, "Two Discoveries at Tel Dan," IEJ 30 [1980]: 89–98; also Uehlinger, "Eine anthropomorphe Kultstatue des Gottes von Dan?," 91–95; idem, "Anthropomorphic Cult Statuary," 117–18). Although Biran remained adamant that the installation was not an olive press but was used for water libations (Biblical Dan, 177), L. Stager and S. Wolff have made a compelling case for its interpretation as an olive press. They also explain oil production at Area T as an example of the "temple commodities" that were prevalent in the ancient Near East ("Production and Commerce in Temple Courtyards: An Olive Press in the Sacred Precinct at Tel Dan," BASOR 243 [1981]: 95–102; see also O. Borowski, "A Note on the 'Iron Age Cult Installation' at Tel Dan," IEJ 32 [1982]: 58).

24. The best evidence for the occupation of Area T during the Bronze Age is a revetment wall that runs beneath the T-North podium and eventually joins the corner of a structure (Biran et al., Dan I, 46; see also Ben-Dov, Dan III, 154–73). While this revetment and foundation, which date to the MB IIA, are not necessarily cultic in nature, they have led D. Ilan to express the opinion that "the foundations of the Iron

Age 'high place' rest upon those of a Middle Bronze Age Migdal Temple" ("Northeast-ern Israel in the Iron Age I," 1:60 n. 20, 212 n. 81). Biran expresses the same opinion in his preliminary reports (see "Tel Dan," *IEJ* 20 [1970]: 118; idem, "Tel Dan," *BA* 37 [1974]: 41–42).

Besides this revetment wall, evidence of pre–Iron Age cultic activity at Area T is limited to a bronze figurine of a smiting goddess, which, according to Biran, was dis-covered "on the banks of the spring" several years before the first excavations at Dan in 1966 (*Biblical Dan*, 161, ill. 119, pl. 24; see also Ben-Dov, *Dan III*, 154). The bronze figurine is rather small (11 cm high) and depicts a goddess striding forward with her right arm raised in a smiting gesture and her left arm stretched forth. Although this pose might be associated with Resheph, O. Negbi has shown that the figure's long belted robe and Hathor hairstyle suggest an Egyptian female deity ("A Canaanite Bronze Figurine from Tel Dan," *IEJ* 14 [1964]: 270–71; pl. 56: A–B; see also idem, *Canaanite Gods in Metal: An Archaeological Study of Ancient Syro-Palestinian Figurines* [Tel Aviv: Tel Aviv University, Institute of Archaeology, 1976], 84–86; fig. 98 [1627]). Unfortu-nately, every other example of this type lacks a dated archaeological context, so that the example from Tel Dan can be dated only tentatively. Based on the chronology of male figurines in a smiting pose, Negbi has proposed the second half of the second millennium B.C.E. as a probable date for the figurine (*Canaanite Gods in Metal*, 86; see also H. Seeden, *The Standing Armed Figurines in the Levant* (Munich: Beck, 1980), 109, no. 1721; for a proposed later date, see P. Moorey and S. Fleming, "Problems in the Study of the Anthropomorphic Metal Statuary from Syro-Palestine before 330 B.C.," *Levant* 16 [1984]: 75).

Another Bronze Age artifact is a headless Egyptian statuette that was discovered in secondary use in a late Israelite wall (Biran, "Tel Dan, 1979, 1980," *IEJ* 31 [1981]: 105; pl. 19: B; see also Biran, *Biblical Dan*, ill. 120; and Ben-Dov, *Dan III*, 155). Accord-ing to the analysis of B. Brandl and A. Ophel, the statue "belongs to a group of statu-ettes of the personal or private category that was common in the Egyptian Middle Kingdom and in the 18th Dynasty," and based on the name Seti inscribed on the statue, they favor a New Kingdom date (cited in Biran, *Biblical Dan*, 161). A. Schul-man, however, argues for a Middle Kingdom date on stylistic grounds ("An Enigmatic Egyptian Presence at Tel Dan," in *Festschrift Jürgen von Beckrath zum 70. Geburtstag am 19. Februar 1990* [Hildesheimer Ägyptologische Beiträge 30; Hildesheim: Gersten-berg, 1990], 240 n. 8; see also J. Vandier, *Les Grandes Époques, La Statuaire*, vol. 3 of *Manuel d'Archéologie Égyptienne* [6 vols.; Paris: Picard, 1958], 233; pl. 78:6). In light of its discovery in a later wall, however, its precise date is of little consequence, since we cannot be sure that the statuette's original use during the Middle or New Kingdom took place at Tel Dan, and even if we could, the statuette is not an obvious cultic arti-fact and sheds no light on Area T's cultic status in the Bronze Age.

Another artifact that must be eliminated from this discussion is a fragment of another Egyptian statue, namely, the left arm and shoulder of a basalt block statue (Biran, *Biblical Dan*, 161). In his analysis of the fragment, which measures 17 cm high × 14.5 cm wide × 11 cm thick and is inscribed on three sides, A. Schulman has noted

periods,[25] makes a compelling case for the site's cultic status during Strata III–II.

Despite this evidence, one structure remains the subject of some debate, namely, the large podium in T-North. It is certainly true that this structure is the area's most problematic; over the centuries existing levels were cleared before new construction, such that no stratification remained atop the structure. We are left only with the podium's foundation walls, whose deep fills contained a little pottery but few complete vessels and few indications of the cultic practices associated with the building. This short-age of data has led some to argue that the podium was not a cultic build-ing at all but an administrative building or a palace.[26] No one disputes the structural similarities between the Area T podium and these other public buildings of the Iron Age IIB,[27] but method of construction is not by itself a sufficient criterion for identifying the function of a structure. Similarity in construction does not equal singularity of function, since a common

---

that such block statues first appeared in Egypt in the Middle Kingdom, but they per-sist longer after that period well into the first millennium B.C.E. Moreover, based on his examination of the writing, Schulman favors a later date "from the latter Third Intermediate Period (Dynasties 25–26, ca. 780–525 B.C.)" ("An Enigmatic Egyptian Presence at Tel Dan," 237–38). This date agrees with the fragment's archaeological context, which Biran reported to Schulman as "a 7th century B.C. Phoenician level" (ibid., 236). Thus the offerings recorded on the fragment cannot be used as evidence for Bronze Age cultic activity at Tel Dan, but it does offer a tantalizing glimpse of Area T during the Assyrian period.

25. The bilingual votive inscription mentioned above (see p. 19; fig. 2) is irrefut-able evidence that Area T functioned as a cult site in these later periods.

26. See, e.g., H. Weippert, *Palästina in vorhellenistischer Zeit* (Handbuch der Archäologie: Vorderasien 2/1; Munich: Beck, 1988), 540; M. Ottosson, *Temples and Cult Places in Palestine* (Uppsala: Universitet, 1980), 96; G. Barkay, "The Iron II–III," in *The Archaeology of Ancient Israel* (ed. A. Ben-Tor; New Haven: Yale University Press, 1992), 312; I. Sharon and A. Zarzecki-Peleg, "Podium Structures with Lateral Access: Authority Ploys in Royal Architecture in the Iron Age Levant," in *Confronting the Past: Archaeological and Historical Essays on Ancient Israel in Honor of William G. Dever* (ed. S. Gitin et al.; Winona Lake, Ind.: Eisenbrauns, 2006), 153–55. So influential is this opinion that other scholars declare flatly that the podium's function is uncertain and controversial (e.g., M. Gleis, *Die Bamah* [BZAW 251; Berlin: de Gruyter, 1997], 16; and W. Zwickel, *Der Tempelkult in Kanaan und Israel: Studien zur Kultgeschichte Palästinas von der Mittelbronzezeit bis zum Untergang Judas* (FAT 10; Tübingen: Mohr Siebeck, 1994], 255).

27. Biran, "Tel Dan," *BA* 37 (1974): 40.

construction method could be employed to diverse ends.[28] Moreover, when the podium is considered with its surrounding structures, which are almost certainly cultic in nature, and with adjacent artifacts, its cultic purpose seems more likely than not.

The following two chapters will offer portraits of Area T in Stratum III and Stratum II, respectively. For each stratum, I will describe section by section the area's spatial practice, namely, its architecture and artifacts, and I will conclude each chapter with a discussion of Area T's conceptual space, namely, the social order and priorities that are expressed in the area's spatial practice. The priorities and concerns that I will suggest are by no means the only possibilities; other interpretations of Area T have been proposed and will be discussed. Because the evidence from Area T is fragmentary, our understanding is likewise fragmentary, and all interpretations are necessarily provisional.

Strata III–II at Tel Dan date to the ninth and the eighth centuries B.C.E., a period that was chosen based on the archaeological and textual data available. Archaeologically, these centuries correspond to strata with some of Area T's best phasing, an advantage that somewhat mitigates the area's complex stratigraphy, which includes Bronze Age, Iron Age, Hellenistic, Roman, and even modern occupation levels. The stratigraphy here is complicated by two main factors: first, Hellenistic foundation trenches that cut through Iron Age structures and disrupted floor levels; and second, the tendency, not uncommon in long-standing cultic centers, to clear and reuse existing floors and structures rather than fill them in. These complications make all the more important two stratigraphic anchors for the Iron Age levels at Area T: first, the travertine "yellow floor," which has been dated to the ninth century B.C.E., and second, a destruction layer that has been attributed to the western campaigns of Tiglath-pileser III in the eighth century B.C.E. The present study is an analysis of the phases between these two archaeological parameters, but even with this relatively controlled data set, the stratigraphy remains complicated. As already

---

28. In his attempt to distinguish an "Omride architecture," I. Finkelstein identified several "architectural concepts"—one being the podium—that were common to northern sites, but importantly he noted that "in each case, these elements, or some of them, were adjusted to the special features/characteristics of the site" ("Omride Architecture," *ZDPV* 116 [2000]: 122). See also G. Lehmann and A. Killebrew, "Palace 6000 at Megiddo in Context: Iron Age Central Hall Tetra-Partite Residencies and the *Bīt-Hilāni* Building Tradition in the Levant," *BASOR* 359 (2010): 13–33.

noted, I have relied heavily on the expertise, unpublished reports, and field notes of the Tel Dan staff, especially Ross Voss, who has excavated at Area T in Tel Dan since 1974 and will publish its Iron Age stratigraphy in a forthcoming final report. The phasing presented here reflects the staff's most recent opinion at the time of my study, but as Yifat Thareani's analysis of the pottery moves toward completion, this assessment will be subject to refinement and change.[29]

---

29. See already J. Greer's tentative revision of Iron Age stratigraphy, which includes two phases for Stratum III ("Dinner at Dan," 40).

2

Area T, Stratum III:
A Ninth-Century b.c.e. Cult Site

2.1 Spatial Practice in Stratum III

Stratum III at Tel Dan refers to the architecture and material remains associated with the so-called yellow floor, which was made of crushed yellow travertine and exposed in several sections of Area T.[1] In this way it became a common denominator; sections of exposed yellow floor could be linked together to provide a coherent snapshot of Area T after it was installed. The pottery sealed beneath the floor dates to the end of the tenth century b.c.e. and beginning of the ninth century b.c.e. and provides a *terminus post quem* for the yellow floor.[2] Then working back from the

---

1. See A. Biran, *Biblical Dan* (Jerusalem: Israel Exploration Society/Hebrew Union College–Jewish Institute of Religion, 1994), 184; also Biran et al., *Dan I*, 32, 40, 47. Yellow travertine is prevalent in the north Hula Valley, where Dan is situated (see A. Heimann and E. Sass, "Travertines in the Northern Hula Valley, Israel," *Sedimentology* 36 [1989]: 95–108). Thus the stones for the Stratum III buildings would have been quarried locally and dressed on-site. The travertine chips that resulted from this process then became the chief component of the new "yellow" floor.

2. See Biran, "The Temenos at Dan," *EI* 16 (1982): 33–41, figs. 24–27 (Hebrew). These plates show some of the pottery that belong to Stratum IVA at Area T. Based on parallels with Hazor X–IX, Megiddo VA–IVB and Ta'anach IIb, this pottery should be dated to the Iron IIA (see Z. Herzog and L. Singer-Avitz, "Sub-Dividing the Iron Age IIA in Northern Israel: A Suggested Solution to the Chronological Debate," *TA* 33 [2006]: 163–95). Especially significant for our study is the pottery from loci 725, 2093, and 2094, which were sealed beneath the yellow floor (Biran, "Temenos at Dan," figs. 24: 6–8; 26: 1–4; and 27: 1–2, 6) and provide our best evidence for its date.

Of course, the yellow floor is not without its problems. Most importantly, very little material was found that could be considered contemporaneous with the floor. Because it was reused in subsequent centuries as late as the Hellenistic period, the pot-

eighth-century-B.C.E. destruction level of Stratum II as a *terminus ante quem*, it seems likely that the two intervening phases, which are associated with the yellow floor, date to the ninth century B.C.E. Until the final report on the Iron Age pottery and stratigraphy is able to confirm or correct this dating, I will proceed on the assumption that the Stratum III yellow floor dates to the ninth century B.C.E. Therefore, the following sections represent the spatial practice of Area T during this century: the architecture and artifacts of the sacred precinct as well as some tentative suggestions on some of the cultic practices that may be associated with them.

2.1.1. T-NORTH

T-North contains perhaps the best-known structure of Area T, namely, the monumental square podium. I have already noted the podium's poor state of preservation, but valuable information may still be gathered from the surviving foundation walls.

Most importantly, we know that in Stratum III the structure underwent a major renovation that included the new use of ashlar masonry.[3]

---

tery found above the floor is usually fill containing Early Bronze, Middle Bronze, Iron, and Hellenistic sherds (cf. L.2352). The problem posed by this paucity of contemporary pottery has recently been amplified by E. Arie's attempt to eliminate Stratum III altogether in favor of a single stratum (Stratum III–II) that dates to the middle of the eighth century B.C.E. ("Reconsidering the Iron Age II Strata at Tel Dan: Archaeological and Historical Implications," *TA* 35 [2008]: 6–64). He also redates Stratum IVA, attributing it to the invasion of Hazael, and posits an occupation gap at Tel Dan from the mid-tenth to the mid-ninth centuries B.C.E. (ibid., 32–34).

His conclusion is based on the apparent absence of Stratum III pottery and apparent similarities between pottery from Stratum IVA and II, but both arguments are flawed because they are based *only* on the pottery that has been published. Arie himself acknowledges this problem (ibid., 7) but does not reckon with how severely it limits his reconstruction. The pottery from Stratum III is not absent; most of it simply has not yet been published. Moreover, D. Ilan has suggested that the pottery published in Biran's 1982 article ("Temenos at Dan") as "Stratum IV" probably spans Strata IVA–III (personal communication). (This would explain why some of the pottery resembles Stratum II). Ultimately, Tel Dan's Iron II stratigraphy and chronology must depend on the analysis and publication of its complete corpus by Y. Thareani. Until then, any revision of Biran's chronology, such as Arie's argument for an occupation gap in the early ninth century B.C.E. or the compression of Strata III and II, is far from conclusive.

3. Throughout his publications, Biran refers to this ashlar podium as "Bamah B" (see Biran, *Biblical Dan*, 184–87; idem, "Temenos at Dan," 20–25; Biran et al., *Dan I*,

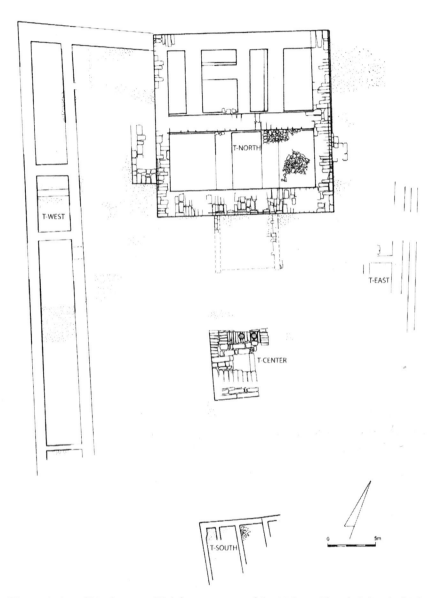

Figure 4. Area T in Stratum III (plan courtesy of the Nelson Glueck School of Biblical Archaeology, Hebrew Union College/Jewish Institute of Religion).

39–41, fig. 1.35), a designation I have abandoned for reasons already stated (see p. 21 n. 19). An additional problem with this designation is the problem of the so-called Bamah A, which likely was not a platform at all but was built as a foundation to support the new Stratum III construction.

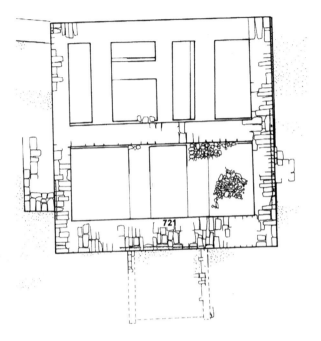

Figure 5. T-North in Stratum III (plan courtesy of the Nelson Glueck School of Biblical Archaeology, Hebrew Union College/Jewish Institute of Religion).

Ashlar blocks were used in the southern wall (W.721) and the eastern and western walls as far as their northern corners, and all three walls were faced with bossed stones.[4] In the northwestern corner the lowest course of the bossed ashlars met the yellow floor (L.2352) and thus confirmed that their installation is contemporary with the floor. In fact, the travertine debris that makes up the floor most likely came from fragments that were chipped away when the ashlar stones were dressed on-site.[5]

---

4. Because the ashlar blocks were reused in later periods, it is impossible to know how high the bossed stones of the façade would have risen, but we can at least note that the podium's eastern and western walls have survived with one more course than the southern wall, so that we can reconstruct another course of ashlars on the façade, if not more. A comparison of this reconstructed course with the present surface of the podium reminds us again how much of the interior is lost and underscores the near complete absence of floors.

5. The same process occurred in T-Center when the ashlar temenos wall was built in Stratum II (see L.2319).

This new stonework was supported by an enormous foundation of rough ashlar blocks (W.7702) that were laid above an earlier basalt foundation. According to Biran's interpretation the rectangular platform (ca. 18 × 7 m) formed by these large blocks constituted the earliest structure in T-North, which he called "Bamah A" and assigned to Stratum IVA.[6] However, the results of a probe (L.9159) dug in the southern half of the platform suggest otherwise. According to this probe, the earliest Iron Age cultic platform was an 18-m² basalt structure, and W.7702 was installed later in Stratum III as a foundation for the new ashlar construction, especially the bossed southern wall W.721 (see fig. 6).[7] This reassessment demonstrates a remarkable continuity between the original basalt platform and the Stratum III podium: both were about 18 m². Furthermore, a ninth-century-B.C.E. date for W.7702 is consistent with the introduction of ashlar masonry elsewhere at Tel Dan[8] and at other northern sites, where it is one of the principal characteristics of Omride architecture.[9]

Unfortunately, it is impossible to know if the T-North podium supported any sort of superstructure. In an early account of Area T, Biran described the building as an "open-air acropolis," and in his accompanying isometric reconstruction, he depicted a simple platform with no superstructure.[10] This depiction has proven influential and has been reprinted as recently as 2003,[11] but this reconstruction must be reconsidered in light

---

6. See Biran, *Biblical Dan*, 165–85, ills. 143–44; Biran et al., *Dan I*, fig. 1.34.

7. The probe sought to determine the relationship between W.7702 and interior wall 8234, but progress was interrupted by a massive basalt construction, namely, W.8758. This basalt wall runs east-west behind the ashlar facing of W.721 and is most likely the terminus of the platform's interior north-south walls. This information has led R. Voss to conclude that the earliest cultic building in T-North was a basalt structure, which measured ca. 18 m square and featured W.8758 as its southern wall. This interpretation of the probe is described in his unpublished report titled "The High Place, March 1988" (p. 4). I am grateful to Mr. Voss for sharing this report with me.

8. For a similar reassessment of the ashlar platform in T-Center, see pp. 38–39.

9. See I. Finkelstein, "Omride Architecture," *ZDPV* 116 (2000): 122.

10. Biran, "Dan, Tel," *EAEHL* 1:319, 321; the same drawing appears in J. Laughlin, "The Remarkable Discoveries at Tel Dan," *BAR* 7.5 (1981): 30. However, later isometric drawings included a superstructure (Biran, *Biblical Dan*, ills. 149, 163).

11. W. Dever, "Religion and Cult in the Levant: The Archaeological Data," in *Near Eastern Archaeology: A Reader* (ed. S. Richard; Winona Lake, Ind.: Eisenbrauns, 2003), 384 fig. 97. In this same essay, Dever remarks that Dan consisted of "a monumental outdoor stepped stone altar (undoubtedly the biblical 'High Place') and an adjacent multiroomed structure (perhaps the biblical *liškāh*)" (p. 388). Both statements are

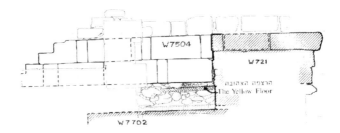

Figure 6. Section (looking west) of W.7702 and W.721 (section courtesy of the Nelson Glueck School of Biblical Archaeology, Hebrew Union College/Jewish Institute of Religion).

of compelling evidence that the extant platform did support a superstructure. For one thing, the sheer size of the foundation walls (1.9 m) exceeds the thickness needed to reinforce a fill. For another, the plan of these interior walls provides some clues for a superstructure. Although foundation walls alone cannot be used to reconstruct a building, it is significant that the wall, which divided the platform lengthwise (W.8223), was rebuilt in Stratum III with ashlar blocks (new wall 8110). If this wall's *only* function was to reinforce the foundation fill, there would be no reason to rebuild at all, let alone with massive ashlars.

At the same time that this dividing wall was rebuilt, the foundation walls in the southern half of the platform's interior (8234 and 8232) were covered over, but the northern walls (8107, 8213, 8217, 8205) were rebuilt. This selective rebuilding suggests that the southern half of the podium perhaps was used as an open courtyard. Unfortunately, no floors survived that might confirm or disprove this possibility; in fact, only one floor was found inside the podium at all, and it was dated to the seventh century B.C.E. based on comparison of its blue plaster with similar floors from the same time.[12] It lay well below even the surviving courses of the ashlar wall and was possibly a basement floor. This meager floor tells us very little about the occupation of the podium but still deserves mention since it was

---

problematic: the first because he seems to be referring to the podium, which has never been identified as an altar; and the second, because Biran in almost every instance used the term *liškâ* to describe the northernmost room in T-West, not the entire series of rooms.

12. See L.9162.

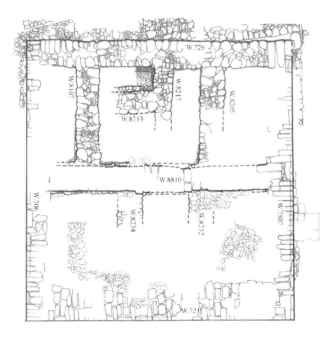

Figure 7. Interior walls of the podium (plan courtesy of the Nelson Glueck School of Biblical Archaeology, Hebrew Union College/Jewish Institute of Religion).

found south of the interior ashlar wall and shows that at least in the last part of the Iron II period this space was actively occupied.

Although we cannot rule out other reconstructions, such as the "open-air acropolis," the evidence presented here suggests that the front half of the podium was an open courtyard, while its back half would have supported a superstructure.[13] Furthermore, it seems likely, though not certain, that this superstructure would have followed the plan of the interior foundation walls, with the new east-west ashlar wall supporting a façade behind which was a series of rooms. As for ascending the podium in Stratum III, access seems to have been available on the western wall and also on the eastern wall,[14] and it cannot be ruled out that there was some sort of

---

13. See Z. Herzog, *Archaeology of the City: Urban Planning in Ancient Israel and Its Social Implications* (Tel Aviv: Emery and Claire Yass Archaeology Press, 1997), 222.

14. Evidence for access points consists of two stone platforms, one on each side of the podium measuring 1.5 × 2.5 m and both abutting the yellow floor (see L.2665, 2666, 2667, 2668; also Biran, *Biblical Dan*, 189). This interpretation is followed by I.

approach, perhaps a ramp, on the southern wall, which was removed when the Stratum II staircase was built.[15]

2.1.2. T-CENTER.

Like T-North, this section of Area T underwent substantial changes in Stratum III.[16] Our dating for these changes is based on the survival of several patches of the yellow travertine floor that were exposed on the northern, western, and southeastern sides of the central platform[17] and that allow us to date certain constructions in T-Center. In particular, Stratum III witnessed the addition of a two-layer ashlar platform, which was set atop an earlier platform of basalt boulders.[18] Biran interpreted the ashlar platform as a parallel construction to the massive W.7702 in T-North and therefore assigned it also to Stratum IVA.[19] But just as W.7702 more likely belongs to Stratum III, so there is likewise strong evidence for assigning the ashlar platform in T-Center to Stratum III.[20] If this is the case, then T-North and T-Center indeed feature parallel constructions but in different periods from those Biran had proposed: both sections featured square

---

Sharon and A. Zarzecki-Peleg, who take the approach as support for their typology of lateral-access podiums ("Podium Structures with Lateral Access: Authority Ploys in Royal Architecture in the Iron Age Levant," in *Confronting the Past: Archaeological and Historical Essays on Ancient Israel in Honor of William G. Dever* [ed. S. Gitin et al.; Winona Lake, Ind.: Eisenbrauns, 2006], 53 n. 30), and it is quite possible, even probable. Yet without further evidence, conclusions must remain tentative.

15. For a description of this staircase, see pp. 68–70.

16. One architectural addition that should not be assigned to Stratum III is the temenos wall that will eventually surround the T-Center altar platform in Stratum II. In an early article, Biran misattributed this wall to Stratum III ("Temenos at Dan," 24; cf. fig. 4), but later publications rightly included the temenos wall with Stratum II (Biran, *Biblical Dan*, 203, ill. 163; Biran et al., *Dan I*, fig. 1.36). Unfortunately, Z. Zevit resurrected the mistake by reproducing the erroneous Stratum III plan from Biran's 1982 article instead of the corrected plan of later publications (*The Religions of Ancient Israel: A Synthesis of Parallactic Approaches* [London: Continuum, 2001], fig. 3.31).

17. See loci 2086, 2156, 2324, 2334, and 2500.

18. See L.2091.

19. See Biran, *Biblical Dan*, 168, 173, and ills. 143–44; Biran et al., *Dan I*, fig. 1.34.

20. According to R. Voss's most recent stratigraphic analysis, there are two walls associated with the earlier basalt platform (W.7807 and W.7615) that have been cut by the introduction of the new ashlar blocks.

basalt platforms in Stratum IVA over which ashlar platforms were built in Stratum III.

The bottom layer of the T-Center platform measures 5 × 5.6 m and consists of large travertine slabs. Above it is a layer of blocks that extends the platform to the north and the east. Because many of the blocks were robbed in antiquity, the platform's exact dimensions have not been determined, but it seems likely that its northern edge is represented by W.7593, which is a foundation course of headers that forms a corner with a channel (W.7602A) found beneath eastern W.7613.[21] The most interesting aspect of this northern wall 7593 is the two plastered circles set atop it. They are each 50 cm in diameter and set 1 m apart and are aligned with the large podium in T-North. Biran noted their symmetry by pointing out that the midpoint between the circles corresponds to the midpoint of the podium's

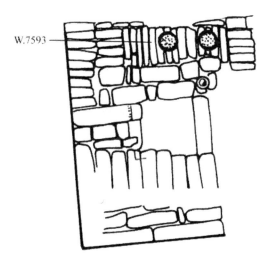

Figure 8: T-Center platform in Stratum III (plan provided courtesy of the Nelson Glueck School of Biblical Archaeology, Hebrew Union College/Jewish Institute of Religion).

21. This is the analysis of R. Voss in his unpublished "High Place Report, March 1988" (p. 25). The only alternative for the platform's northern wall is W.7591, but a probe beneath this wall (L.9040) yielded pottery that dated it and the eastern wall 7613 after Stratum III. Also significant is the fact that W.7593 and W.7591 were built on different lines, suggesting different building phases.

southern face.²² These circles became all the more intriguing when during the 1980 season a basalt column base measuring 50 cm in diameter was found in secondary use (see fig. 9).²³ Its patterned register is reminiscent of the ornate column bases discovered at Tell Tayinat in southeastern Turkey and suggests an Iron II date for the Tel Dan base.²⁴ Biran's suggestion that this base was originally located in one of the platform's plastered circles is a logical and attractive interpretation.

The plaster was probably not used as a mortar for the bases, since a column usually rests on a rock slab that prevents it from sinking.²⁵ With two courses of travertine blocks beneath them, the columns of the T-Center platform were in no danger of sinking.²⁶ More likely, the plaster simply marked the placement of the columns,²⁷ which may not have always stood in T-Center but were erected on certain occasions.²⁸ According to this

<hr />

22. Biran, *Biblical Dan*, 191; for a photograph of one of the plastered circles, see ibid., ill. 150.

23. See Biran et al., *Dan I*, 44, fig. 1.43a.

24. See R. Haines, *Excavations in the Plain of Antioch II: The Structural Remains of the Later Phases* (OIP 95; Chicago: University of Chicago Press, 1971), 37–66. Of the numerous column bases that were found at this site, eight featured a double register of a pattern similar to that of the Area T base. In five of these, the registers and the torus of each were undecorated (ibid., pls. 68c–d; 89a; 116b; 117a), while in three the upper register was decorated and the torus of each featured a guilloche (ibid., pls. 75a–b; 116a; see also C. McEwan, "The Syrian Expedition of the Oriental Institute of the University of Chicago," *AJA* 41 [1937]: 9–13; figs. 4, 8). Also noteworthy is the throne fragment that features this architectural element in relief and that interestingly shows it as a *capital* rather than a base (Haines, *Excavations in the Plain of Antioch II*, 41; pl. 118; McEwan, "Syrian Expedition of the Oriental Institute," fig. 12); perhaps the Tel Dan example is in fact a capital. Further examples of the decorated type were found at Zinjirli (see G. Jacoby, "Das Gebäude K," in *Ausgrabungen in Sendschirli IV* [Mittheilungen aus den orientalischen Sammlungen 14; Berlin: Reimer, 1911], 293–94, abb. 201–2). The only datable column bases from Tell Tayinat were the three decorated ones, which belong to the site's Second Building Period at the beginning of the eighth century B.C.E. (see Haines, *Excavations in the Plain of Antioch II*, 64–66).

25. See G. R. H. Wright, *Ancient Building in South Syria and Palestine* (2 vols.; Leiden: Brill, 1985), 1:369–73, 423–34; cf. the pillars in the South Room of T-West, discussed below (p. 87).

26. It is possible that the plaster was used to level the surface beneath the pillars, which would have been uneven from the roughly hewn blocks.

27. Biran et al., *Dan I*, 40; cf. Biran, "Tel Dan, 1975," *IEJ* 26 (1976): 55.

28. See 2 Kgs 10:25–27, which describes how Jehu's officers, once inside the

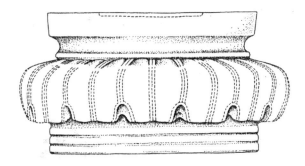

Figure 9. Column base from Area T at Tel Dan (drawing courtesy of the Nelson Glueck School of Biblical Archaeology, Hebrew Union College/Jewish Institute of Religion).

understanding, the plaster was left so that the columns could be set up each time in the same location and with the same alignment.[29]

Even if we accept this interpretation, the function of the ashlar platform in T-Center remains uncertain. Because in the next stratum it will support a sacrificial altar (see p. 72), it is natural to suppose that the platform served a similar purpose in Stratum III, but evidence supporting this assumption is rather meager. The artifact most suggestive of a cultic purpose is a four-horned incense altar that was found beside the platform and showed substantial burn marks. Its prominent horns and block form suggest a ninth-century-B.C.E. date,[30] which would correspond with Stratum III. However, the date is not certain, nor is the altar's association

---

temple of Baal, retrieved the temple's *maṣṣēbôt* from its inner room (reading *dĕbîr* with LXX[L] [Gr. *tou naou*] instead of MT's *'îr*), where it was stored while it was not in use.

29. Here we should also remember storerooms, such as Locus 2081 at Megiddo, which was full of cultic equipment being stored for later usage (see D. Ussishkin, "Schumacher's Shrine in Building 338 at Megiddo," *IEJ* 39 [1989]: 170–72; O. Negbi, "Israelite Cult Elements in Secular Contexts of the 10th Century B.C.E.," in *Biblical Archaeology Today, 1990: Proceedings of the Second International Congress on Biblical Archaeology, Jerusalem, June–July 1990* [ed. A. Biran and J. Aviram; Jerusalem: Israel Exploration Society, 1993], 221–30).

30. Its precise measurements are 39 × 39.5 × 40.5 × 41 cm, and its total height is 35 cm with its horns accounting for the top 3 cm. The dish of the altar slopes up 3.5 cm. For the dating of the altar, see the typology established by S. Gitin ("Incense Altars from Ekron, Israel and Judah: Context and Typology," *EI* 20 [1989]: 61*; cf. A. Biran, "An Israelite Horned Altar at Dan," *BA* 37 [1974]: 106–7).

with the platform. Since it was found in secondary usage and because an incense altar is a moveable piece of cultic equipment, the altar's findspot is not necessarily its original location, and its primary context is uncertain.[31]

In addition to this altar, T-Center in Stratum III included several deposits of bone and ash that were found near the platform.[32] Five deposits, dating from the late tenth century B.C.E. to the early eighth century B.C.E., have been analyzed recently by Jonathan Greer as part of his larger study of Area T's faunal remains.[33] Here I will only cite a few of Greer's analyses and recommend his forthcoming book, which includes a synthetic discussion of cultic feasts at Tel Dan and in biblical depictions. In general, the bones from Tel Dan have yielded "numerous examples of bones of sheep, goat, and cattle from Area T that bore marks associated with slaughter, processing, and consumption activities."[34] At T-Center, in particular, sheep and goats represent 82 percent of the identified bones, while large cattle represent 17 percent (with "Other" species accounting for the remaining 1 percent).[35] Some of Greer's most intriguing insights are the contrasts he has drawn between the bones from T-Center to two bone deposits found in T-West. Their comparison shows that T-Center had a higher percentage of cattle bones than was found at T-West and also a higher percentage of meat-bearing long bones.[36] From this evidence Greer concludes T-Center was the site of cultic feasting: "people enjoyed meat-based meals in a communal setting in the courtyard area, and deposited the remains from these events close to the large center altar structure. ... The feasts would have been charged with religious significance imparted from their enactment within the sanctuary."[37] (The faunal evidence from

---

31. See Biran, *Biblical Dan*, 203.

32. Although it was suggested in early reports that the center of the platform also served as a pit (see A. Biran, "Tel Dan, 1976," *IEJ* 26 [1976]: 204), excavators later concluded that the depression was the result of slabs that had been robbed in antiquity (see Biran et al., *Dan I*, 40).

33. J. Greer, "Dinner at Dan: A Biblical and Archaeological Exploration of Sacred Feasting at Iron II Tel Dan." This work is forthcoming in Brill's Culture and History of the Ancient Near East series, though all citations here refer to Greer's unpublished dissertation.

34. Ibid., 41.

35. Ibid., 53–54.

36. Ibid., 54, 62.

37. Ibid., 78–79.

T-West will be discussed further in §3.1.3.4 below, and I will also revisit Greer's work in my discussion of Stratum III's conceptual space.)

There is one, final, noteworthy artifact that was found beside the southernmost pit, namely, the torso of a male figurine, made of faience and holding a lotus flower in front of his chest (see fig. 10).[38] H. Weippert regards the piece as part of the influx of Egyptian faience during the ninth century B.C.E., which led to local manufacture soon thereafter.[39] A close parallel was found at Kition, which is slightly smaller and later (ca. 600–450 B.C.E.) but also better preserved.[40] The figurine is suggestive; perhaps, like its Kition parallel,[41] the Dan figurine was a votive offering. We cannot

Figure 10. Male torso holding lotus flower (photos courtesy of the Nelson Glueck School of Biblical Archaeology, Hebrew Union College/Jewish Institute of Religion).

---

38. The figurine measures 6.2 cm high, 5.2 cm wide (max), and 3 cm thick; see A. Biran, "Two Discoveries at Tel Dan," *IEJ* 30 [1980]: 97, fig. 6; idem, *Biblical Dan*, pl. 29; ill. 142; idem, "Temenos at Dan," 29–30, fig. 18; Uehlinger, "Eine anthropomorphe Kultstatue des Gottes von Dan?," 93–94, abb. 3. Uehlinger thinks the figurine is holding a scepter, but similar figurines from Cyprus indicate that it is probably a lotus flower (see M. Yon, *Salamine de Chypre V: Un depôt de sculptures archaïques* [Paris: Boccard, 1974], 107–13). The lotus flower is an artistic motif that originated in ancient Egypt and is attested in the Levant as early as the Middle Bronze Age; it is a symbol of regeneration and fertility (see S. Schroer, *In Israel gab es Bilder: Nachrichten von darstellender Kunst im Alten Testament* [OBO 74; Fribourg: Universitätsverlag; Göttingen: Vandenhoeck & Ruprecht, 1987], 55–57).

39. Weippert, *Palästina in vorhellenistischer Zeit*, 648–49.

40. See G. Clerc et al., *Fouilles de Kition II: Objets égyptiens et égyptisants* (Nicosia: Department of Antiquities, Cyprus, 1976), 139, pls. 12–13; V. Karageorghis, "Chronique des fouilles et découvertes archéologiques à Chypre en 1966," *Bulletin de Correspondance Hellénique* 91 (1967): 323–24, fig. 119.

41. See Clerc et al., *Fouilles de Kition II*, 118; Karageorghis, "Chronique des fouilles," 324.

be sure, however, and with its primary context unclear, we cannot know how, if at all, it was associated with the platform.

2.1.3. T-West

T-West in Stratum III consisted of a series of rooms running north to south (see fig. 11). Before looking at each room, a few remarks are in order about the section in general. First, T-West experienced much less reuse in later periods than has been observed in T-Center and T-North. Its worst intrusion came from the Hellenistic temenos wall (W.705), whose foundation trench cut through earlier walls and floors, but this wall also left most of T-West *outside* the temenos and thus relatively undisturbed during the Hellenistic period and subsequent occupations of the area. Moreover, because T-West sits at a slightly lower elevation than the rest of Area T, the Hellenistic builders found it easier simply to cover over previous phases than to clear them; thus many more were left intact.

Second, the reuse of certain wall lines in T-West over multiple periods demonstrates substantial architectural continuity in the section. For example, basalt wall 8511 (1.85 m thick) represented the northern end of T-West from the tenth through the eighth century B.C.E. This basalt foundation supported a mud-brick wall,[42] which extended eastward from T-West up to the northwestern corner of the podium, thus providing an important link between the two sections.[43] Running southward from W.8511 were two parallel walls made of basalt and dolomite fieldstones. These 1.1-m-thick walls provided the western and eastern boundaries for the rooms of T-West and gave the rooms a standard width of 3.5 m in Stratum III. Even when a new eastern wall was built during Stratum II, the rooms' width remained uniform.

---

42. Some of its mud bricks were preserved in L.2840.

43. Unfortunately, the precise relationship between W.8511 and the T-North podium cannot be established. Because the wall was cut by the foundation of the Stratum III ashlar wall 706, it stops just short of the platform's corner. It is unclear whether this gap was used as a passageway or would have been filled in with mud brick. R. Voss favors the latter, pointing out that if it was a passageway, we would expect the yellow floor to have continued through the gap. (Patches of the yellow floor were found with both W.8511 and W.706). Its absence—indeed, the lack of any kind of threshold—should be taken as evidence that the gap was most likely filled in.

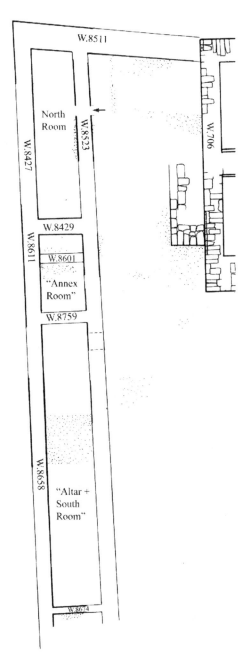

Figure 11. T-West in Stratum III (plan courtesy of the Nelson Glueck School of Biblical Archaeology, Hebrew Union College/Jewish Institute of Religion).

In what follows I will describe each room from north to south, using names that were initially created for the rooms as they were found in Stratum II. In most cases these designations pose no problem, since, as noted above, several wall lines were reused, but in cases where a significant redivision of rooms has occurred between Stratum III and Stratum II, I will clarify these changes.

2.1.3.1. The North Room[44]

Besides wall 8511 discussed above, this room was bound on the west by W.8427 (= W.8611) and on the east by W.8523. The room's southern wall was W.8429, a partition wall that remained in use until the Assyrian period. These walls resulted in a space that measures 13 m long and 3.5 m wide. Patches of the yellow travertine floor were traced to the eastern face of W.8523 and also to its western face,[45] and they allow us to date this phase of the North Room to Stratum III. These patches on either side of W.8523 likely were parts of a continuous pavement that extended from T-North into the rooms of T-West, and for this reason we should probably imagine that the North Room's main entrance passed through its eastern wall. Such a location would best facilitate the expansion of the yellow floor, and it also comports with the eastern entrance found in subsequent periods. Still the possibility of a second entrance through the northern wall cannot be ruled

---

44. This is the room that Biran called the *liškâ*, or "chamber" (A. Biran, "Tel Dan, 1984," *IEJ* 35 [1985]: 188–89; idem, "The Dancer from Dan, the Empty Tomb and the Altar Room," *IEJ* 36 (1986): 179 n. 17; idem, *Biblical Dan*, 212). In later articles, however, especially in popular journals, the term was applied to other rooms as well (e.g., H. Shanks, "Avraham Biran—Twenty Years of Digging at Tel Dan," *BAR* 13.4 [July/Aug 1987]: 18–20; Biran, "Sacred Spaces: Of Standing Stones, High Places and Cult Objects at Tel Dan," *BAR* 24.5 [1998]: 40–41). This word's use in the Hebrew Bible suggests that such chambers could be used for multiple purposes. Biran cites several illustrative examples, not all of equal weight (*Biblical Dan*, 212–13). The most interesting are 1 Sam 9:22–25 and Jer 35:4, which depict the *liškâ* as a place where food and wine were consumed. Less instructive are 2 Chr 31:11, which has the advantage of linking the term with the Jerusalem temple but comes from a late source and depicts *liškôt* simply as storerooms for the overflow of cultic contributions, and Neh 13:9, another late text that again depicts the chambers as cultic storerooms. Given its variety of functions in the biblical evidence, the term *liškâ* seems to complicate more than it clarifies, and so I have chosen to refer to the room simply as the North Room.

45. See loci 9036 and 9037. In fact, the cards for these loci note that the patches met mud-brick debris that was left over from W.8523's superstructure.

out, since in the seventh century B.C.E. an enlarged North Room features an ashlar ramp through its northern wall (W.8418). If a similar entrance existed in Stratum III, however, it would have been much more modest; the lack of any sort of threshold associated with W.8511 indicates that such an entrance would have been a simple wooden door or the like set on top of the basalt foundation wall.

Immediately south of the North Room and sharing with it W.8429 is a small space (1.5 m long) where a patch of yellow travertine floor was traced to its western wall (W.8611), thus confirming the space's usage in Stratum III. No artifacts were found in this space, and so its function is unknown.

2.1.3.2. The "Annex Room"

This section discusses the room between east-west walls 8601 and 8759, which in Stratum II will constitute the "Annex Room."[46] Because this space underwent major renovations in later periods, little evidence from Stratum III has survived. Indeed, its southern wall (W.8759) was removed at the end of Stratum II and could only be inferred from section drawings and comparison of fills.[47] These walls give us the room's size (4.5 m × 3.5 m), and a basalt cobblestone floor (L.2849), which is associated with north-south W.8523,[48] offers a small glimpse of this room in Stratum III. But with this limited exposure we cannot know how far the basalt floor extended, and with so few finds we know even less about the function of the room in this period.

2.1.3.3. The "ImmadiYaw Room"

Although this room is not situated in the series of rooms—it is located to the west of the Annex Room, sharing with it W.8611—it is considered

---

46. As will be discussed below, this name refers to the fact that in Stratum II the room was connected to the Altar Room to its south. However, because there is no evidence in Stratum III that the Annex Room was annexed to another room, I have put this name and others in quotes.

47. I would like to thank G. Cook of the Hebrew Union College for this information and explanation.

48. According to the locus card for L.2849, this basalt floor was covered with occupational debris that included pottery dating to the ninth century B.C.E. This debris, in turn, was sealed with a clay floor, which was covered in the black ash that represents the eighth-century-B.C.E. destruction layer (cf. L.2832).

part of T-West. Its name comes from the stamped jar handle that was found in a Stratum II phase of this room and will be discussed in the next section. For now we can note that in Stratum III this room featured a 10-cm-thick floor made of dolomite pebbles. In addition to pottery, the occupational debris above this floor included gray ash and bones. East-west walls 8615 and 8610 were built in this period; they rested on top of the pebble floor and survived until the room's destruction at the end of the eighth century B.C.E.

2.1.3.4. The "Altar + South Room"

As is clear from the heading of this section, the last room of Stratum III T-West comprises a space that in the next stratum will be divided into two rooms. The southern wall of the room (W.8674[49]) was located almost 22 m south of the room's northern wall W.8759, making it by far the largest room in Stratum III T-West. The yellow travertine floor was found in this room, and parts of it were connected to the room's western wall (W.8658).[50] Because this floor will be reused in the next stratum, none of the materials associated with it can definitively be assigned to Stratum III. Like the other rooms of T-West, our knowledge of the "Altar + South Room" in this period is rather limited.

This is also the case for the space west of the Altar + South Room. Between the room and the later Roman fountain house, excavators exposed some walls and floors with pottery dating to the ninth century B.C.E. (see L.9094). Among this pottery, there was even an incense burner, which suggests that this space was integrated into the cultic activity of Area T.

A final point to mention about T-West in Stratum III is that it yielded a substantial number of animal bones, which have been studied by P. Wapnish and B. Hesse and, more recently, by J. Greer.[51] The faunal remains from T-West consist of two bone deposits, one dating to the late ninth/early eighth century B.C.E. and the other dating to the mid-eighth

---

49. Originally this wall was numbered W.8662 (see the locus card for L.9089), but later this number was reassigned to a wall in Area T, and the Stratum III partition wall received a new number—W.8674.

50. See L.9022, L.9023, L.9087.

51. See Greer, "Dinner at Dan"; and P. Wapnish and B. Hesse, "Faunal Remains from Tel Dan: Perspectives on Animals Production at a Village, Urban and Ritual Center," *Archaeozoologica* 4.2 (1991): 9–86.

century B.C.E. Because the evidence for sacrificial activity in T-West is based especially on the latter group, I will save our full discussion of the faunal remains for the next chapter on Stratum II at Tel Dan (see below, pp. 81–82). But here I will note that, some differences between the two deposits notwithstanding, the faunal evidence suggests that the slaughter, processing, and consumption of animals took place in T-West in both Strata III and II.

2.1.4. T-SOUTH

In the phases prior to Stratum III this section consisted of a complex of rooms that flanked a street leading north toward the podium in T-North (see L.2504). This pre-Stratum III phase is best known for the olive oil installation and the so-called Pool Room, which both lay on the eastern side of this street and shared a wall.[52] In Stratum III, however, both rooms were sealed over with plaster floors, which yielded no clues about their new functions. The east-west wall between the rooms (W.7809) remained in use, as did the street to their west (see L.2336), but the renovations

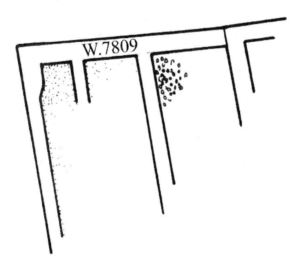

Figure 12. T-South in Stratum III (plan provided courtesy of the Nelson Glueck School of Biblical Archaeology, Hebrew Union College/Jewish Institute of Religion).

---

52. For more on the "Pool Room" and the olive oil installations, see above, p. 7 n. 16 and p. 26 n. 23, respectively.

included the division of the rooms into three spaces divided by two new partition walls. The resulting three rooms were approximately the same size, but they also yielded very little material remains, due to the extensive intrusions of later periods, some of which will be discussed below.

2.1.5 T-East

Because it has been excavated the least, this section of Area T is certainly the most fragmentary. Several walls were uncovered, one of which (W.7577) was associated with the Stratum III yellow floor. This evidence shows that the eastern part of Area T was in use during this period, but further excavations notwithstanding, we are unable to assess how it functioned within the sacred precinct.

2.2. Conceptual Space in Stratum III

In light of these descriptions of Area T's spatial practice in Stratum III, I will conclude this chapter with some remarks on the area's conceptual space. As discussed in chapter 1, conceptual space refers to the mental blueprint of a particular space, the conceptual design according to which the space was organized. Moreover, conceptual space concerns the social and political contexts that underlie this mental blueprint. The conceptual space suggested here is of course speculative and in no way represents the last word on the complex intersection of cult, politics, and social interaction that took place at Tel Dan. Nonetheless, I think the following reconstruction, which proposes verticality, symmetry/duality, and accessibility as three organizing principles for Area T, offers a cogent account of the area's conceptual space.

2.2.1. Verticality

The architecture in Area T accentuates the verticality that is already a feature of Tel Dan's topography. Just to reach Area T, worshipers would have ascended from the city gate to the top of the site's mound, where the sanctuary is located. This slope continues even in the sacred precinct and leads ultimately to the podium in T-North, which seems to have been the area's primary focus. Besides exhibiting the most and the finest ashlar masonry,[53] the podium's size (ca. 18 m^2) and its location at the crest of the mound make it a dominating presence, the crowning structure of not only Area T but the entire site of Tel Dan. Its stature grows all the more if we restore its robbed ashlar courses and imagine the superstructure that was likely built atop its foundation walls. Such verticality established a ritual distance between the worshipers and the object(s) of worship and was an organizing principle for ancient Near Eastern temples, in which resident deity was usually housed in an elevated chamber. For example, the cellas of Mesopotamian temples, especially ziggurats, and Egyptian temples were often elevated from the rest of the temple space.[54] Likewise, this tendency is apparent in the design of the Jerusalem temple[55] and likely accounts for the frequent use of mountains for theophanies and divine residences in the Hebrew Bible and the ancient Levant.[56] For these reasons, I am inclined to regard the T-North podium as the divine abode of the deity (or deities) worshiped at Tel Dan. It is tempting here to agree with Biran that the gold calf of Jeroboam ben Nebat was set up here (1 Kgs 12:28–29),[57] but our present data can neither support nor reject this conjecture. While a divine image is certainly not out of the question[58] and the evidence of multiple rooms atop the podium is suggestive, for now the question of the deity's dwelling there must remain unanswered.[59]

---

53. The central platform also featured ashlar blocks, but they do not show any of the bossing that was found on the southern face of the podium.

54. See J. Baines, "Palaces and Temples of Ancient Egypt," *CANE* 1:309–14; and M. Roaf, "Palaces and Temples in Ancient Mesopotamia," *CANE* 1:429–31.

55. See J. Z. Smith, *To Take Place: Toward Theory in Ritual* (Chicago: University of Chicago Press, 1987), 57.

56. See R. Clifford, *The Cosmic Mountain in Canaan and the Old Testament* (HSM 4; Cambridge: Harvard University Press, 1972). One notable exception to this tendency is the tabernacle, which was organized horizontally (see M. George, *Israel's Tabernacle as Social Space* [SBLAIL 2; Atlanta: Society of Biblical Literature, 2009], 128–29).

57. Biran, *Biblical Dan*, 165, 168; cf. R. Albertz, *A History of Israelite Religion in the Old Testament Period* (trans. J. Bowden; 2 vols.; Louisville: Westminster John Knox, 1994), 1:144–46.

58. See N. Na'aman, "No Anthropomorphic Graven Image: Notes on the Assumed Anthropomorphic Cult Statues in the Temples of YHWH in the Pre-exilic Period," in *Ancient Israel's History and Historiography: The First Temple Period*, vol. 3 of *Ancient Israel and Its Neighbors: Interaction and Counteraction* (3 vols.; Winona Lake, Ind.: Eisenbrauns, 2006), 311–38, esp. 332; repr. from *UF* 31 (1999).

59. R. Albertz has argued that cultic activity known from the Hebrew Bible, such

Beyond this ritual purpose, however, elevated architecture, such as the podium, represents an ordering principle for its surrounding buildings. For example, the northern wall of T-West (W.8511) was built in line with the northern wall of the podium, and the columns of T-Center seem to have been placed according to the midpoint of the podium's southern face. The podium's singularity is not unlike Lefebvre's description of Greek acropolis:

> At the highest point of the acropolis, the temple presided over and rounded out the city's spatio-temporal space. Built in no image, the temple was simply there, "standing in the rocky valley." It arranged and drew about itself (and about the god to which it was devoted) the grid of relations.[60]

Moreover, this power to order surroundings extended, at least in ancient Near Eastern cultures, to the king who built the temple. Such temples, especially their elevated architecture, often symbolized the elevated status of the king and legitimated his rule.[61] The Jerusalem temple, which was located beside the palace atop Mt. Zion, shares in this tradition, in that

as kissing the calf in Hos 13:2 (cf. 1 Kgs 19:18), "presupposes that in certain liturgies the cult symbol could be seen in the open air and possibly could be touched by individuals" (*History of Israelite Religion*, 1:145–46). Likewise, various rituals of procession, which consisted of the divine image "traveling" into the city, show that direct contact (visual or otherwise) with the divine image was not unusual in the ancient Near East (cf. KTU 1.43; 1.91; 1.148:18–22; see T. Lewis, "Syro-Palestinian Iconography and Divine Images," in *Cult Image and Divine Representation in the Ancient Near East* [ed. N. Walls; ASOR Books 10; Boston: American Schools of Oriental Research, 2005], 93–97). These rites show that a divine image atop the podium would be consistent with cultic traditions of ancient Israel and its neighbors.

60. H. Lefebvre, *The Production of Space* (trans. D. Nicholson-Smith; Cambridge: Blackwell, 1991), 249–50.

61. For examples from Egypt, see I. Shaw, "Balustrades, Stairs and Altars in the Cult of Aten at el-Amarna," *JEA* 80 (1994): 109–27; and L. Bell, "The New Kingdom 'Divine' Temple: The Example of Luxor," in *Temples of Ancient Egypt* (ed. B. Shafer; Ithaca, N.Y.: Cornell University Press, 1997), 127–84. Examples from Mesopotamia may include Esarhaddon's rebuilding of Esagila and Etemenanki (see B. Porter, *Images, Power, and Politics: Figurative Aspects of Esarhaddon's Babylonian Policy* [Philadelphia: American Philosophical Society, 1993], 41–75). Perhaps also the temple of Nabu in Dur Sharrukin (Khorsabad), which was connected by bridge to the palace of Sargon II (see G. Loud and C. Altman, *Khorsabad, Part II: The Citadel and the Town* [OIP 40; Chicago: University of Chicago Press, 1938], 56–64).

"the legitimacy of the shrine as a House of Yahweh gave legitimacy to the [Davidic] monarchy."[62] The podium at Tel Dan achieves a similar effect by its architectural resemblance to administrative buildings of the Iron Age IIB. Above I argued that these structural similarities do not negate the podium's cultic function but simply show that an architectural design can be used for diverse purposes.[63] From the perspective of conceptual space, however, the podium's resemblance to Palace 1723 at Megiddo,[64] Palace A at Lachish,[65] or the palace at Samaria[66] is significant for the political connotations that the podium's design encodes.

The most likely political context for interpreting this significance is the Omride dynasty, which ruled the northern kingdom in the first half of the ninth century B.C.E. This supposition is based primarily on the dating of Stratum III to the same century, but it is also significant that massive podiums and ashlar masonry have been identified as two defining characteristics of Omride architecture.[67] Moreover, the Tel Dan stela indicates that the site played a strategic role in the Omrides' administration of the northern kingdom (cf. 1 Kgs 20:34).[68] With this sociopolitical

---

62. C. Meyers, "Temple, Jerusalem," *ABD* 6:361.

63. See pp. 28–29 above.

64. See R. Lamon and G. Shipton, *Megiddo I: Seasons of 1925–34, Strata I–V* (OIP 42; Chicago: University of Chicago Press, 1939), 8–11; D. Ussishkin, "King Solomon's Palace and Building 1723 in Megiddo," *IEJ* 16 (1966): 179–86; idem, "King Solomon's Palaces," *BA* 36 (1973): 94–101; Z. Herzog, "Settlement and Fortification Planning in the Iron Age," in *The Architecture of Ancient Israel from the Prehistoric to the Persian Periods* (ed. A. Kempinski and R. Reich; Jerusalem: Israel Exploration Society, 1992), 251.

65. O. Tufnell, *Lachish III: The Iron Age* (London: Oxford University Press, 1953), 78–86; and more recently, R. Reich, "Palaces and Residencies in the Iron Age," in *The Architecture of Ancient Israel from the Prehistoric to the Persian Periods*, 208. Alternatively, D. Ussishkin referred to the buildings as "palace-forts" ("Excavations at Tel Lachish—1973–1977," *TA* 5 [1978]: 27).

66. N. Franklin, "Samaria: From the Bedrock to the Omride Palace," *Levant* 36 (2004): 200; idem, "Correlation and Chronology: Samaria and Megiddo Redux," in *The Bible and Radiocarbon Dating: Archaeology, Texts and Science* (ed. T. E. Levy and T. Higham; London: Equinox, 2005), 316–18; Z. Herzog, "Settlement and Fortification Planning in the Iron Age," 249–50; idem, *Archaeology of the City*, 229–30.

67. Finkelstein, "Omride Architecture," 121–25.

68. See N. Na'aman, "The Northern Kingdom in the Late Tenth-Ninth Centuries BCE," *Proceedings of the British Academy* 143 (2007): 406; A. Mazar, "The Spade and the Text: The Interaction between Archaeology and Israelite History Relating to the

context in mind, it may be possible to speculate further on the ideological aims of Area T, in particular its podium that looks so much like a palace. Besides simply projecting legitimacy, as is true for almost all monumental architecture,[69] the Omrides may have intended their construction of Area T to foster a sense of unity in their kingdom. It is well known that the population of the northern kingdom was quite heterogeneous during the Iron Age. D. Ilan has shown that the Iron I occupation at Tel Dan was a "very mixed bag of material culture attributes,"[70] and A. Faust has described the northern kingdom in the Iron II as a "plural society ... in which several ethnic groups existed."[71] In light of this heterogeneity, archaeologists have interpreted the monumental architecture at northern sites as attempts to unify the region's mixed populations under the authority of the Omride dynasty.[72] At Tel Dan this effort at consolidation

———

Tenth-Ninth Centuries BCE," *Proceedings of the British Academy* 143 (2007): 160. Most commentators identify Hazael as the author of the stela's inscription and interpret it as "propaganda boasting of Hazael's victories on the northern border of Israel" (W. Schniedewind, "Tel Dan Stela: New Light on Aramaic and Jehu's Revolt," *BASOR* 302 [1996]: 85; see also I. Kottsieper, "The Tel Dan Inscription [*KAI* 310] and the Political Relations between Aram-Damascus and Israel in the First Half of the First Millennium BCE," in *Ahab Agonistes: The Rise and Fall of the Omri Dynasty* [ed. L. Grabbe; LHB/OTS 421; London: T&T Clark, 2007], 118; V. Sasson, "The Old Aramaic Inscription from Tell Dan," *JSS* 40 [1995]: 13–14; P. McCarter, *Ancient Inscriptions: Voices from the Biblical World* [Washington, D.C.: Biblical Archaeological Society, 1996], 86–90). This interpretation presupposes that Dan was a prominent city during the Omride dynasty and therefore a meaningful place to erect such a stela. Arie's alternative interpretation of the stela as Hazael's "celebration of the construction of the city of Dan" is unconvincing ("Reconsidering the Iron Age II Strata at Tel Dan," 35).

69. See Sharon and Zarzecki-Peleg, "Podium Structures with Lateral Access," 161.

70. Ilan, "Northeastern Israel in the Iron Age I," 1:148.

71. Faust, "Ethnic Complexity in Northern Israel during Iron Age II," *PEQ* 132 (2000): 21; see also Finkelstein, "Omride Architecture," 131–33.

72. Faust, "Ethnic Complexity," 21; Finkelstein, "Omride Architecture," 132; see also idem, "City-States to States: Polity Dynamics in the 10th–9th Centuries B.C.E.," in *Symbiosis, Symbolism, and the Power of the Past: Canaan, Ancient Israel, and Their Neighbors from the Late Bronze Age through Roman Palaestina, Proceedings of the Centennial Symposium, W. F. Albright Institute of Archaeological Research and American Schools of Oriental Research, Jerusalem, May 29–31, 2000* (ed. W. Dever and S. Gitin; Winona Lake, Ind.: Eisenbrauns, 2003), 79–81; H. Williamson, "Tel Jezreel and the Dynasty of Omri," *PEQ* 128 (1996): 46–50. Meyers has shown that the Jerusalem temple served a similar purpose for the various constituencies of the Davidic dynasty ("Temple, Jerusalem," 360–61).

seems to have included new religious architecture that would exalt the site's cult and also reinforce the authority of the dynasty responsible for its renovation. Furthermore, within Area T the podium in T-North, presiding over the sacred precinct and giving order to its various buildings, exemplifies this process of consolidation, whereby the Omrides sought to unify the various constituencies of their kingdom.

2.2.2. SYMMETRY AND DUALITY

Area T and several of its buildings seem to have been constructed according to a single north-south axis. This symmetry was mentioned earlier, where I noted that the midpoint between the two columns of the T-Center platform is the same as the midpoint of the podium. Therefore, if we imagine a line running through those two midpoints, we see that T-North and T-Center are aligned on the same axis. (Unfortunately, T-East remains unexcavated, so we cannot know if the same axis is shared by it and T-West.) This preference for symmetry is also apparent in the podium and the central platform, which are both squares. As such, both buildings produce transversal axes, running east-west across each construction; in the podium this axis is actualized by east-west W.8810. The intersections of these auxiliary axes with the principal axis are not exactly square, but still their rough coordination suggests that T-North and T-Center—most likely the two foci of cultic activity—were built in relation to each other and according to a preference for symmetry that seems to have ordered the cultic space (see fig. 13).

Such alignment is significant, or, to use G. Wightman's word, "purposive," since "there are all sorts of ways in which these spaces can be juxtaposed without any of their axes coinciding."[73] The challenge, of course, is to ascertain what that purpose might be. One starting place might be the recognition by Lefebvre and others that symmetries in spatial order stand for certain dualities that are constitutive of the space.[74] From a structuralist perspective, such duality may represent cultural or social oppositions that exist between the various groups that occupy a space.[75] Others noting the

---

73. G. Wightman, *Sacred Spaces: Religious Architecture in the Ancient World* (ANESS 22; Leuven: Peeters, 2007), 962.

74. Lefebvre, *Production of Space*, 170–75, 180–88.

75. See S. Kunin's structuralist analysis of the tabernacle in which he identifies a pattern of such oppositions whose ultimate purpose is the establishment of a strong

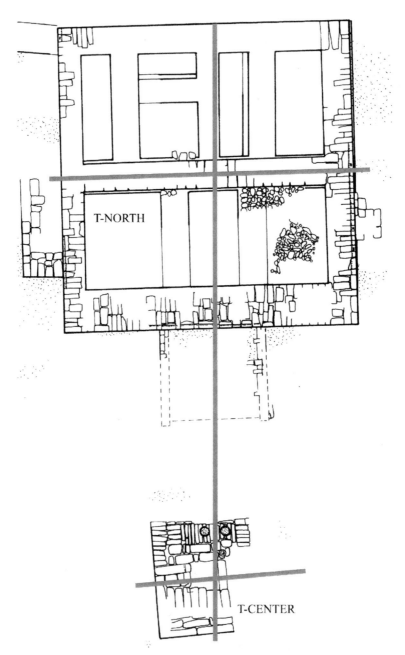

Figure 13. Axes of Area T in Stratum III (after plan provided by the Nelson Glueck School of Biblical Archaeology, Hebrew Union College/Jewish Institute of Religion).

significance of symmetrical design include J. Z. Smith, who emphasizes that the dualisms produced by symmetry encode a hierarchical ranking.[76] A concrete example of this kind of ranking may be O. Negbi's observation that among the Canaanite cult sites of the Bronze Age, urban temples are monumental and symmetrical, while temples on the periphery are smaller and unsymmetrical.[77]

It is impossible to know if any of these meanings associated with symmetrical design apply to Area T in Stratum III, but the link between symmetry and duality does underscore again the importance of the two column bases in T-Center, which are a key part of the area's symmetry.[78] The use of columns or pillars in sacred precincts is hardly unique to Tel Dan. In some instances they simply served a functional use, namely, supporting a roof. In these cases the columns do not mark the site of cultic activity but create a (permeable) barrier to the primary focus of the temple.[79] Indeed, the best stylistic parallels for the Tel Dan column base were all found in a transitional space rather than within the building itself. This is true for the nonreligious *bīt ḫilāni* buildings at Tell Tayinat and Zinjirli[80]

---

external boundary (*God's Place in the World: Sacred Space and Sacred Place in Judaism* [London: Cassell, 1998], 14–17, 28).

76. Smith, *To Take Place*, 41. In this regard, Lefebvre notes that insofar as spatial symmetries seem to reflect symmetries from the natural world, the ranking is likewise regarded as "natural" and inevitable (*Production of Space*, 171–72).

77. Negbi, "Levantine Elements in the Sacred Architecture of the Aegean at the Close of the Bronze Age," *ABSA* 83 (1988): 356.

78. Cf. the comments of C. Graesser, who in his study of "standing stones" (Heb. *maṣṣēbôt*) remarks on paired stones that "the duality of the stones ... seems rather to stem from a feeling for symmetry, and perhaps from imitation of the use of pairs of other objects before entryways, such as guardian winged beasts, pillars, etc." ("Studies in *maṣṣēbôt*" [Ph.D. diss., Harvard University, 1969], 180–81).

79. As G. Wightman has noted, "columns and pillars served to bound space in the manner of a wall, yet at the same time to render the boundary visually, and sometimes functionally, permeable" (*Sacred Spaces*, 957). For examples in the Levant, see the Fosse Temple at Lachish and temples 4040 and 2048 at Megiddo. The two rows of columns at Shechem had a similar effect, but there is no niche or pedestal within the temple; its sacrificial altar stood in the forecourt outside (see L. Stager, "The Fortress-Temple at Shechem and the 'House of El, Lord of the Covenant,'" in *Realia Dei: Essays in Archaeology and Biblical Interpretation in Honor of Edward F. Campbell, Jr. at His Retirement* [ed. P Williams and T. Hiebert; Atlanta: Scholars Press, 1999], 232).

80. This statement applies to the column bases found in situ at Tell Tayinat (Building I, Floor 3) and Zinjirli (Gebäude K) and probably also for the unprovenienced

and also for the two temples discovered at Tell Tayinat.[81] Further examples of external columns marking a temple threshold include the fortress
temple at Shechem,[82] the temple at 'Ain Dara,[83] the Phoenician temple at
Kition,[84] and the description of the Solomonic temple in 1 Kgs 7:15–22.[85]
Based on these parallels, a case could be made that the T-Center platform
and its columns marked a transitional space between the entrance to Area
T and the podium in T-North. According to this interpretation, the columns were not themselves the focus of cultic offerings but rather served to
differentiate space in the forecourt before the large podium, which was the
primary focus of Area T's cultic space.

However, there is also a case to be made that the columns marked the
site of ritual activities and may have even been the focus of them. For one
thing, there are the faunal remains from T-Center, which likely indicate
the consumption of ritual meals around the platform, and there is ample
evidence from archaeology and from the Hebrew Bible, which suggests
that freestanding columns or pillars played an important role in the cult

---

bases at the former site; excavators restored their probable locations on the porches of
Building I, Floor 1, and Building IV, Floor 2 (see Haines, *Excavations in the Plain of
Antioch II*, 42, 51; pls. 97; 102).

81. The first of these is Building II, which is a tripartite temple; its columns
were in antis and sat atop double-lion column bases, only one of which is preserved
(see Haines, *Excavations in the Plain of Antioch II*, 53–55; pls. 80–81; 100b; see also
McEwan, "Syrian Expedition of the Oriental Institute," 13–14; figs. 6–7). The second
temple has been discovered only recently, but a report and plan published online
depict a temple with a porch that was approached by a staircase. In the middle of the
porch was a single basalt column, decorated like the other bases from the site; two
brick piers separated the porch from the cella (T. Harrison and J. Osborne, "Building
XVI and the Neo-Assyrian Sacred Precinct at Tell Tayinat," *JCS* 64 [2012]: 125–43).

82. See Stager, "Fortress-Temple at Shechem," 233.

83. See A. Abū 'Assāf, *Der Tempel von 'Ain Dārā* (Damaszener Forschungen 3;
Mainz am Rhein: Zabern, 1990), 14–15; J. Monson, "The New 'Ain Dara Temple: Closest Solomonic Parallel," *BAR* 26.3 (2000): 23–24; idem, "The 'Ain Dara Temple and the
Jerusalem Temple," in *Text, Artifact, and Image: Revealing Ancient Israelite Religion*
(ed. G. Beckman and T. Lewis; BJS 346; Providence: Brown Judaic Studies, 2006), 288.

84. See V. Karageorghis, *Kition: Mycenaean and Phoenician Discoveries in Cyprus*
(London: Thames & Hudson, 1976), 98; G. R. H. Wright, *Ancient Building in Cyprus*
(2 vols.; Leiden: Brill, 1992), 1:113, 216.

85. See E. Bloch-Smith, "'Who Is the King of Glory?': Solomon's Temple and
Its Symbolism," in *Scripture and Other Artifacts: Essays on the Bible and Archaeology
in Honor of Philip J. King* (ed. M. Coogan et al.; Louisville: Westminster John Knox,
1994), 19.

itself. In some cases, such as the Late Bronze temples from Hazor (Area H) and Kamid el-Loz, pillars were featured within the cellas and were found beside pits that contained various cultic implements.[86] Other examples of pillars found within cellas include the fortress temple at Shechem,[87] Temples 4040 and 2048 at Megiddo,[88] and the Fosse Temple at Lachish.[89] This cultic usage is further supported by the number of monoliths, or "standing stones," that have been found beside altars at Arad,[90] Kition,[91] and in the gate area of Tel Dan itself.[92] In the Hebrew Bible such standing stones are called *maṣṣēbôt* and are depicted with a variety of functions, not least as cultic objects that are closely connected to other cultic equipment, such as altars and *'ăšērîm* (sacred poles).[93] In a few examples from the Hebrew Bible, *maṣṣēbôt* even seem to represent deities, as in the *maṣṣēbat habba'al*

---

86. For Hazor, see Y. Yadin et al., *Hazor III–IV: An Account of the Third and Fourth Seasons of Excavation, 1957–1958* (Jerusalem: Israel Exploration Society; Hebrew University of Jerusalem, 1989), 245; Y. Yadin, *Hazor: The Head of All Those Nations with a Chapter on Israelite Megiddo* (London: Oxford University Press, 1972), 84. For Kamid el-Loz, see M. Metzger, "Arbeiten im Bereich des 'spätbronzezeitlichen' Heiligtums," in *Bericht über die Ergebnisse der Ausgrabungen in Kāmid el-Lōz in den Jahren 1971 bid 1974* (ed. R. Hachmann; Saarbrücker Beiträge zur Altertumskunde 32; Bonn: Habelt, 1982), 17–29, esp. 24–26.

87. See G. E. Wright, "The Fluted Columns in the Bronze Age Temple of Baal-Berith at Shechem," *PEQ* 97 (1965): 66–84; Stager, "Fortress-Temple at Shechem," 228–49.

88. See A. Kempinski, *Megiddo: A City-State and Royal Centre in North Israel* (Materialen zur Allgemeinen und Vergleichenden Archäologie 40; Munich: Beck, 1989), 176, 183; fig. 45:4, 10.

89. See D. Ussishkin, *The Renewed Archaeological Excavations at Lachish (1973–1994) I* (5 vols.; Tel Aviv: Emery and Claire Yass Publications in Archaeology, 2004), 224–26.

90. Y. Aharoni, "Excavations at Tel Arad: Preliminary Report on the Second Season, 1963," *IEJ* 17 (1967): 247–48.

91. Karageorghis, *Kition*, 98.

92. Multiple sets of standing stones were discovered in Area A, two of which were found alongside evidence of cultic activity (see Biran, "Sacred Spaces," 42–45).

93. See E. LaRocca-Pitts, *"Of Wood and Stone": The Significance of Israelite Cultic Items in the Bible and Its Early Interpreters* (HSM 61; Winona Lake, Ind.: Eisenbrauns, 2001), 205–28; E. Bloch-Smith, "Will the Real *Massebot* Please Stand Up: Cases of Real and Mistakenly Identified Standing Stones in Ancient Israel," in Beckman and Lewis, *Text, Artifact, and Image*, 64–79; Zevit, *Religions of Ancient Israel*, 256–62. Still important as well is the seminal work of C. Graesser, "Standing Stones in Ancient Palestine," *BA* 35 (1974): 34–63.

mentioned in 2 Kgs 3:2 and 10:25–27.[94] Perhaps then the columns at Tel Dan represented two deities who were worshiped in Area T in Stratum III, as some have proposed for the pair of stones that were found inside the cella of the Arad temple.[95] If so, then the symmetry that structures Area T's religious architecture may have been a way to reinforce the dual deities who presided over the sacred precinct.

Altogether the symmetry and duality, which seem to be an organizing principle for Area T in Stratum III, offer several interpretive possibilities. Although it is tempting to speculate on the symbolic significance of the area's multiple symmetries, the two column bases represent our most concrete example of the duality that is evident in Area T. Archaeological parallels indicate that sometimes such columns were themselves objects and other times they simply marked transitional space, though the two roles need not be mutually exclusive. Based on the biblical description of *maṣṣēbôt*, it is not impossible that columns within a sacred precinct could function as cultic objects in their own right but also serve a more practical purpose of establishing boundaries with the precinct.[96]

2.2.3. ACCESSIBILITY

Even as we recognize the monumentality of Area T as a projection of political authority, Stratum III also seems to be characterized by its openness and accessibility. The stratum is remarkable for its lack of physical restrictions on movement, and besides the T-North podium, which presides imperiously over the sacred precinct, most sections of Area T appear to have been accessible to worshipers. The rooms of T-West all face open to the courtyard, and the central platform was open on all sides, with pavement found to its south and east, suggesting that people gathered in the courtyard around it. Indeed, this is the picture that has emerged from J. Greer's faunal analysis, which suggests that communal feasts were held in the courtyard around the platform. According to his reconstruction:

---

94. See T. Lewis, "Divine Image and Aniconism in Ancient Israel" (review of Tryggve N. D. Mettinger, *No Graven Image? Israelite Aniconism in Its Ancient Near Eastern Context*), *JAOS* 118 (1998): 41–42.

95. Zevit, *Religions of Ancient Israel*, 168.

96. Indeed, I will argue in a subsequent chapter that the pillars and stones mentioned in Exod 24:4 and 1 Kgs 18:31–32 serve as cultic equipment as well as boundary markers (see p. 140).

"People apparently dined with vessels typical of a domestic assemblage. The variety within each type (various styles of cooking pots, jugs, bowls, etc.) may suggest a less regulated environment in which these feasters brought their own 'mess kits,' rather than utilizing mass-produced wares upon arrival in the precinct."[97]

This picture of communal feasting compares favorably with certain biblical descriptions of communal sacrifices, such as the *šĕlāmîm* sacrifice, which functioned as a common meal shared by the offerer, the priest, and YHWH (see Lev 3:1–17),[98] and Greer has shown that the order of sacrifice prescribed in the Priestly literature is compatible with the cultic space of Area T.[99] Moreover, the overall accessibility of Area T is consistent with the Priestly description of the tabernacle: each space featured a preeminent structure (the tabernacle proper and the T-North podium) fronted by a courtyard in which communal worship by priests and nonpriests alike took place.[100] The comparison of these two sacred spaces also reiterates the point made above that an open and accessible worship space should not imply the absence of regulation. For example, the tabernacle courtyard was an inclusive worship space,[101] but the bronze altar within the courtyard, though not physically demarcated, was nonetheless restricted to the priesthood, whose approach to the altar required the same preparations as the tabernacle itself (Exod 30:20; Lev 21:17–23).[102] Similarly, the relative openness of Area T's architecture does not mean that movement around the sacred precinct was unregulated; indeed, it is likely that officiants monitored the cultic activity. This management of the cultic area, however it existed, is not (yet) expressed in the architecture of Area T. Insofar as spatial arrangement can indicate how worshipers interacted with a cultic

97. Greer, "Dinner at Dan," 79.

98. See M. Modéus, *Sacrifice and Symbol: Biblical* Šĕlāmîm *in a Ritual Perspective* (ConBOT 52; Stockholm: Almqvist & Wiksell International, 2005).

99. Greer, "Dinner at Dan," 100–103.

100. See W. Propp, *Exodus 19–40* (AB 2A; New York: Doubleday, 2006), 498–99; George, *Israel's Tabernacle as Social Space*, 71–75.

101. See George's discussion of the Israelite "congregation" (Heb. *ʿēdâ*) as an inclusive category that maximized participation in the tabernacle cult (*Israel's Tabernacle as Social Space*, 112–19; contra M. Haran, *Temples and Temple-Service in Ancient Israel: An Inquiry into the Character of Cultic Phenomena and the Historical Setting of the Priestly School* [Oxford: Clarendon, 1978], 184–87).

102. See Propp, *Exodus 19–40*, 501; S. Olyan, *Rites and Rank: Hierarchy in Biblical Representations of Cult* (Princeton: Princeton University Press, 2000), 23.

space, the temple complex in Stratum III suggests a worship space that was characterized by accessibility and openness.

This aspect of Area T marks an important contrast with the biblical descriptions of the tabernacle and the Jerusalem temple and recommends caution in how we use their arrangement of cultic space to understand the spatial dynamics of Area T at Tel Dan.[103] The tabernacle and the Jerusalem temple are characterized by a tripartite division, which in the tabernacle is evident in the three gradations of holiness that divide it into most holy, holy space, and court space.[104] In the Jerusalem temple this tripartite arrangement is represented by the division of the temple itself into the "holy of holies" (Heb. *dĕbîr*), the main hall (Heb. *hêkāl*), and the porch (Heb. *'ûlām*).[105] This arrangement is consistent with other Levantine temples, such as Buildings II and XVI from Tell Tayinat and the temple at 'Ain Dara, which are examples of the temple *in antis* tradition.[106] According to S. Mazzoni, this tradition, which is indigenous to Syria and the Levant, is characterized by the following features: "isolation of the building, long central room, entrance from the short side facing the adyton and cult image, sequence of access and further occasional subdivision of rooms."[107] Yet none of these defining characteristics of the temple *in antis* seem to be present in Area T; rather the sacred precinct at Tel Dan seems to have more in common with the open-air sanctuaries of Phoenicia, which "typically consisted of a paved, open, elevated

---

103. Greer's comparison of the dimensions of Area T and the Jerusalem temple is a good example of this cautious approach, which considers potential correspondence between the two but also acknowledges the gaps in our understanding of each ("Dinner at Dan," 92–99).

104. See George, *Israel's Tabernacle as Social Space*, 71–75; Haran, *Temples and Temple-Service*, 149–88.

105. Spatial divisions likely continued outside the temple proper into the courtyard (see Olyan, *Rites and Rank*, 21).

106. For Building II at Tell Tayinat, see Haines, *Excavations in the Plain of Antioch II*, 53–58; for Building XVI, see T. Harrison and J. Osborne, "Building XVI," 125–43; for the 'Ain Dara temple, see Monson, "The 'Ain Dara Temple and the Jerusalem Temple," 273–99. Finally, for the langhaus tradition, in general, see A. Mazar, "Temples of the Middle and Late Bronze Ages and the Iron Age," in *The Architecture of Ancient Israel from the Prehistoric to the Persian Periods* (ed. A. Kempinski and R. Reich; Jerusalem: Israel Exploration Society, 1992), 161–87.

107. Mazzoni, "Syrian-Hittite Temples and the Traditional *in antis* Plan," in *Kulturlandschaft Syrien: Zentrum und Peripherie; Festschrift für Jan-Waalke Meyer* (ed. J. Becker et al.; Münster: Ugarit-Verlag, 2010), 359.

courtyard or *temenos*, enclosing a cultic installation of some sort (i.e. a betyl, altar, or shrine (*naiskos*). Where feasible, it was located on high ground—on a mountain peak or ridge, or on the summit of a neighbouring hill."[108] A classic example of this architectural style is the temple at 'Amrit, which compares favorably with the religious architecture found at Area T.[109] Although its sixth-century-b.c.e. date is significantly later than Stratum III at Tel Dan, the 'Amrit temple, especially its altar surrounded by an enclosed, open-air courtyard, represents an architectural tradition that can be traced back to the ninth-century-b.c.e. Phoenician temple at Kition.[110] Their comparison suggests that the reconstruction of cultic life at Tel Dan ought not begin with the Jerusalem temple or the tabernacle and their concentric gradations of sanctity but rather with the tradition of open-air sanctuaries of the northern Levant, not only in Phoenician sanctuaries but also among the open-air cult places in Israel, such as Mt. Ebal and the so-called Bull Site.[111]

Although, even among these Israelite open-air sanctuaries, Area T stands out for its unusual arrangement and the quality of its construction,[112] these shrines may offer our best opportunity for assessing the religious character of the temple complex at Tel Dan. For example, R. Albertz has argued that the open-air sanctuaries of prestate Israel were "visible and accessible to all" and that the cult at these sites is marked by a "decentralized character, which brought it near to the people."[113] This interpreta-

---

108. G. Markoe, *Phoenicians* (Berkeley and Los Angeles: University of California Press, 2000), 126.

109. See M. Dunand and N. Saliby, *Le Temple d'Amrith dans la Pérée d'Aradus* (Bibliothèque Archéologique et Historique 121; Paris: Geuthner, 1985). Its comparison to Area T has already been suggested by Wightman (*Sacred Spaces*, 193) and Lehmann and Killebrew ("Palace 6000 at Megiddo in Context," 28).

110. See W. Mierse, *Temples and Sanctuaries from the Early Iron Age Levant* (HACL 4; Winona Lake, Ind.: Eisenbrauns, 2012), 118–19, 223–24; Karageorghis, *Kition*, 100–101, 118–19 (fig. 18).

111. Mierse, *Temples and Sanctuaries*, 149–50. For an analysis of Mt. Ebal, see R. Hawkins, who suggests that the best parallels for the building on Mt. Ebal are the so-called *gilgalim*, the open-air, possibly religious, enclosures that dot the Jordan Valley (*The Iron Age I Structure on Mt. Ebal: Excavation and Interpretation* (BBRSup 6; Winona Lake, Ind.: Eisenbrauns, 2012), 118–22, 150. For the "Bull Site," see A. Mazar, "The 'Bull-Site': An Iron Age I Open Cult Place," *BASOR* 247 (1982): 27–42.

112. Mierse, *Temples and Sanctuaries*, 193–94, 198.

113. Albertz, *History of Israelite Religion*, 1:85. Cf. Zevit's characterization of

tion is consistent with the contrasting political landscapes of the northern and southern kingdoms. Unlike the southern kingdom, where the
temple and palace compound projected a powerful and lasting image of
centralized authority, political power in the northern kingdom remained
diffused among several important cities. This decentralization is apparent
from the foundations of the northern kingdom, as Jeroboam I supports
tribal interests against Rehoboam's exploitative policies (1 Kgs 12:16),[114]
and the career of the former attests the various cities that played key roles
in northern politics: Jeroboam's kingship is prophesied by a Shilonite (1
Kgs 11:29–31; 12:15), but he is made king in Shechem (1 Kgs 12:1, 20),
where he established a capital; later he builds up Penuel as a stronghold in
the Transjordan (1 Kgs 12:25).[115] Under his successors the capital will be

---

northern cultic centers as "autonomous, decentralized, politically neutralized" (*Religions of Ancient Israel*, 449).

114. The question of Jeroboam ben Nebat's role in the secession of the northern tribes is a difficult one. Parts of 1 Kgs 11–12 suggest that he was recognized as a
leader of these tribes before he became their king. According to 1 Kgs 11:26–28 he
had originally been in charge of the corvée (*sēbel*) of the house of Joseph but later
"raised his hand against the king," a phrase that denotes insurrection (cf. 2 Sam 18:28;
20:21). Unfortunately, the account of this event has been syncopated by vv. 29–39,
a later insertion that has left the description of the revolt rather thin on details. The
rest of his role in the secession can only be inferred from the negative depiction of
Rehoboam, who in 1 Kgs 12:1–19 vulgarly refuses to lessen the corvée (*mas*) of the
northern tribes. It is reasonable to assume that Jeroboam's revolt in some way paralleled the complaints of the northern tribes, and he was chosen as their leader because
he had already shown himself sympathetic to their cause. This evidence of Jeroboam's
early political career is admittedly meager, but its positive view of Jeroboam probably represents an early tradition, especially when we compare it with the negative
depiction in 1 Kgs 14:1–18 and the rest of the Deuteronomistic History (see C. Evans,
"Naram-Sin and Jeroboam: The Archetypal *Unheilsherrscher* in Mesopotamian and
Biblical Historiography," in *Scripture in Context II* [ed. W. Hallo et al.; Winona Lake,
Ind.: Eisenbrauns, 1983], 114–25; see also M. Sweeney, *I and II Kings: A Commentary*
[OTL; Louisville: Westminster John Knox, 2007], 159).

115. Two of these cities—Shechem and Penuel—were associated with the
Canaanite deity El. According to Judg 9:46, Shechem was the site of the house of El-
Berith (cf. Gen 33:20; see T. Lewis, "The Identity and Function of El/Baal Berith," *JBL*
115 [1996]: 415–16), and in the case of Penuel, its link to El is suggested by its very
name ("the face of *'ēl*"). This association with El touches on the debate regarding the
basis of Jeroboam's religious policies. Some argue that the golden calves he installed
at Dan and Bethel stood for Yahweh (or Baal) and that these northern sanctuaries
were alternative sites for Yahweh-worship (see L. Bailey, "The Golden Calf," *HUCA*

moved to Tirzah (1 Kgs 15:33) and ultimately to Samaria (1 Kgs 16:23–24). In the analysis of H. Niemann, this peripatetic kingship reflects the political fragmentation of the northern kingdom in contrast to the centralized power at Jerusalem.[116]

This diffusion of political power is mirrored in the religious sphere and explains why the northern kingdom had two national sanctuaries at Dan and Bethel. J. Olivier, for example, has written that the founding of Dan and Bethel as cult centers is evidence that the northern kingdom "favoured an egalitarian and decentralized society to the hierarchical power structure so typical of the capital."[117] Similarly B. Halpern has called "the location of [Dan and Bethel] at the northernmost and southernmost extremes of the land … a tonic against regional dissatisfaction with the central government."[118] It is in this context of decentralized political and religious authority that we should view the openness that distinguished Area T in Stratum III. Although the expenditure and monumentality of this stratum's architecture project the prestige of the Omride dynasty, its accessibility preserves the pluralistic tradition of the northern kingdom in contrast to the sacral hierarchies and gradations of holiness that are depicted in the tabernacle and the Jerusalem temple traditions of the Hebrew Bible.[119]

In conclusion, I have argued for three different organizing principles that are constitutive of Area T's conceptual space during Stratum III: verticality, symmetry, and accessibility. The identification of these principles

---

42 [1971]: 97–115), while others argue that Jeroboam's actions represent an attempt to reassert the old Canaanite deity El, who was often depicted with bull imagery (see F. M. Cross, *Canaanite Myth and Hebrew Epic: Essays in the History of the Religion of Israel* [Cambridge: Harvard University Press, 1973], 73–75).

116. H. Niemann, "Royal Samaria—Capital or Residence? or: The Foundation of the City of Samaria by Sargon II," in Grabbe, *Ahab Agonistes*, 184–207.

117. J. Olivier, "In Search of a Capital for the Northern Kingdom," *JNSL* 11 (1983): 131. See, however, the critique of this position by W. Toews (*Monarchy and Religious Institution in Israel under Jeroboam I* [SBLMS 47; Atlanta: Scholars Press, 1993], 76–86).

118. B. Halpern, "Levitic Participation in the Reform Cult of Jeroboam I," *JBL* 95 (1976): 32.

119. Cf. Albertz's argument that Bethel, another northern cult place, "seems to have been closer to the popularistic worship on the cultic high places from the time before the state than to the national cult in Jerusalem (*History of Israelite Religion*, 1:145).

is based on my analysis of the architecture and artifacts from Stratum III as well as a consideration of the larger religious, political, and social developments of the ninth century B.C.E. I think that these principles, though speculative, represent a cogent, hopefully compelling, interpretation of that priorities and concerns that produced the sacred space we find at Area T in Stratum III.

3

AREA T, STRATUM II:
AN EIGHTH-CENTURY B.C.E. CULT SITE

3.1. SPATIAL PRACTICE IN STRATUM II

Stratum II at Tel Dan is defined by a destruction layer that was exposed in Areas A, B, and T. As we shall see in the description below, the layer was most pronounced in T-West, where more phasing has been preserved. This destruction has been connected to the second western campaign of Tiglath-pileser III, although admittedly neither the Hebrew Bible (see 2 Kgs 15:29) nor the Assyrian royal annals mention Dan as a casualty of this campaign.[1] Yet even if Tiglath-pileser was not responsible for the conflagration, an eighth-century-B.C.E. date for the stratum is confirmed by the pottery found in the debris.[2] Therefore, Stratum II in Area T should be dated to this century and to the kingship of Jeroboam II, whose long reign over the northern kingdom (787–748 B.C.E.) corresponds with this period. As in the previous chapter, I will describe section by section the spatial practice of Area T, which will include the architecture and artifacts from

---

1. This absence in the textual record has been discussed by W. Dever ("Archaeology and the Fall of the Northern Kingdom: What Really Happened?," in *"Up from the Gates of Ekron": Essays on the Archaeology and History of the Eastern Mediterranean on Honor of Seymour Gitin* [ed. S. Crawford; Jerusalem: W. F. Albright Institute for Archaeological Research; Israel Exploration Society, 2007], 83–84).

2. This pottery is published in A. Biran, *Biblical Dan* (Jerusalem: Israel Exploration Society/Hebrew Union College–Jewish Institute of Religion, 1994), figs. 167–68; D. Pakman, "Late Iron Age Pottery Vessels at Tel Dan," *EI* 23 (1992): 230–34, figs. 1–3 (Hebrew); and Biran, "The Dancer from Dan, the Empty Tomb and the Altar Room." *IEJ* 36 (1986): 185, fig. 14. See also E. Arie, "Reconsidering the Iron Age II Strata at Tel Dan: Archaeological and Historical Implications." *TA* 35 (2008): 30–31.

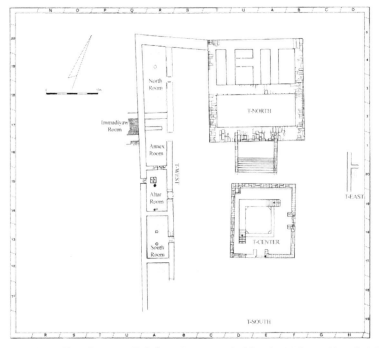

Figure 14. Area T in Stratum II (after plan provided by the Nelson Glueck School of Biblical Archaeology, Hebrew Union College/Jewish Institute of Religion).

Stratum II as well as some suggestions of the cultic practices that may be indicated by these material remains.

3.1.1. T-North

Again the massive podium's poor state of preservation limits our perspective on the building's superstructure and how it may have changed from Stratum III to Stratum II. We do know that the substructure remained unchanged and, more importantly, that some key features of the podium continued into the latter stratum. In particular, the major renovation of Stratum III, which was defined by the introduction of ashlar masonry in T-North and elsewhere, remained intact in Stratum II.

One significant change in Stratum II that is archaeologically discernible is the construction of a new large staircase against the podium's southern wall. This staircase measured 8 m wide and was composed of worked fieldstones, except for its lateral walls (W.722 and W.7504), which were made of ashlar blocks. Moreover, when this staircase was removed, an ear-

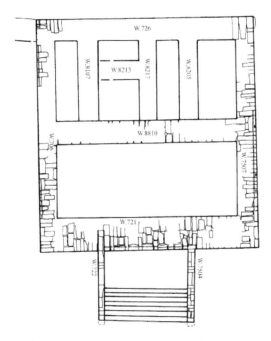

Figure 15. T-North in Stratum II (after plan by of the Nelson Glueck School of Biblical Archaeology, Hebrew Union College/Jewish Institute of Religion).

lier staircase was exposed (see W.7703), which was smaller (6.2 m wide) and built on a slightly different alignment (see fig. 16). Both staircases have been dated to Stratum II based on the pottery found within the stone fill of the staircase and the fact that the staircases postdate the yellow floor of Stratum III (the larger staircase cutting through it).[3] This staircase marks

---

3. Sharon and Zarzecki-Peleg argue that this staircase was not built until the Hellenistic period, but their misrepresentation of the evidence makes their case untenable. In several publications, beginning with the 1977 preliminary report, Biran described his excavation of the staircase in this way: "Eight steps were found, each about 0.20–0.27 m. high. Three additional steps were found rising from the middle of the eighth step to 0.60 m. above the top of the lateral walls. These upper steps underwent much rebuilding and repairs and were covered by remains of the Roman period of the fourth century A.D. When we removed the upper rows of the steps, Hellenistic and Roman pottery was found. In the seven lower steps, however, only Iron Age pottery was discovered" (A. Biran, "Tel Dan, 1977," *IEJ* 27 [1977]: 244; see also Biran et al., *Dan I: A Chronicle of the Excavations, the Pottery Neolithic, the Early Bronze Age and the Middle Bronze Age Tombs* (Jerusalem: Nelson Glueck School of Biblical Archaeology, Hebrew

an important change in the accessibility of the podium. As noted above (p. 37), access in Stratum III was most likely available on the western and eastern walls; likely there was also an approach on the southern wall that was removed to build the later staircase. In any case, by Stratum II the approaches on the eastern and western walls were covered over, leaving the new monumental staircase on the southern wall as the only entry to the podium.

Furthermore, the two Stratum II phases of the staircase reveal a subtle difference in orientation. The earlier, 6.2-m-wide staircase was built perpendicular to the southern face of the podium, as W.7703 and its parallel demonstrate. By contrast, the orientation of the later staircase, which is wider (8 m) and features ashlar blocks, is less than perpendicular with the podium; instead its perpendicularity occurs in relation to the central platform construction and its northern temenos wall (W.7505). Such an adjustment can be interpreted in several different ways. Possibly, as the space between the central platform and the podium became increasingly occupied, the relationship between the two sections had to be realigned, and the staircase was most easily adjusted to accommodate a new arrangement—certainly it was easier to modify than the podium's foundation.

Alternatively, this adjustment could indicate a shift in the focus of Area T in general. From the area's earliest Iron Age levels the podium has been the area's focal point. In the previous chapter I emphasized its importance

---

Union College–Jewish Institute of Religion, 1996), 41–42; Biran, "The Temenos at Dan," *EI* 16 [1982]: 24 [Hebrew]). The misrepresentation of this evidence by Sharon and Zarzecki-Peleg includes the following statement: "the excavators maintain that, when they removed the frontal staircase, they found Hellenistic pottery beneath only the lowermost three stairs. The published plans and photographs, however, do not show any noticeable differences in the construction of the frontal staircase or banister walls" ("Podium Structures with Lateral Access: Authority Ploys in Royal Architecture in the Iron Age Levant," in *Confronting the Past: Archaeological and Historical Essays on Ancient Israel in Honor of William G. Dever* [ed. S. Gitin et al.; Winona Lake, Ind.: Eisenbrauns, 2006], 155). This description is mistaken on two counts: first, it was the uppermost three stairs, *not* the lowermost three stairs, which yielded the Hellenistic and Roman pottery; and second, it is incorrect to say that there are no noticeable differences in construction in the staircase or the banister. The cross-section published in Biran's 1982 article clearly shows that top three steps were not part of the stone fill that composed the other eight steps (Biran, "Temenos at Dan," 22–23, fig. 7). Of course, any conclusions must await the analysis of the pottery found within this stone fill, but for now Biran's preliminary analysis remains viable; Sharon and Zarzecki-Peleg's challenge to his dating of the podium staircase is unconvincing.

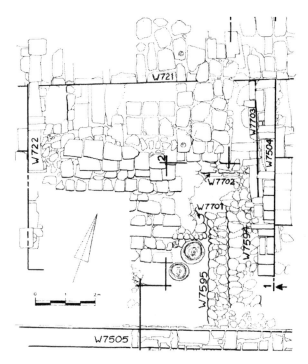

Figure 16. Two phases of the podium staircase (plan courtesy of the Nelson Glueck School of Biblical Archaeology, Hebrew Union College/Jewish Institute of Religion).

as the keystone of Stratum III's architecture, but even in the earlier Stratum IVA the podium anchored the cultic area.[4] However, the realignment of the podium's staircase may suggest that in Stratum II the center of gravity has shifted from the podium in T-North to the central platform in T-Center and that the latter structure has begun to determine the area's spatial arrangement. In the next section I will present evidence from T-Center itself that shows its increased prominence in Stratum II, but already here in T-North the coordination between the podium's monumental staircase and the T-Center altar *rather than* the T-North podium suggests a shift in the architectural arrangement of Area T.

---

4. In this stratum the pathway leading into Area T ended at the podium, and the central storerooms were set along the southern face of the structure. Moreover, the path's enclosure wall (W.718 [=W.7711]) terminated at the podium's southwestern corner.

3.1.2. T-Center

Like T-North, T-Center in Stratum II reveals several continuities from the previous stratum as well as several important changes. First of all, while the ashlar platform remained the focal point of the section, a new wall (W.7591) seems to have been added on its northern side, and this addition likely eclipsed the two columns that had been a prominent feature of the previous stratum. This northern wall lies in line with a staircase that was built at the platform's northeastern corner and that survives with two steps (W.7714). A matching staircase was built in the southwestern corner and survives with five steps (W.7614).[5] Perpendicular to the latter staircase is a stone bench (W.7612) that runs along the southern edge of the platform.[6] These staircases provide evidence that in Stratum II the ashlar platform was the foundation of another structure, most likely a monumental altar that was ascended by these two staircases.

These staircases also help us estimate the size of the altar; if we assume that they were its northern and western limits and that the altar did not extend past the southern bench (W.7612), we can imagine its size to be ca. 5 × 5 m. A large altar horn (51 cm high and 36 cm long) that was found in the Roman fill atop the platform may have been part of this monumental altar, but we cannot be sure (see fig. 18).[7] Its association with the Stratum II altar is attractive, especially in light of the large horned altar from Iron Age Beersheba;[8] but without a secure date, we can only speculate.

---

5. Interestingly, the bottoms of the staircases roughly correspond with the two bone-filled favissae (L.2155 and L.2395) that belong to Stratum III (see above, p. 42).

6. According to Voss's unpublished 1988 report, "both steps and bench are set directly on the Phase 3 [= ninth century b.c.e.] ashlar platform." Other evidence for this dating comes from pottery found beneath a thick, white travertine floor that was traced to walls 7613 and 7713.

7. The horn was found when excavators removed the balk that abutted the stairs of W.7614 of the central platform (Biran et al., *Dan I*, 45). Cf. the one-eighth of a sphere found at Megiddo, which the excavators interpreted as an altar horn with a height and width of 50 cm (R. Lamon and G. Shipton, *Megiddo I: Seasons of 1925–34, Strata I–V* (OIP 42; Chicago: University of Chicago Press, 1939), 24, fig. 31b).

8. The Beersheba altar featured four horns and has been assigned to Stratum II, which Y. Aharoni dated to the eighth century b.c.e. ("The Horned Altar of Beer-sheba," *BA* 37 [1974]: 2–6). Although Y. Yadin attempted to reassign this stratum to the seventh century b.c.e. ("Beer-sheba: The High Place Destroyed by King Josiah," *BASOR* 222 [1976]: 5–17), Aharoni's dating has been confirmed by the similarities of

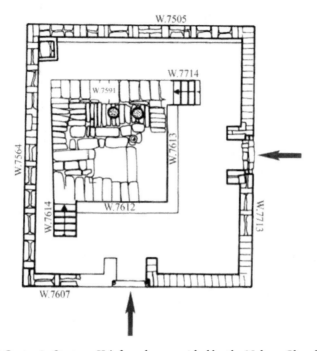

Figure 17. T-Center in Stratum II (after plan provided by the Nelson Glueck School of Biblical Archaeology, Hebrew Union College/Jewish Institute of Religion).

Another major architectural change in Stratum II is the addition of a temenos wall around the central altar. This wall has been assigned to Stratum II based on two factors: first, pottery sherds found beneath a floor (L.2319) that was traced from the eastern side of the platform (W.7613) to the eastern wall of the temenos (W.7713); and second, two loci (L.2324 and L.2500) that show the ashlar blocks of the temenos cutting through the Stratum III yellow floor. The wall measured 14 m north-south and 13 m east-west and was supported by a foundation of sunken ashlar blocks—two courses under the northern wall and one course everywhere else. Furthermore, it was built with headers and stretchers, the latter showing evidence of shallow bossing. As with the

Stratum II's material to Lachish Stratum III, which was destroyed by Sennacherib in 701 B.C.E. (see O. Borowski, "Hezekiah's Reforms and the Revolt against Assyria," *BA* 58 [1995]: 150–51; L. Fried, "The High Places [*bāmôt*] and the Reforms of Hezekiah and Josiah: An Archaeological Investigation," *JAOS* 122 [2002]: 447–48).

Figure 18. Large altar horn from Area T (photo courtesy of the Nelson Glueck School of Biblical Archaeology, Hebrew Union College/Jewish Institute of Religion).

ashlar walls of the podium, however, the finely dressed blocks of the altar temenos were robbed during the Hellenistic and Roman occupation of the site. For this reason, only one course of the wall has been preserved, except for the northern wall (7505), where four courses survived intact.

This enclosure would have been entered by one of two entrances: one in the eastern wall and one in the southern wall, each measuring 1.6 m wide. The thresholds of the entrances stepped down into the temenos area, and on either side were ashlar doorjambs that projected 0.80 m into the enclosure. These entrances correspond with two staircases found on the eastern and southern sides of the altar platform, and in the northwestern corner of the temenos wall was a stone installation that measured 1.4 × 1 m and featured a flagstone pavement. It was framed by two ashlar slabs, which cornered with the temenos walls to create a square receptacle, perhaps a bothros for the deposit of refuse. Less than one meter south of this paved receptacle, the square four-horned incense altar discussed above was found (see pp. 41–42). There we determined that the altar was probably part of the Stratum III assemblage, but it is likely that the altar, like many other features of that stratum, was reused in Stratum II. Needless to say, this new temenos wall and its accompanying features had a significant impact on the spatial organization of Area T, and this impact will be discussed in the section below on Stratum II's conceptual space.

3.1.3. T-West

T-West in Stratum II consists primarily of five excavated rooms, all of which were significantly enlarged in this period. In prior strata the rooms were 3.5 m wide, but in this new phase, the eastern wall of these rooms (W.8523–8607) was removed, covered with a white travertine floor, and replaced by a new wall (W.8430–7716–8609–8856) that increased the width of the rooms to 4.6 m.

3.1.3.1. The North Room

This room's northern wall (W.8511) and western wall (W.8427 = W.8611) remained in use from the previous period, and between them was a thin white plaster floor, which sealed over the previous eastern wall (W.8523). As just noted, the new eastern wall (W.8430) enlarged the room by over a meter. The southern limit of the North

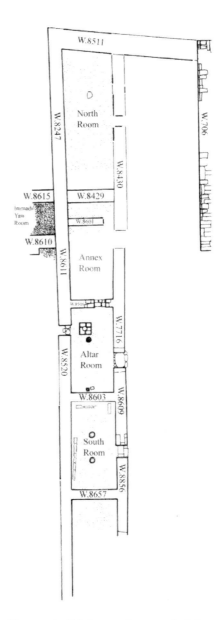

Figure 19. T-West in Stratum II (after plan provided courtesy of the Nelson Glueck School of Biblical Archaeology, Hebrew Union College/Jewish Institute of Religion).

Room (W.8429) remained the same.[9] In the center of the room atop the white plaster floor were burnt bricks that will be observed in other rooms of T-West. There, as here, the bricks mark the eighth-century-B.C.E. destruction layer.

In Stratum II there was certainly an entrance through the eastern wall, which featured a threshold and ashlar doorjambs, and again we must consider a possible passage through the northern wall, though this wall still lacks any evidence of a threshold. In later periods the North Room's northern entrance will become much more prominent, as it features an ashlar ramp and is surrounded by a flagstone pavement. In Strata III–II, however, the eastern wall should be regarded as the main entrance and probably the only one.

Immediately south of the North Room is the same small space (1.5 m long) that was observed in Stratum III, and although the space's function still remains uncertain, it is worth noting that the yellow travertine floor continues to be used in Stratum II. This reuse is clear since the floor was found immediately beneath a destruction layer of burnt mud bricks (L.9014).[10]

3.1.3.2. The Annex Room

The southern wall of this enigmatic space (W.8601) also served as the northern wall of the Annex Room, which joined W.8611 (= 8427) to the west and W.8430 to the east. Its southern wall comprised walls 8516 and 8506, between which was a passage to the Altar Room. Besides this entrance, it is likely that there was also an entrance through the eastern wall. A break appears in W.8430, and immediately east of this break is a pavement and ashlar blocks that cut the Stratum III yellow floor. It is possible that this ashlar construction was built in the eighth century B.C.E.

---

9. Southern wall 8405, like W.8401, was constructed in the seventh century B.C.E. as part of the rebuilding that also included W.82005 and W.8418, which enlarged the room northward.

10. A potential discrepancy was found in the locus card for L.9014, where it was written that walls 8430 and 8429 cut this destruction layer, but elsewhere these same walls had been dated to the eighth-century-B.C.E. phase of T-West. Upon consultation with R. Voss, it was determined that W.8430 should still be understood as an eighth-century-B.C.E. construction and that the disturbance of the destruction layer in L.9014 should be attributed to a secondary phase of W.8430, or more likely to the leveling that preceded the construction of L.2770.

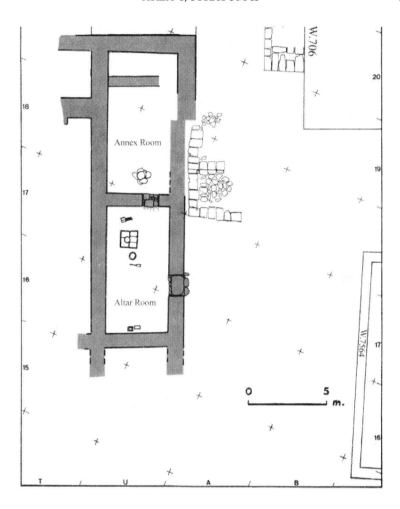

Figure 20. Annex Room with reinforced pavement (plan courtesy of the Nelson Glueck School of Biblical Archaeology, Hebrew Union College/Jewish Institute of Religion).

to augment the floor in front of the Annex Room. This reinforcement suggests that the entrance received frequent use and had to be strengthened to accommodate the heavy traffic. Unfortunately, we cannot know for sure since the Hellenistic temenos (W.705) cut through precisely this corner of the structure.

The room yielded two floors, one around the northern wall (L.9008) and the other around the room's southern limit (L.2832). The latter was a clay floor into which was set a round basalt slab surrounded by smaller flagstones, and this floor was covered with black ash and burnt debris that continued through the southern passage.[11] Within this destruction layer were found several metal objects, namely, an iron crescent-shaped blade, a rhomboid iron stand, a perforated lead tablet, an iron arrowhead, an iron handle, a bronze fibula, a bronze handle, and a bronze ring.[12] At this point, the function of these objects and also of the basalt slab is uncertain, though it is likely that these artifacts, especially the iron blade, should be interpreted in light of the faunal analysis that will be discussed below (see pp. 81–82).[13]

3.1.3.3. The ImmadiYaw Room

The ImmadiYaw Room lies outside the main series of rooms in T-West, to the west of the Annex Room, sharing with it W.8611. Its other walls included W.8615 to the north and W.8610 to the south; its western wall was removed in a later phase. This room is remarkable for several reasons: first, it provided some of the best evidence of the Assyrian destruction. Locus 9024 consists of burnt mud brick that had collapsed from its surrounding walls; beneath this debris was found a pottery assemblage dating to the eighth century B.C.E.[14] The most important find within this assemblage was a stamped jar handle bearing the name 'ImmadiYaw (l'mdyw), which joins two other impressions of the same name found at Dan: the first in Area B during the 1974 excavation, and the second on an

---

11. Benches 8424 and 8425 and wall 8525 rest on top of this ash layer and therefore date later.

12. The locus card for L.2832 records the blade and the iron stand. The other objects were described by R. Voss in his unpublished "Area T 1985 Report" (p. 11). One object that must be excluded from the Stratum II is the blue faience die that Biran considered as part of this assemblage (see Biran, *Biblical Dan*, 199, fig. 157; pl. 37; idem, "Dancer from Dan," 179, fig. 10). In fact, the die was found atop compact clay floor (L.2830) that covered an ashlar threshold. The metal objects described above were found beneath this threshold in the layer of black ash and debris associated with the eighth-century-B.C.E. destruction.

13. See J. Greer, "Dinner at Dan: A Biblical and Archaeological Exploration of Sacred Feasting at Iron II Tel Dan" (Ph.D. diss., Pennsylvania State University, 2011), 66.

14. See Pakman, "Late Iron Age Pottery Vessels," 232, fig. 2:2 (Hebrew); Biran, *Biblical Dan*, 207, ill. 165.

eighth-century-B.C.E. flagstone pavement in the center of the city (Area M, Locus 8321).[15]

3.1.3.4. The Altar Room

Of the rooms in T-West the Altar Room has received the most attention, due mostly to the three altars discovered there and the various objects associated with them. But before discussing these finds, it will be helpful to address the room's boundaries. Three of its four walls featured an entrance: with the Annex Room to its north it shared walls 8506 and 8516 as well as the passage between them; on its western side was a passage through wall 8611 = 8520 that entered the northern half of the room, and on its eastern side was a passage through wall 7716 = 8608 that entered the southern half of the room. The eastern and western entrances had basalt thresholds, while the passage to the Annex Room consisted of compacted clay.[16] Only the room's southern wall (W.8603) had no entrance.

The Stratum II floor is a mix of new and reused floors. In the northern part of the room the Stratum III yellow floor was cut away to an even earlier plaster floor, most likely to create a level surface on which to set the room's main altar. Surrounding this altar was a new white plaster floor

---

15. These seals are published as no. 692 in N. Avigad and B. Sass, *Corpus of West Semitic Stamp Seals* (Jerusalem: Israel Academy of Sciences and Humanities/Israel Exploration Society, 1997), 255. The 1974 seal was first published by Biran in "A Mace-Head and the Office of Amadiyo at Dan," *Qadmoniot* 21 (1988): 16 (Hebrew); see also idem, *Biblical Dan*, 201.

In addition to "Amadiyo," Biran also read the name as ʿImadiyau (*ESI* 6 [1987/1988]: 47), then later as *ImmadiYo* (*Biblical Dan*, 199–200). Of these, the former most accurately represents the theophoric element of the name, since in the eighth century B.C.E. a final mater *waw* could only stand for /û/. Most likely, *-yw* is a northern dialect of an original *-yahū*, which after the syncope of the *heh* became *-yau* and finally *-yaw* (cf. the Samaria ostraca). In southern dialects, by contrast, the *heh* is retained, and the original theophoric *-yahū* becomes *-yāhû* (see Cross, *Canaanite Myth and Hebrew Epic*, 61 n. 62).

Biran took the name to mean "God is with me" and compared it with one of the ostraca from Ḥorvat ʿUza, which reads ʿmdyhw . bn . zkr. (This name shows the southern *-yāhû* ending.) Interestingly, the name occurs (as ʿmdyhw) in three other stamp seals, and in two of the instances the name belongs to a woman (see Avigad and Sass, *Corpus of West Semitic Stamp Seals*, nos. 40, 41, and 590).

16. The passage between the Annex Room and the Altar Room will not feature an ashlar threshold until the seventh century B.C.E. (see L.2830 and L.2832).

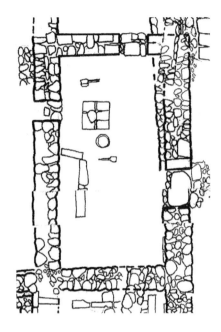

Figure 21. Altar Room in Stratum II (plan courtesy of the Nelson Glueck School of Biblical Archaeology, Hebrew Union College/Jewish Institute of Religion).

that extended southward until it met the sloping yellow floor that was reused in the southern part of the Altar Room, just as it had been in the Annex Room.

The name "Altar Room" comes from the discovery of the five-block square altar in the room's northern half as well as two incense altars that were found against its southern wall. The square altar measured 1.03 × 1.03 m and 27 cm high and was set on top of the plaster floor that was exposed when the yellow travertine floor was stripped away (see fig. 22). It included a flat, round basalt stone on top of its five travertine blocks.[17] Its identification as an altar is based on the traces of heavy burning on the ashlars' surface[18] as well as the discovery of an ash-filled pot that had been sunken into the floor just 20 cm away from the square altar.[19] This jar contained burnt sheep and goat bones as well as a fine gray ash, distinguishable from the black destruction ash found elsewhere in the room.[20]

17. See Biran, "Dancer from Dan," 182, fig. 11.

18. The locus card for L.2844 describes the altar's surface as "fired orange and grey from heavy burning on top of the stone."

19. For a photograph and drawing of the jar, see Biran, *Biblical Dan*, 195, ill. 153; idem, "Dancer from Dan," 183, fig. 12. A second jar was found beneath the white plaster floor in a context described as a "burnt area" (see L.2881), and although this broken jar dates to an earlier period, its discovery suggests a tradition of sacrificial burning in this room (Biran, "Dancer from Dan," 187 n. 25).

20. This information came from neutron activation of the ashes (see Biran, "Dancer from Dan, the Empty Tomb," 183, 187 nn. 23–24; idem, *Biblical Dan*, 195). For the distinction between the gray ash in the jar and the black destruction ash, see the card for L.2844.

Of this jar and its contents P. Wapnish and B. Hesse have written that "it is difficult to see how bone ashes, collected and placed in carefully positioned jars in a room with an altar that is located in a sacred precinct can reflect other than ritual activities involving animals, namely sacrificing and eating."[21] Moreover, they conclude that because the faunal remains in T-West contrast sharply with contemporaneous areas at Tel Dan, its bones are probably indicative of ritual sacrifice.[22] Related to this sacrificial activity is the evidence Wapnish and Hesse provide for the processing of animal skins in T-West. This

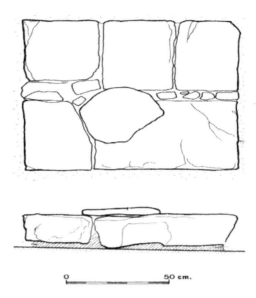

Figure 22. Square altar (drawing courtesy of the Nelson Glueck School of Biblical Archaeology, Hebrew Union College/Jewish Institute of Religion).

evidence consists of the high percentage of slaughter debris, such as toes and cranial fragments,[23] from which Wapnish and Hesse conclude that the animal sacrifice in these two rooms may have been "associated with the processing of skins, the consumption of ritual meals, and the storage of remains of burnt offerings."[24]

Jonathan Greer's recent analysis of two bone deposits from the Altar Room has shed further light on the ritual activities that took place in T-West, including some significant contrasts between the bones found

---

21. P. Wapnish and B. Hesse, "Faunal Remains from Tel Dan: Perspectives on Animals Production at a Village, Urban and Ritual Center," *Archaeozoologica* 4.2 (1991): 36, 47. Although Biran first interpreted the Altar Room's square altar as an incense altar ("Dancer from Dan," 183), he later accepted that it was probably used for animal sacrifice (*Biblical Dan*, 195).

22. Wapnish and Hesse, "Faunal Remains from Tel Dan," 47.

23. Ibid., 35, 45; table 8.

24. Ibid., 47.

there and those from T-Center.[25] For example, while sheep and goat bones predominate in both parts of Area T, Greer has shown that there is a slightly higher percentage of sheep and goat in T-West compared to T-Center, where bones from large cattle are more prevalent.[26] Also there is a slightly higher percentage of "Other" taxa represented in T-West, including deer, birds, and equids.[27] Moreover, his analysis has confirmed the initial conclusion of Wapnish and Hesse that T-West was also the site of skin processing. Here there was a significantly higher percentage of phalanges, which "were more likely left attached to skins and were not present as meat."[28] From these faunal remains Greer reconstructs the following picture of cultic activity in T-West: "As in the courtyard, sheep, goats, and cattle were likely killed within the precinct close to the western chambers before being gutted, skinned, and disarticulated. Some portions, notably from a higher percentage of sheep and goats compared to the courtyard, were then likely burned up on the small altar of the 'altar room' or disseminated."[29]

The remaining artifacts from the Altar Room should probably be interpreted in light of this picture. For example, three iron shovels were discovered around the altar: two 70 cm to its north and another 1.05 m to its south (see fig. 23).[30] The first two shovels are similar in length: 54 and 55 cm long, consisting of handles that measure 37 and 40 cm and blades that are 15 and 17 cm long, respectively, and 12 cm wide. Both shovels have hooked handles, so as to be hung on the wall; indeed, one of them still had an iron ring through its hook, and another bronze ring (5 cm diameter) and a bronze stud were found nearby.[31] The third shovel, even

---

25. Age of death among animals is not included among these contrasts. Although the initial study of the bones from Area T suggested a higher percentage of young animals (Wapnish and Hesse, "Faunal Remains from Tel Dan," 35; Tables 6, 10–11), Greer's reanalysis does not show a significant difference in the age of animals' death ("Dinner at Dan," 54–55).

26. Greer, "Dinner at Dan," 54.

27. Ibid. To these taxa we might add the two gazelle toes, two donkey metapodials, and paws from a bear and a lion, which were included in Wapnish and Hesse's initial study ("Faunal Remains from Tel Dan," 46).

28. Greer, "Dinner at Dan," 62, 70.

29. Ibid., 81.

30. Ibid., 181–83, fig. 13. For a photograph, see Biran, Biblical Dan, pl. 33.

31. See locus card for L.2844.

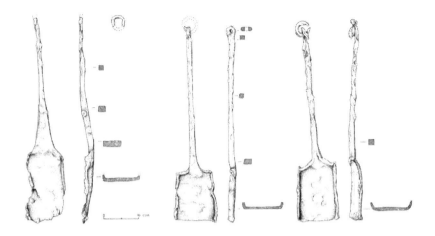

Figure 23. Three iron shovels from the Altar Room (drawings courtesy of the Nelson Glueck School of Biblical Archaeology, Hebrew Union College/Jewish Institute of Religion).

with its broken handle, was the longest at 58 cm, with a blade measuring 19.5 × 11 cm.

Similar shovels have been found in Palestine from earlier periods,[32] and two more have come from bronze hoards from Cyprus, one of which contained numerous cult objects, including an incense burner and a portable hearth.[33] This parallel, as well as the proximity of the Tel Dan shov-

---

32. At Megiddo, a bronze shovel was found in Area D-D of Stratum VIIA (Late Bronze); see G. Loud, *Megiddo II, Seasons of 1935–39*, vol. 2 (OIP 62; Chicago: University of Chicago Press, 1948), pl. 283:2, and G. E. Wright, "Solomon's Temple Resurrected," *BA* 4 (1941): 29–30, fig. 9. At Beth Shemesh a copper shovel was discovered in city debris during the 1928 season; see E. Grant, *Beth Shemesh: Progress of the Haverford Archaeological Expedition* (Haverford, Pa.: Biblical and Kindred Studies, 1929), 137; and E. Grant and G. E. Wright, *Ain Shems Excavations (Palestine)*, Part 5 (Haverford, Pa.: Biblical and Kindred Studies, 1939), 154.

33. Clandestine excavations account for both hoards. For the hoard of cultic objects, see V. Karageorghis, "A Late Cypriote Hoard of Bronzes from Sinda," *RDAC* (1973): 75, pl. 8: 4. The other hoard consisted of smithy and agricultural tools; see A. Murray, *Excavations in Cyprus* (London: Trustees of the British Museum, 1900), 16, fig. 25: 1461–63; C. Schaeffer, *Enkomi-Alasia: Nouvelles Missions en Chypre 1946–1950* (Paris: Librairie C. Klincksieck, 1952), 1:28–31, pl. LXIV: 8-10; and H. Catling, *Cypri-*

els to the square altar and the jar full of burnt bones, suggests that the shovels served a cultic function in the Altar Room. With the dish (1–2 cm deep) created by their flanged sides, perhaps the shovels were used

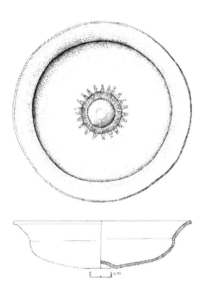

to clear sacrificial remains from the altar or to transfer coals from it.[34] As Biran noted, this is how shovels are used in biblical descriptions of the tabernacle (Exod 27:3; 38:3; Lev 10:1) and of the Jerusalem temple (1 Kgs 7:40, 45, 50; 2 Kgs 25:14–15; Jer 52:18–19), where the *yā'eh* and *maḥtâ* function as containers for transporting ashes from an altar.[35]

Another metal object from the Altar Room is the small (16 cm diameter) bronze carinated bowl that was discovered 1.5 m east of the stone altar.[36] It is 5 cm deep with an omphalos base surrounded by a lotus flower design.

Figure 24. Bronze bowl from the Altar Room (drawings courtesy of the Nelson Glueck School of Biblical Archaeology, Hebrew Union College/ Jewish Institute of Religion).

This bowl has recently been the focus of a study by J. Greer, who compares it to Assyrian drinking bowls from the same time period and concludes from these parallels

ote *Bronzework in the Mycenaean World* (Oxford: Clarendon, 1964), 278–81. Both hoards have been dated to ca. 1200 B.C.E.

34. See J. Greer, "An Israelite *mizrāq* at Tel Dan?," *BASOR* 358 (2010): 36–40; R. Kletter and I. Ziffer, "Incense-Burning Rituals: From Philistine Fire Pans to the Improper Fire of Korah," *IEJ* 60 (2010): 166–87.

35. Biran, *Biblical Dan*, 192. We should note that in some passages the *maḥtâ* is used to collect coals from the altar, and then incense is put on the coals within the shovel (Lev 16:12; Num 16:17–18). In these cases, the *maḥtâ* functions not as a container for transporting ashes but becomes a vessel for offering incense. However, it is unlikely that the shovels in the Altar Room functioned in this way. The two incense altars in the room probably received whatever incense was offered, and the shovels were associated with the sacrificial altar.

36. See Biran, *Biblical Dan*, 196–98, ill. 154; pl. 34; see also idem, "Dancer from Dan," 181, fig. 15.

that the Tel Dan bowl was used for cultic offerings.[37] More specifically, he argues that the bowl should be identified with the biblical *mizrāq*, which was part of the Altar Room's "altar kit" (cf. *kĕlê hammizbēaḥ* [Exod 38:3; Num 4:14]). Such kits are known from the descriptions of the tabernacle (Exod 27:1–8; 38:1–7; Num 4:13–15) and the Jerusalem temple (1 Kgs 7:40, 45, 50) and, in addition to the *mizrāq*, typically include pots (*sîrôt*), shovels (*yā'îm*), forks (*mizlāgōt*), and fire pans (*maḥtōt*). Given the pot and shovels found in the Altar Room, Greer has argued that this cultic assemblage is an archaeological example of an altar kit,[38] and the kit's *mizrāq* would have been used for collecting and sprinkling the blood of sacrificial victims.[39]

There are two other features of the Altar Room that deserve mention, namely, the two smaller incense altars that were found against the northern face of the southern wall. The first measured 44 cm high[40] and was made of yellow travertine; its slightly concave top measures 20×20 cm^2 with some evidence of a 10-cm-wide band, but near the bottom the altar flares out to 23 cm (fig. 25). The other altar is made of a blue travertine and stands 30 cm high (fig. 26).[41] Its top measured 23×23 cm, was recessed 2 cm, and featured a flat band on two sides. Both altars showed signs of burning, especially the smaller of the two, which had fine gray ash in its recessed dish, and have been identified as incense altars.[42]

---

37. Greer, "An Israelite *mizrāq* at Tel Dan?," 27–45.

38. Ibid.," 38.

39. See W. Gilders, *Blood Ritual in the Hebrew Bible: Meaning and Power* (Baltimore: Johns Hopkins University Press, 2004), 65.

40. Originally its height was listed as 0.52 m (Biran, "Dancer from Dan," 187) but was later corrected to 44 cm (idem, *Biblical Dan*, 196).

41. The height of this altar was also originally erroneous. It was first listed as 0.20 m (Biran, "Dancer from Dan," 187) but later corrected to 30 cm (idem, *Biblical Dan*, 196).

42. See S. Gitin, "Incense Altars from Ekron, Israel and Judah: Context and Typology," *EI* 20 (1989): 61*. Elsewhere Gitin notes that the designation of these and similar altars as incense altars does not exclude the possibility that substances besides incense were offered on them (idem, "New Incense Altars from Ekron: Context, Typology and Function," *EI* 23 [1992]: 44*–45*; see also P. Daviau, "Stone Altars Large and Small: The Iron Age Altars from Ḫirbet el-Mudēyine (Jordan)," in *Bilder als Quellen = Images as sources: Studies on ancient Near Eastern Artefacts and the Bible Inspired by the Work of Othmar Keel* (OBO; eds. S. Bickel et al.; Fribourg: Academic Press; Göttingen: Vandenhoeck & Ruprecht, 2007), 125–49.

Figure 25. Yellow travertine incense altar (photo courtesy of the Nelson Glueck School of Biblical Archaeology, Hebrew Union College/Jewish Institute of Religion).

Figure 26. Blue travertine incense altar (photo courtesy of the Nelson Glueck School of Biblical Archaeology, Hebrew Union College/ Jewish Institute of Religion).

Of final note is a small installation along the western wall of the room. It was built with three large, flat stones: the first was a plastered ashlar, which abuts the room's western wall (W.8520) on one side and corners with a long basalt fieldstone on the other. The basalt stone is followed by an unplastered ashlar slab. Together these stones created a small niche (0.5 × 2.4 m), which is described as a "receptacle" in the 1985 and 1986 season reports of Area T, but its purpose remains unclear.

3.1.3.5. The South Room

The South Room is directly south of the Altar Room and shares its northern wall (W.8603) with it. While the room's eastern wall (W.8609) is clear, its western wall is more complicated. Sometime during the eighth century B.C.E., W.8658 was replaced by the pilastered W.7568, and the latter's relationship with the room's southern wall (W.8657) suggests that it was used in Stratum II.[43] One noteworthy feature of the South Room is the group of ashlar orthostats, which lined its walls.[44] It has been suggested that they served as benches, but it is also possible that they were built to insulate the room from water. After all, the fountain house is directly west of the room, and if the space between the orthostats and the walls were lined with mud bricks, they may have shielded the room from flooding. Like the Altar Room to its north, the South Room yielded a substantial destruction layer, especially around its southern wall and the orthostats that lined the western wall. The floor beneath this ash featured two flat basalt stones, set 2.5 m from each other. These stones were likely bases for pillars that supported a roof (see L. 9087).

Finally, it is necessary to mention a section of Area T that was discovered at the end of the 1986 season and that came to be called Area T1. This new area is located 14 m west of T-West and features a covered water channel that was built of stone. This channel was traced for 12 m, but it remains unclear if the channel was meant to bring water to, or away from, Area T. According to the excavators, the debris atop the channel roof provided evidence for two phases. The first phase was "a 0.2 m thick burnt layer, which contained fragments of bowls, small bowls, cooking pots, store jars

---

43. See the discussion appended to the locus card of L.9087.
44. These orthostats are numbered W.8604 (east), W.8605 (north), and W.8653 (west).

and a pithos, all dating from the 9th to the early 8th centuries BCE."[45] The later phase consisted of building remains, including floors on which was found a destruction layer that was 1.2 m deep in some places. This layer contained the collapsed walls and ceiling of the building as well as "many pottery fragments—store jars (some whole), jugs, craters, cooking pots and bowls, as well as a basalt bowl—dated to the second half of the 8th century BCE. A bull figurine, probably part of a kernos, and an anthropomorphic figurine with a prominent nose were also found in the debris."[46] Biran attributed this latter destruction layer to the campaign of Tiglathpileser III in 732 B.C.E., which is a reasonable assumption. A more difficult question, which for now must remain unanswered, is how this building in Area T1 functioned in relation to the springs of the Dan River and also to the sacred precinct in Area T proper.

3.1.4. T-South

The complex of three rooms described in Stratum III remained in use with new plaster floors. North of this complex, in the room that once contained the olive oil press, excavators found a subfloor network of flues, each 10–12 cm wide and some containing bits of charcoal and ash. Rising to the clay floors, the flues converged at two bowl-shaped furnaces (30 cm diameter and 20 cm deep) that were set into the floor. Although they were first identified as tabuns, excavators later abandoned this interpretation, after a more conventional tabun was discovered a few meters east of the furnaces (L.2546). The function of these furnaces remains unknown.

Further complicating the situation is T-South's uncertain stratigraphy. While the features described here are certainly post-Stratum III, the section yielded very little pottery, and none of the destruction has been helpful for identifying Stratum II. Hopefully, the relationship of T-South to the rest of Area T will be clarified once the area's stratigraphy has been worked out.

---

45. A. Biran, "Tel Dan—1989," *ESI* 9 (1989): 87; see also Biran et al., *Dan I*, 50; Biran, *Biblical Dan*, 204.

46. Biran, "Tel Dan—1989," 87; for pottery drawings, see Pakman, "Late Iron Age Pottery Vessels," 230–34; figs. 1–3.

3.1.5. T-EAST

This part of Area T continues to be the most fragmentary. Although some walls can be assigned to Stratum II, the data presently available are not adequate to draw even preliminary conclusions.

3.2. CONCEPTUAL SPACE IN STRATUM II

The changes to Area T in Stratum II affected the organization of its cultic architecture in several important ways. Beyond simply observing these changes, a consideration of the stratum's conceptual space seeks to identify some of the religious, political, and social priorities that underlie them. Accordingly, the following section tries to locate the Stratum II sacred precinct within the larger political and religious realities of the eighth century B.C.E. and suggests two concepts that may be part of the mental blueprint that produced the stratum's sacred space. In particular, I think the concept of centralization and the overlapping of distinct cultic spheres may be regarded as two organizing principles for Area T in Stratum II. As I noted in my discussion of Stratum III's conceptual space, such principles are necessarily speculative, but I hope they will provide a cogent, if not compelling, analysis of the complex interplay of religion and politics at Tel Dan in the eighth century B.C.E.

3.2.1. CENTRALIZATION

One of the most important changes to Area T in Stratum II is the new prominence of T-Center. In part, this shift can be demonstrated simply by comparing the size of T-North and T-Center. In the preceding Stratum III there was no question that the podium dominated Area T; with its large size and height it presided over the entire cultic area and also displayed the finest masonry of all the area's buildings. In this same period, the central platform was a relatively modest structure. Although it was made of ashlar blocks, they were not worked as carefully as those that made up the podium. In Stratum II, by contrast, the importance of T-Center becomes more pronounced, and it even seems to have eclipsed the podium as the architectural center of Area T. The addition of the temenos wall increased its cultic area to more than double the size of the Stratum III platform, and the wall itself featured bossed ashlars, which previously had only been observed on the T-North podium. Despite this enlargement, the T-Center altar enclosure remains smaller than the T-North podium, but the expansion of the former still would have had a diminishing effect on the latter. For one thing, the temenos wall obstructed the approach to the podium. Whereas in Stratum III the T-Center platform was only a slight impediment before the T-North podium, the northern temenos wall effectively cut the space in front of the podium in half.

Further evidence of the T-Center's new prominence may be the new axis that runs diagonally through the altar temenos, dividing it into right triangles with corresponding staircases at the right angles. This new orientation is demonstrated by the two entrances to the temenos, which are both set 6 m from its southeastern corner.[47] Unlike in the previous stratum, in which the podium was the architectural keystone for Area T's building and the central altar enclosure was aligned with its north-south axis, now the altar is oriented to the southeast. Moreover, the staircases abutting the altar and the smoke rising from the elevated altar have lent T-Center a verticality that was previously reserved for the T-North podium. Whereas in Stratum III the podium stood alone at the apex of Area T, these new vertical elements in T-Center would have preempted some of the podium's prominence.

These features of the altar enclosure, which indicate its new prominence, also reveal another difference from the previous stratum. Unlike Stratum III, in which the cultic area was characterized by its openness and accessibility, Stratum II shows some limitations to access. This change is most apparent in T-Center. In the previous stratum, its platform was accessible from all sides, and the pavement found on its eastern and southern sides suggested that the area accommodated religious gatherings. Such assemblies would have been effectively curtailed by the addition of the temenos wall, which restricted access to entrances on just two sides of the enclosure. Exactly how passage through these entrances was regulated is impossible to know, though several compelling suggestions have been offered. Z. Zevit, for example, has proposed that sacrificial "animals were first presented before priests at the southern entrance [of T-Center], slaughtered, flayed, and butchered somewhere in the large courtyard, and

47. The entrances' southeastern orientation is clear from the builders' attempt to create diagonal symmetry, even though the temenos wall is not exactly square (14 × 13 m). Instead of building the entrances in the middle of the walls, they built them precisely 6 m from the southeastern corner and thus preserved the orientation established by the altar and staircases.

the blood and sacrificial parts then presented at the western [*sic*] entrance."[48] Alternatively, J. Greer has argued that the architecture of Area T is consistent with the sequence of rituals prescribed in the Priestly literature. He imagines that an offerer would slaughter his sacrifice on the southern end of the altar and then hand over to a priest the portions to be offered; when the burnt offering was complete, the priest would deposit the ashes nearby the altar.[49] While both reconstructions are plausible, from the perspective of conceptual space the key point is the temenos wall itself and what it suggests about the design of Stratum II. Namely, it testifies that in Stratum II a new effort has been made to exclude certain persons from the central altar.[50] Already we have seen that the T-Center altar complex achieved new prominence in Stratum II, and it is very likely that these two changes are related: as the central altar was elevated in status, access to it became more restricted. In this way, the temenos represents a sacral hierarchy that was relatively absent in the architecture of Stratum III. This correlation of status and access is a familiar phenomenon at cult places ancient and modern[51] but is relatively new to Area T. This new boundary of the temenos wall divided the cultic area that had been used for communal gatherings and restricted access to the T-Center altar. It is possible that the low wall was nothing more than crowd control and is unrelated to questions of cultic status, but more likely the area inside the temenos was reserved for religious specialists only, and the wall was built as a physical expression of this differentiation.[52] This gradation not only indicated varying degrees of holiness but also established a religious hierarchy according to one's degree of access.

This transformation in cultic architecture is not inconsistent with the political and religious centralization that occurred in the northern kingdom during the eighth century B.C.E. Indeed, a likely explanation for this change is the resurgence of the northern kingdom under the reigns of Joash

---

48. Z. Zevit, *The Religions of Ancient Israel: A Synthesis of Parallactic Approaches* (London: Continuum, 2001), 190.

49. Greer, "Dinner at Dan" 100–103.

50. See Zevit, *Religions of Ancient Israel*, 190.

51. See G. Wightman, *Sacred Spaces: Religious Architecture in the Ancient World* (ANESS 22; Leuven: Peeters, 2007), 929–52.

52. Zevit writes that the space inside the temenos "was of a higher degree of holiness than the extramural courtyard" and also "may have been restricted to officiants alone" (*Religions of Ancient Israel*, 190).

(ca. 802–787 B.C.E.) and Jeroboam II (787–748 B.C.E.) and the concomi-
tant expansion of royal bureaucracy. It is well-known that this period was
one of unprecedented prosperity for Israel. The western campaigns of the
Assyrian king Adad-nirari III at the turn of the eighth century B.C.E. sent
Damascus into a steady decline and released Israel from Aramean hegemony. This Assyrian pressure is clear from the inscriptions of Adad-nirari
III[53] and can also be inferred from certain Aramean inscriptions that show
the constriction of Damascus's authority.[54] These inscriptions provide the
context for interpreting the biblical reports that describe the reclamation
of territory by Joash and Jeroboam II. According to 2 Kgs 13:25, Joash

---

53. The campaigns against Damascus are recounted in three inscriptions (*RIMA*
3 A.0.104.6–8; cf. *COS* 2:274–77) and also in the Assyrian Eponym Chronicle (see
J.-J. Glassner, *Mesopotamian Chronicles* [SBLWAW 19; Atlanta: Society of Biblical Literature, 2004], 168–71). The latter attest several western campaigns between 805 and
796 B.C.E., while the former are usually dated to ca. 796 B.C.E. (For an explanation of
this dating in light of the problematic "fifth year" mentioned in the Saba'a inscription [*RIMA* 3 A.0.104.6], see W. Pitard, *Ancient Damascus: A Historical Study of the
Syrian City-State from the Earliest Times until Its Fall to the Assyrians in 732 B.C.E.*
[Winona Lake, Ind.: Eisenbrauns, 1987], 161–65). These three inscriptions describe
the subjugation of the Damascene "lord" (Akk. ᵐ*ma-ri-i*'), who probably should be
identified with Bar-Hadad, son of Hazael (see Pitard, *Ancient Damascus*, 165–66), and
one of them—the Tell el-Rimah Stele (*RIMA* 3 A.0.104.7)—also mentions "Joash of
Samaria" (Akk. ᵐ*iu-'a-su* kur *sa-me-ri-na-a-a*) as a tributary. Although this payment
may seem to contradict the burgeoning independence of the northern kingdom under
Joash, several have argued that the tribute should be interpreted as Israel's recognition
of Assyria as its deliverer (see M. Cogan and H. Tadmor, *II Kings: A New Translation
with Introduction and Commentary* [AB 11; New York: Doubleday, 1988], 152). In any
event, after the death of Adad-nirari III in 782 B.C.E. the Assyrians were preoccupied
with the Urartian threat, as the Eponym Chronicle attests (see Glassner, *Mesopotamian
Chronicles*, 170–71), and the northern kingdom was able to reclaim its lost territory.

54. We have already noted that the inscriptions of Adad-nirari III refer to Bar-
Hadad, son of Hazael, as "lord" and in the one is called the "king of Damascus" (*RIMA*
3 A.0.104.8:15–16). Likewise in the Zakkur inscription (ca. 800 B.C.E.) he is referred
to as the "king of Aram" (*mlk. 'rm* [*KAI* 202:4]). In subsequent inscriptions, however,
the ruler of Damascus is afforded no such status. A stele of Shalmaneser IV from 773
B.C.E., for example, records tribute from Ḥadiiāni but only calls him the Damascene
(*RIMA* 3 A.0.105.1:6). Moreover, J. Fitzmyer has shown that the phrase "all Aram"
(*'rm klh*) from the Sefire inscriptions (*KAI* 222A:5) probably refers to the empire of
Mati"il of Arpad (*The Aramaic Inscriptions of Sefire* [BibOr 19; Rome: Pontifical Biblical Institute, 1967], 62). If true, this treaty from the mid-eighth century B.C.E. would
offer further evidence of Damascus's decline, which benefited the king of Arpad as
well as Jeroboam II.

was able to defeat Bar-Hadad, son of Hazael, a victory that "curtailed Ara-maean expansion and paved the way for a complete reversal by Jeroboam II."[55] This advance by Jeroboam II is described in 2 Kgs 14, which reports that "he restored the boundaries of Israel from Lebo-hamath to the Sea of Arabah" (v. 25) and also restored Damascus and Hamath (v. 28).[56]

However, my interest in these two kings is less concerned with the spread of Israel's hegemony during their reigns than with the social and political repercussions of their achievement. In particular, I am interested in the increased social stratification and the expansion of officialdom throughout the northern kingdom that resulted from the relative pros-perity of the eighth century B.C.E.[57] Important evidence for this burgeon-ing bureaucracy is the corpus of sixty-three ostraca from Samaria, which date to the reign of Jeroboam II and record the receipt of select com-modities, such as refined oil and aged wine.[58] However one understands the movement of these commodities, the discovery of these receipts in an administrative center of Samaria provides a glimpse of the northern kingdom's fiscal organization and implies a bureaucratic class that man-aged its operation.[59]

---

55. Cogan and Tadmor, *II Kings*, 149. The biblical text also specifies Aphek as the site of the battle (1 Kgs 14:17; cf. also v. 22 in LXX[L]), which most locate east of the Sea of Galilee (see A. Rainey and R. Notley, *The Sacred Bridge: Carta's Atlas of the Biblical World* [Jerusalem: Carta, 2006], 216–17). The site would have been a logical place to staunch the Aramean advance and accords with the biblical report of Transjordanian territory lost to Hazael (2 Kgs 10:32–33).

56. For information on these geographical designations and further comments on Jeroboam II's reign, see Cogan and Tadmor, *II Kings*, 160–64. On the relationship of these verses to Amos 6:14, see B. Halpern, "The Taking of Nothing: 2 Kings 14.25, Amos 6.14 and the Geography of the Deuteronomistic History," in *The World of the Aramaeans* (ed. P. Daviau et al.; 3 vols.; JSOTSup 324–26; Sheffield: Sheffield Aca-demic Press, 2001), 1:186–204.

57. For a discussion of officialdom and of various models of social differentiation as applied to ancient Israel, see I. Jaruzelska, *Amos and the Officialdom in the Kingdom of Israel: The Socio-Economic Position of the Officials in the Light of the Biblical, the Epigraphic and Archaeological Evidence* (Seria Socjologia 25; Poznań: Uniwersytetu im. Adama Mickiewicza w Poznaniu, 1998), 14–23.

58. See P. McCarter, *Ancient Inscriptions: Voices from the Biblical World* [Wash-ington, D.C.: Biblical Archaeology Society, 1996], 103–4; I. Kaufman, "The Samaria Ostraca: An Early Witness to Hebrew Writing," *BA* 45 (1982): 229–39.

59. See Jaruzelska, *Amos and the Officialdom*, 115–18.

Another instructive set of data from this period is the corpus of personal seals and seal impressions that proliferated in the eighth century B.C.E. I. Jaruzelska has discussed many of the seals from this period and argued that their prevalence attests to increased activity of officials in the economic sphere.[60] This evidence is especially important for our study of Tel Dan, where several seal impressions have been discovered, including one in Area T (Stratum II) that belonged to ʿImmadiYaw.[61] Unfortunately, we can only speculate on this tantalizing seal and its owner's position at Tel Dan, but it does imply that the growing bureaucracy of the eighth century B.C.E. played a role in the sacred precinct at Tel Dan.[62] Such bureaucracy is also found in the book of Amos, which recounts the confrontation between the prophet and Amaziah, the priest of Bethel (Amos 7:10–17).[63] This episode shows just how closely the priesthood was aligned with the royal interests during the reign of Jeroboam II, and it is also important to note that the confrontation revolves around Amaziah's authority to expel from the sanctuary at Bethel. In this passage, as at Area T in Stratum II, access to certain parts of the sacred precinct has become a method of social differentiation.

This brief survey of the political developments during the eighth century B.C.E. is intended to provide a context for interpreting the architectural changes made to Area T in this same period. The consolidation achieved by Joash and Jeroboam had a profound effect on the administration of the northern kingdom, which we can observe in the proliferation of written sources, especially the Samaria ostraca and personal seals. They reflect a new centralization in the northern kingdom and also a burgeoning bureaucracy that functioned throughout the kingdom. This official apparatus was also prevalent in the religious sphere, and in my opinion, this social reorganization can help explain the changes in cultic architecture in Stratum II at Tel Dan. My analysis of this stratum has shown

---

60. Ibid., 121–32.

61. See above, p. 78.

62. Cf. the seal belonging to "Zekaryaw, the priest of Dor" ([lz]kryw / khn dʾr), which likewise attests to the participation of cultic functionaries in the centralization that took place in the eighth century B.C.E. As N. Avigad has written, the fact that Zekaryaw requires a seal for his priestly service speaks to the expansion of his duties: "In carrying out his office, the priest sometimes depended on the use of a seal. Our seal must have belonged to a priest of some consequence whose duties were not restricted to ritual acts" (N. Avigad, "The Priest of Dor," *IEJ* 25 [1975]: 104).

63. For a full discussion of this passage, see below, pp. 149–51.

that the addition of the temenos wall around the central altar effectively restricted access both to the altar and to the podium in T-North. These changes indicate an official presence at Area T that was responsible for the maintenance of the cultic area and the imposition of these architectural restrictions, and the fact that these impositions occurred in the eighth century B.C.E. suggests that they should be interpreted as part of the expanding officialdom of the northern kingdom.

3.2.2. OVERLAPPING CULTIC SPHERES

Another spatial feature of Area T in Stratum II seems to be the division of the area into two distinct cultic spheres. Comparison of T-West and T-Center/T-North suggests a fundamental division between the two areas of the sacred precinct. The differences are apparent not only in the architecture of the two spheres, especially with respect to size, building material, and access, but also in their material remains. By examining these differences I hope to show that Area T was designed to accommodate a range of cultic activities, ranging from large, communal religious gatherings in T-Center/T-North to smaller, more family-oriented religious occasions in T-West. In this way, the sacred precinct at Tel Dan attests the interface of both types of cultic celebrations, which are often regarded as dichotomous modes of religious experience.

3.2.2.1. Size

From the standpoint of sheer size, there is no question that the T-North podium and the T-Center altar dominate Area T. All of the T-West rooms are about 4.5 m wide and range in length from 6.5 to 12 m, with its central room—the Altar Room—measuring 4 × 8 m. These rooms are dwarfed by the T-North podium, which measures around 18 × 18 m; its staircase (6.2 m wide) alone almost matches the size of the Annex Room. The T-North podium's stature grows all the more when we consider its prominent place at the top of the area's natural slope and the probability that it supported a superstructure. The central altar commanded a similar attention. Although smaller (5.6 × 5 m) than the podium, the addition of the temenos wall around the altar more than doubled the structure's overall size.

Yet while the altar complex expanded, the rooms of T-West changed very little: they were slightly widened and in some places redivided, but compared to the development of T-Center, they remained modest in size.

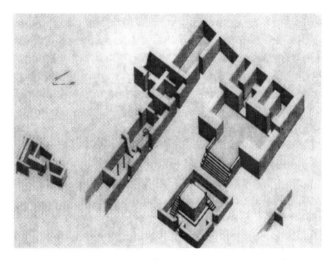

Figure 27. Isometric reconstruction of Area T in Stratum II (plan courtesy of the Nelson Glueck School of Biblical Archaeology, Hebrew Union College/Jewish Institute of Religion).

This contrast is also apparent in the sizes of their respective altars. If the central altar was the size of its ashlar base, then at 5.6 × 5 m it would be five times larger than the 1-m² sacrificial altar in T-West.[64] The monumental podium in T-North and the altar complex in T-Center dominated the sacred precinct.

3.2.2.2. Building Materials

In his list of archaeological indicators of ritual, C. Renfrew thrice cites expenditure and the investment of wealth as relevant to the composition of cultic space,[65] and I think that Area T can be divided according to this criterion. Even though the Altar Room and its neighboring rooms exhibit fine construction, they do not show the same investment of resources and expertise as is found in T-North and T-Center. For example, the podium, the altar platform, and its temenos were built *predominantly* with ashlar

---

64. If the large altar horn discovered in later fill belongs to the T-Center altar, it would provide further perspective on the difference in scale. At 51 cm high and 36 cm long, this horn alone is almost a quarter of the size of the entire of the T-West altar.

65. See Indicators 5, 15, and 16 in C. Renfrew and P. Bahn, *Archaeology: Theories, Methods and Practice* (3rd ed.; London: Thames & Hudson, 2000), 409.

blocks, and their blocks were often finely dressed; only in these sections were bossed ashlars found. This situation is reversed in the western rooms. Here the walls were built primarily with fieldstones of basalt and dolomite. When ashlar blocks are found, they are usually roughly hewn blocks; the few dressed blocks were reserved for doorjambs and thresholds.

This contrast is also apparent in the incense altars found in the two sections. According to S. Gitin's typology of incense altars, all of the incense altars found at Tel Dan are removed from the prominent horns and well-formed shafts of the tenth-century-B.C.E. altars from Megiddo, but distinctions can be found within the Dan corpus itself: the four-horned altar found inside the altar temenos, which features well-defined horns, represents an earlier stage of development than the two found in the Altar Room, which are hornless and show only slight decoration on their sides.[66] This point of comparison, taken together with the more general comparison of building materials, suggests that the T-North podium and the T-Center altar enclosure received a greater investment of resources and expertise than the series of rooms in T-West.[67]

3.2.2.3. Access

Finally, there seems to be a contrast between T-Center/T-North and T-West with respect to their accessibility. While the new temenos wall in T-Center was not especially tall, it was certainly high enough to establish a boundary, especially if the three to four ashlar courses were topped by mud brick. The enclosure had entrances, of course, but they were located on the southern and eastern walls, away from the pathway that approached from the south.[68] We cannot be sure if this was the only way into the sacred precinct, since the eastern side of Area T remains unexcavated, but for worshipers who took this path, which led along the western side of the temenos wall, access to the central altar would not be immediately avail-

---

66. Gitin, "Incense Altars," 61*.

67. A similar division of building materials has been noted in Temple I at Hattusha-Boğazköy, where the ceremonial chambers featured granite while the surrounding structures were built of limestone (see H. Akurgal, *The Art of the Hittites* [New York: Abrams, 1962], 102).

68. This road, identified in T-South, is the only known entry to the sacred precinct. However, we cannot rule out another possible entry on the unexcavated east side of Area T.

able. The entrances to the altar complex were built opposite of this southern approach and thus limited direct access to the altar.[69]

We also noted above that a similar impediment was created between the T-Center altar and the T-North podium. While we cannot know how the space between these two structures was used in earlier strata, we observed that the erection of the T-North podium's monumental staircase and the raising of the temenos wall in T-Center cut this space at least in half. It is likely that even before these obstructions, access to this part of Area T was restricted and simply not reflected in the architecture. In Stratum II, however, this spatial limitation is made concrete. By contrast, direct access seems to have been available to all the rooms of T-West. Again if we take the southern approach as the main entry into the area, we can imagine that worshipers entering the sacred precinct would encounter—indeed would be unable to avoid—these entrances immediately on their left. In his assessment of these rooms, Z. Zevit argues that the multiple entrances to the Altar Room "formed a passage between the area to the west of the cultic center and the yellow court," and for this reason "its degree of holiness was less than that of other areas in the center."[70] Certainly, the accessibility of T-West stands in contrast to the central altar and suggests a conceptual division between the two spaces.

These contrasting cultic spaces suggest that Area T was the site of both large religious gatherings in the courtyard around the T-Center altar and smaller-scale worship that would have taken place in the rooms of T-West. Significantly, this division of Area T into two cultic spheres is also represented in the faunal evidence. In the above descriptions of spatial practice in Stratum II, I have already cited some of the results of J. Greer's analysis of this evidence, from which he concludes that T-West and T-Center represent two distinct spheres of activity.[71] The courtyard around the altar featured large cultic feasts, while the rooms of T-West were the site of smaller feasts as well as related activities, such as the processing of skins.

---

69. As M. Parker Pearson and C. Richards have noted, "physical barriers, such as walls or earthworks, mark differences in domains and thus restrict and control access between them. By physically dividing up and demarcating space we may classify and control places and relationships more readily" ("Ordering the World: Perceptions of Architecture, Space and Time," in *Architecture and Order: Approaches to Social Space* [London: Routledge, 1996], 24).

70. Zevit, *Religions of Ancient Israel*, 190.

71. Greer, "Dinner at Dan," 72–82.

Such a spatial arrangement is hardly unique to Tel Dan but is found at many major temples in the ancient Near East, which featured a main sanctuary as well as subsidiary chapels that were smaller and often more accessible to worshipers.[72] Among the examples from ancient Mesopotamia, we can note the Kitîtum temple, which dates to the Old Babylonian period. Its main sanctuary occupies the western part of the temple complex and includes its own courtyard, while in the northeastern corner of the complex, immediately behind its main gate, was a smaller temple dedicated to Ninshubura.[73] Closer in time to the Tel Dan temple were the Neo-Assyrian temple of Nabu at Nimrud and the temple of Nabu at Dur Sharrukin, which both featured double sanctuaries as their primary cultic space but also had ancillary chapels in more accessible areas of their temple complexes.[74] Finally, the Neo-Babylonian temple to Marduk in Babylon included several small chapels in addition to the main cult rooms.[75] Further evidence for subsidiary chapels comes from the temples in ancient Egypt, where it was common practice during the New Kingdom for laypersons to erect so-called contra shrines, which abutted the walls of several temples at Karnak.

---

72. In his scheme of sacral hierarchy, G. Wightman regards the cult object and the main cella as primary and secondary spaces, respectively, and subsidiary chapels and shrines as tertiary space (*Sacred Spaces*, 932).

73. See T. Jacobsen, "The Mesopotamian Temple Plan and the Kitîtum Temple," *EI* 20 (1989): 79*–91*. He writes that "from the gate room one passed into the courtyard of the small temple of Ninshubura who, as a servant deity, sukkal, would suitably have the lower platform which was devoted to menial tasks, as her domain. The cella in the west wing is a single cella, as befits a minor deity like Ninshubura" (p. 83*).

74. Like the Kitîtum temple, the main sanctuary (NT 4 and NT 5) of the Nabu temple (called Ezida) at Nimrud was insulated from the rest of the temple complex, while its ancillary chapels (NTS 1, NTS 2, and possibly the "Throne Room") were located adjacent to the forecourt (see M. Mallowan, *Nimrud and Its Remains* [3 vols.; New York: Dodd, Mead & Co., 1966], 1:231–41). Similarly, at Dur Sharrukin the "inner temple" (Rooms 21–25) was set apart inside the temple complex, but a more modest shrine (Room 14) was immediately accessible from the forecourt (see G. Loud and C. Altman, *Khorsabad, Part II: The Citadel and the Town* [OIP 40; Chicago: University of Chicago Press, 1938], 56–64).

75. The main cult rooms have been identified with rooms that lie behind Rooms 21, 18, and 15. As for small chapels within the temple complex, the excavators suggested several possibilities, such as Rooms 23, 32, 35, and 37, but only Room 12, which faces the courtyard, can be identified with certitude (see F. Wetzel and F. Weissbach, *Das Haupttheiligtum des Marduk in Babylon, Esagila und Etemenanki* [WVDOG 59; Leipzig: Hinrichs, 1938] 4–13).

Through these shrines, which sometimes replicated architectural elements from the temples themselves, the lay public was able to participate in the temple's worship.[76] A similar impulse can be seen in the Middle Kingdom, when private votive chapels were built near major temples, such as the Osiris temple at Abydos.[77]

Thus it comes as no surprise that a state sanctuary like Tel Dan should include a monumental altar as well as a more modest cult room with its own small sacrificial altar. Because Tel Dan was a state-sponsored cult center in the northern kingdom, scholars have naturally associated its sacred precinct with major religious festivals. Such occasions would have included an assembly of worshipers and therefore required a cultic area that was commensurate with its public character. The biblical *ḥaggîm* immediately come to mind as the sort of religious events that would have been celebrated in T-Center. These festivals usually included large gatherings, as we know from the frequent mention of "solemn assemblies" (*'aṣṣěrōt*) present at them,[78] and also communal sacrifices (cf. Exod 32:5–6). For example, the dedication of the temple in 1 Kgs 8, which coincided with the Feast of Tabernacles (vv. 2, 65), describes sacrifices made at the altar in the temple courtyard in the presence of the king, priests (v. 3), elders (vv. 1, 3), and a great assemblage (*qāhāl gādôl*, v. 65).[79] This descrip-

---

76. See P. Brand, "Veils, Votives, and Marginalia: The Use of Sacred Space at Karnak and Luxor," in *Sacred Space and Sacred Function in Ancient Thebes* (ed. P. Dorman and B. Bryan; SAOC 61; Chicago: Oriental Institute of the University of Chicago, 2007), 60–61; also C. Routledge, "Parallelism in Popular and Official Religion in Ancient Egypt," in *Text, Artifact, and Image: Revealing Ancient Israelite Religion* (ed. G. Beckman and T. Lewis; BJS 346; Providence: Brown Judaic Studies, 2006), 223–38.

77. See W. Simpson, *The Terrace of the Great God at Abydos: The Offering Chapels of Dynasties 12 and 13* (Publications of the Pennsylvania-Yale Expeditions to Egypt 5; New Haven: Peabody Museum of Natural History of Yale University; Philadelphia: University Museum of the University of Pennsylvania, 1974), 1–16; also J. Richards, *Society and Death in Ancient Egypt: Mortuary Landscapes of the Middle Kingdom* (Cambridge: Cambridge University Press, 2005), 38–45.

78. See especially Amos 5:21, a polemic against the northern kingdom in which the prophet equates *ḥaggîm* with *'aṣṣěrōt*, and Ps 42:5, which refers to the "crowd celebrating the festival" (*hāmôn ḥōgēg*). See also Lev 23:36; Deut 16:8.

79. Most scholars agree that vv. 1–13 and 62–66 of this chapter represent a pre-Deuteronomistic tradition. See M. Weinfeld, *Deuteronomy and the Deuteronomic School* (Winona Lake, Ind.: Eisenbrauns, 1992), 250; V. Hurowitz, *I Have Built You an Exalted House: Temple Building in the Bible in Light of Mesopotamian and Northwest*

tion is instructive because it describes the multiple constituencies involved in major religious events.[80]

The rooms of T-West, however, suggest that the Tel Dan temple was not only the site of public festivals but also of small-scale worship that has often been designated "family religion." Beginning with R. Albertz's groundbreaking study of personal piety in ancient Israel, scholars have shown increasing interest in this subdiscipline of Israelite religion, which examines the cult practices that took place in the *Lebensraum* of the family.[81] This trend is also apparent in recent archaeological studies that focus on cultic practices within domestic contexts[82] and also on certain household activities, such as food and textile production, which may have had

---

Semitic Writings (JSOTSup 115; Sheffield: Sheffield Academic Press, 1992), 260–77; M. Cogan, *I Kings* (AB 10; New York: Doubleday, 2000), 290–93.

80. This plurality is also apparent in Mesopotamian descriptions of temple dedications (see Hurowitz, *I Have Built You an Exalted House*, 274–75). For example, according to Ashurnasirpal II, he concluded his dedication of the palaces and temples at Kalah with a banquet that served thousands of guests (*RIMA* 2 A.0.101.30)

81. R. Albertz, *Persönliche Frömmigkeit und offizielle Religion* (Calwer Theologische Monographien 9; Stuttgart: Calwer, 1978). Subsequent studies include K. van der Toorn's *Family Religion in Babylonia, Syria, and Israel: Continuity and Changes in the Forms of Religious Life* (SHANE 7; Leiden: Brill, 1996); E. Gerstenberger's *Theologies in the Old Testament* (trans. J. Bowden; Minneapolis: Fortress Press, 2002), 25–91; and most recently, R. Albertz's monumental *Family and Household Religion in Ancient Israel and the Levant* (Winona Lake, Ind.: Eisenbrauns, 2012), which was cowritten with R. Schmitt.

82. For example, household shrines have been identified at Tel Masos, Tell el-Far'ah (North), Beersheba, and Tell Halif. See C. Meyers, "Household Religion," in *Religious Diversity in Ancient Israel and Judah* (ed. F. Stavrakopoulou and J. Barton; London: T&T Clark, 2010), 118–34; B. Nakhai, *Archaeology and the Religions of Canaan and Israel*, 190–91; also E. Willett, "Women and Household Shrines in Ancient Israel" (Ph.D. diss., University of Arizona, 1999), 101–65; H. Weippert, *Palästina in vorhellenistischer Zeit* (Handbuch der Archäologie: Vorderasien 2/1; Munich: Beck, 1988), 409. In addition to these sites, W. Dever identifies several more "family shrines" at Ai (Room 65), Khirbet Raddana, Megiddo (locus 2081 [mistakenly cited as 2048]), Tel Rehov, Tel Amal, Samaria (locus E 207), Lachish (Room 49), and Tell Beit Mirsim (*Did God Have a Wife? Archaeology and Folk Religion in Ancient Israel* [Grand Rapids: Eerdmans, 2005], 110–25), but the contexts of these additional examples are far less certain. For an example from the Transjordan, see P. Daviau's study on Tall Jawa ("Family Religion: Evidence for the Paraphernalia of the Domestic Cult," in *The World of the Aramaeans* [ed. P. Daviau et al.; 3 vols.; JSOTSup 324–26; Sheffield: Sheffield Academic Press, 2001], 2:199–229).

religious significance.[83] In my opinion, the phrase "family religion" best captures the cultic practices at the center of these recent studies,[84] since many of these practices are related to the life cycles of a family (e.g., rites of mourning, healing, and fertility as well as ancestor worship).[85]

A biblical example that may help contextualize the rooms of T-West is the story of Elkanah (1 Sam 1–2), whose *zebaḥ hayyāmîm* exemplifies the purpose, scale, and participants of family religion.[86] Although it is

---

83. See C. Meyers, "From Field Crops to Food: Attributing Gender and Meaning to Bread Production in Iron Age Israel," in *The Archaeology of Difference: Gender, Ethnicity, Class and the "Other" in Antiquity, Studies in Honor of Eric M. Meyers* (ed. D. Edwards and C. McCollough; AASOR 60/61; Boston: American Schools of Oriental Research, 2007), 67–84; S. Ackerman, "Asherah, The West Semitic Goddess of Spinning and Weaving?," *JNES* 67 (2008): 1–29; for more on food preparation and textile production as household activities, see C. Meyers, "Material Remains and Social Relations: Women's Culture in Agrarian Households of the Iron Age," in *Symbiosis, Symbolism, and the Power of the Past: Canaan, Ancient Israel, and Their Neighbors from the Late Bronze Age through Roman Palaestina, Proceedings of the Centennial Symposium, W. F. Albright Institute of Archaeological Research and American Schools of Oriental Research, Jerusalem, May 29–31, 2000* (ed. W. Dever and S. Gitin; Winona Lake, Ind.: Eisenbrauns, 2003), 425–44; and P. King and L. Stager, *Life in Biblical Israel* (Louisville: Westminster John Knox, 2001), 64–67, 146–62.

84. This designation is preferable to "popular religion," which can imply cultic practice that is degenerate or derivative (see R. Albertz, "Family Religion in Ancient Israel and Its Surroundings," in *Household and Family Religion in Antiquity* [ed. J. Bodel and S. Olyan; Malden, Mass.: Blackwell, 2008], 91; and F. Stavrakopoulou, "'Popular' Religion and 'Official' Religion: Practice, Perception, Portrayal," in *Religious Diversity in Ancient Israel and Judah* [ed. F. Stavrakopoulou and J. Barton; London: T&T Clark, 2010], 37–58). The phrases "private religion" and "household religion" are likewise insufficient. The former risks introducing modern conceptions of individuality that are ill-suited for the study of ancient culture (see van der Toorn, *Family Religion*, 3–4), and the latter is unable to account for examples of families worshiping outside their home at local and regional sanctuaries (see below).

85. Albertz, "Family Religion in Ancient Israel," 97–99. "Family" here refers to the social unit denoted by the Hebrew phrase *bêt 'āb*, or "house of the father," which could include multiple generations of relatives as well as various dependents (see J. Schloen, *The House of the Father as Fast and Symbol: Patrimonialism in Ugarit and the Ancient Near East* [Winona Lake, Ind.: Eisenbrauns, 2001], 150; also L. Stager, "The Archaeology of the Family in Ancient Israel," *BASOR* 260 [1985]: 29 n. 9). Here I will follow the model proposed by Schloen, who estimated that the average nuclear family consisted of five persons, the average joint-family *bêt 'āb*, ten persons, and the average *mišpāḥâ*, 120 persons (*House of the Father*, 154–55).

86. See M. Haran, *Temples and Temple-Service in Ancient Israel: An Inquiry into*

celebrated annually at a major cult center, this feast is altogether separate from the national *ḥag* festivals; rather, it is concerned with Elkanah's
annual fulfillment of vows at Shiloh (1 Sam 1:21).[87] The feast is a pri-

---

the Character of Cultic Phenomena and the Historical Setting of the Priestly School
(Oxford: Clarendon, 1978), 304–13; and P. K. McCarter, *I Samuel* (AB 8; Garden City,
N.Y.: Doubleday, 1980), 58.

87. In fact, these verses describe three instances of Elkanah's pilgrimage to
Shiloh: (1) The first (vv. 1–20) reports that Elkanah made this pilgrimage annually
(*miyyāmîm yāmîmâ*) and would take his two wives and their children. Although the
passage mentions two resident priests at Shiloh, Elkanah performs the sacrifice himself (*wayyizbaḥ*) and distributes the meat to his family. (2) The second pilgrimage (vv.
21–23) was made by Elkanah and "his whole house" (*kôl bêtô*), minus Hannah, who
stayed home to nurse Samuel. Here the journey is called the *zebaḥ hayyāmîm*, which
was an opportunity for Elkanah to fulfill his own vow and pay his tithe. This reading
is based on the LXX[BL] of v. 21: *kai tas euchas autou kai pasas tas dekatas tēs gēs autou*)
and LXX[L]. (The latter adds *apodounai pasas* before *tas euchas*.) It is a fuller text than
MT's *wĕ'et-nidrô*, and from it McCarter has reconstructed the following Hebrew Vorlage: *w't ndrw lšlm w't kl m'śrwt 'rṣw*, "and to redeem his vow and all the tithes of the
land" (*I Samuel*, 55). (3) The third pilgrimage (vv. 24–28) took place after Samuel had
been weaned and includes his dedication at Shiloh. Unfortunately, the text here has
been corrupted, but we can still emphasize that Elkanah and Hannah are the principal cultic actors in this sacrifice, and Hannah seems to play an especially important
role. According to the MT, she is the subject of a series of feminine singular verbs and
should be considered, with Elkanah, the plural subject of the verb *wayyišḥaṭû* (v. 25;
also LXX[L]), which describes the actual sacrifice of the calf. In the LXX[B] Elkanah alone
slaughters the bull (*esphaxen*), but both versions agree that Hannah brought her son,
along with the three-year-old bull, flour, and wine, to the temple at Shiloh, since it was,
after all, her vow that occasioned Samuel's dedication (reading LXX *en moschō trieti-
zonti* [< Heb. *bpr mšlš*] against MT *bĕpārîm šĕlōšâ*; see McCarter, *I Samuel*, 56–57).
McCarter has shown that the fuller reading of LXX[B] is preferable and probably itself
consists of a conflation of two variants; the shorter and superior of these variants
includes the plural verb *wyšḥṭw* (ibid., 57).

Finally, I should note my agreement with McCarter and others that the purpose
of this second pilgrimage (reflected in the LXX[B]) was twofold: after Elkanah performed his usual *zebaḥ hayyāmîm*, he and Hannah attended to the fulfillment of her
vow (ibid., 56; see also S. Walters, "Hannah and Anna: The Greek and Hebrew Texts of
1 Samuel 1," *JBL* 107 [1988]: 403; Ackerman, "Household Religion, Family Religion,
and Women's Religion in Ancient Israel," in Bodel and Olyan, *Household and Family
Religion in Antiquity*, 146). The special purpose of the latter is suggested by the fact
that the bull offered is three years old, and likely so is Samuel, since that is the typical
age for a child in ancient Israel to be weaned (see J. Blenkinsopp, "The Family in First
Temple Israel," in *Families in Ancient Israel* [Louisville: Westminster John Knox, 1997],
97–98 n. 42; M. Gruber, "Breast-Feeding Practices in Biblical Israel," in *Motherhood of*

vate affair, presided over by Elkanah (and later, possibly, Hannah), and it seems to have been just large enough for Elkanah, his wives, and his children (see 1 Sam 1:4–5).[88] Indeed, the familial character of the *zebaḥ hayyāmîm* is confirmed by its use elsewhere in 1 Samuel, where it is synonymous with *zebaḥ mišpāḥâ* (20:6, 29). This offering and feast are probably the kind of religious occasion we should imagine took place in T-West. After the animal was slaughtered and offerings were made in the Altar Room, perhaps the family consumed its portion of the meat in one of the other rooms.

It is not my intention to connect these specific biblical examples to Area T at Tel Dan, nor is this the only possible reconstruction. Indeed, Biran identified the T-West rooms as "priestly chambers," or *lĕšākōt*, where "the priests officiated and their garments and the like were deposited."[89] He defined *liškâ* according to its usage in Ezra 8:29 and 1 Chr 9:26, where the term denotes temple storerooms for priests and other cultic personnel,[90] though elsewhere in the Hebrew Bible the *liškâ* is the site of ritual feasting (e.g., 1 Sam 9:22).[91] Another interpretation of the western rooms comes

---

God and Other Studies [Atlanta: Scholars Press, 1992], 69–107; repr. from *JANESCU* 19 [1989]).

88. See S. Ackerman, "Who Is Sacrificing at Shiloh? The Priesthoods of Ancient Israel's Regional Sanctuaries," in *Levites and Priests in Biblical History and Tradition* (ed. M. Leuchter and J. Hutton; SBLAIL 9; Atlanta: Society of Biblical Literature, 2011), 25–43. As the present discussion argues, her assessment of priests' engagement at regional sanctuaries may also be relevant to state-sponsored sanctuaries (ibid., 30).

89. H. Shanks, "Avraham Biran—Twenty Years of Digging at Tel Dan," *BAR* 13.4 (July/Aug 1987): 18. Visitors to the Tel Dan today will notice that signage at the site refers to the rooms of T-West as "priestly chambers."

90. In early reports, this term was used exclusively for the North Room (A. Biran, "Tel Dan, 1984," 188–89; idem, "Dancer from Dan," 179 n. 17; also idem, *Biblical Dan*, 212), but in later articles, especially in popular journals, the term was ascribed to other rooms as well (Shanks, "Avraham Biran," 18–20; Biran, "Sacred Spaces," 40–41). For the prevalence of storerooms in ancient Near Eastern temple complexes, see K. Kitchen, "Two Notes on the Subsidiary Rooms of Solomon's Temple," *EI* 20 (1989): 107*–12*.

91. The difference between this *liškâ* and the *lĕšākōt* of Ezra 8:29 and 1 Chr 9:26 is reflected in the LXX, which translates the former with Gr. *katalyma* ("room") and the latter with Gr. *thēsauros* ("treasury"). Furthermore, these different translations help us recognize another instance of *liškâ* used to denote a room for ritual feasting, namely, 1 Sam 1:18, which takes place at the sanctuary at Shiloh. The LXX[BL] of this verse reports that Hannah, after finishing her conversation with Eli, "went on her way and

from J. Greer, who sees them as the domain of priests, based in part on the higher percentage of right-sided animal portions that were found in the T-West bone deposits.[92] According to his assessment, the western rooms are where priestly portions were awarded, processed, and consumed.

Such a reconstruction of T-West is not incompatible with the picture I have suggested, since family religion does not mean that priests had no role in the cultic activity, only that the family members represent the primary officiants, participants, and beneficiaries, who sometimes collaborated with religious specialists. This is precisely the picture we find in 1 Sam 2:13–16, which reports that "when any man made a sacrifice, the priest's servant would come while the meat was boiling and with a three-pronged fork in his hand. He would thrust it into the pot or kettle,[93] and whatever the fork brought up the priest took for himself. Thus they did for all Israelites who came [to sacrifice to YHWH[94]] at Shiloh." Significantly, this text assumes that "any man" (*kol-'îš*) could come to make a sacrifice at Shiloh as long as he gave a proper portion to the resident priest. Also noteworthy is the fact that the priest himself does not preside over such a sacrifice nor even retrieve the portion himself. The priest sends a servant to take his portion from the offering presided over by the lay worshiper. This text sheds light on the cultic situation at Tel Dan because it shows that family religion and priestly prerogatives were not mutually exclusive but could coexist in the same worship space. It seems plausible that small-scale, family-oriented rites could take place in part of T-West, while the priests could be in the same area, attending to cultic activity and receiving their prebends.

Indeed, my primary interest is the apparently contrasting, but also overlapping, purposes of T-Center and T-West. Whereas the former pro-

---

entered the [LXX[B]: "her"] room [*katalyma*] and ate with her husband." As McCarter has shown, this reading was likely the original, and the shorter MT reading likely resulted from a haplography caused by the similarity of Heb. *ldrkh* ("on her way") and *lškh* ("room") (*I Samuel*, 55). As in 1 Sam 9:22, the term *liškâ* denotes a room within a larger cultic complex that is used for consuming meals.

92. See Greer, "Dinner at Dan," 86–90. Greer connects this preference for right-sided portions to the biblical evidence indicating priests were awarded those portions (cf. Exod 29:27–28; Lev 7:32–33). Additionally, he connects the evidence of skin processing in T-West to the biblical evidence that skins were a form of payment to priests (cf. Lev 7:8).

93. Following 4QSam[a], which lists only two vessels (see McCarter, *I Samuel*, 79).

94. Cf. LXX *thysai kyriō*. See McCarter, *I Samuel*, 79.

vides an archaeological example of an altar temenos and surrounding courtyard whose worship space is large enough for the priestly officials and religious assembly that would be on hand for national religious celebrations, the latter likely served as a place for smaller-scale worship, perhaps cultic activities that are representative of family religion. Although this reconstruction remains hypothetical, it may help contribute to a growing recognition among scholars of the interplay between family religion and "official" religion.[95] Although some still regard them as distinct categories of religious experience,[96] many scholars now recognize that "'official' and 'popular' manifestations of religion co-exist within a complex dynamic relationship, reflecting the dynamism of the cultural system in which religious practice must take place."[97] One part of this coexistence is the prevalence of family religion at public sanctuaries, a phenomenon that for Albertz includes

> all the rites that would have been performed by a family within the sphere of their public cult, in local, regional, or state sanctuaries. Not only family members but also other kin, friends, and neighbors would usually have participated in these celebrations. Examples may have included a sacrificial meal in the sanctuary to celebrate the healing of a family member, so he could be reintegrated into the local community, or a sacrificial meal intended to pay the promissory vows of family mem-

---

95. The scare quotes are an acknowledgment that "official" is a problematic term, which erroneously implies the existence of a stable and normative religious tradition that can be traced through Israel's history, when in fact normative cultic activity is a rather fluid concept in the biblical evidence (see Z. Zevit, "False Dichotomies in Descriptions of Israelite Religion: A Problem, Its Origin, and a Proposed Solution," in *Symbiosis, Symbolism, and the Power of the Past: Canaan, Ancient Israel, and Their Neighbors from the Late Bronze Age through Roman Palaestina, Proceedings of the Centennial Symposium, W. F. Albright Institute of Archaeological Research and American Schools of Oriental Research, Jerusalem, May 29–31, 2000* [ed. W. Dever and S. Gitin; Winona Lake, Ind.: Eisenbrauns, 2003], 230–32). Acknowledging this problem, I think it is still a serviceable term to refer to religious groups who seek to assert their theological and cultic agenda as normative (see J. Berlinerblau, *The Vow and the "Popular Religious Groups" of Ancient Israel: A Philological and Sociological Inquiry* [JSOTSup 210; Sheffield: Sheffield Academic Press, 1996], 29).

96. See, e.g., P. Miller's discussion of "orthodox Yahwism" and "heterodox Yahwism" (*The Religion of Ancient Israel* [Library of Ancient Israel; Louisville: Westminster John Knox, 2000], 47–56).

97. Stavrakopoulou, "'Official' Religion and 'Popular' Religion," 41.

bers. Also the rites having to do with family production ... would have belonged to this outer circle [of family religion].[98]

So far archaeological examples of this interplay between family religion and "official" religion have been limited, but the division of cultic space at Area T between T-West and T-Center/T-North may provide further evidence of the interface.[99] The evidence from Tel Dan suggests that family religion need not be restricted to domestic contexts, nor should a major sanctuary be equated exclusively with "official" religion. Insofar as Area T's overlapping cultic spheres are reflected in its architecture and material remains, as argued above, their correlation should be considered part of the site's conceptual space. The sacred precinct at Tel Dan seems to have been designed to accommodate a variety of cultic activities, ranging from large public festivals to smaller religious celebrations.

In conclusion, I have argued for two organizing principles that are constitutive of Area T's conceptual space during Stratum II: centralization and the overlapping of distinct cultic spheres. These principles represent my attempt to correlate the changes in the spatial arrangement of Area T in Stratum II to other religious and political developments that took place in the eighth century B.C.E., and while they are of course speculative and tentative, the principles offer a cogent argument for some of the priorities and concerns that produced the sacred space we find at Area T in Stratum II.

---

98. Albertz and Schmitt, *Family and Household Religion*, 44. See also Albertz, *History of Israelite Religion*, 1:99–103.

99. Albertz and Schmitt so cite Tel Dan as an example of family religion at a supraregional sanctuary but only cite votive objects as evidence of rituals involving families or individuals (*Family and Household Religion*, 481; see also 237–38).

PART 2
ANALYSIS OF BIBLICAL TEXTS

In part 2 I turn my attention to textual data, which will provide further context for the archaeological data I have analyzed. In this endeavor the Hebrew Bible will play a central role, but even as I am convinced that the biblical text can shed new light on the issues I have addressed, I am also mindful of its pitfalls. For this reason, I will begin part 2 by discussing the biblical texts that are relevant to my discussion of Tel Dan in the Iron IIB period and by explaining my rationale in selecting texts for the present work.

When we think about the biblical traditions concerning Tel Dan, especially its cultic history, the two texts that immediately come to mind are Judg 17–18, which tells the story of the Levite priest who is drafted into the service of the Danites on their way to Laish, and 1 Kgs 12:25–33, which recounts Jeroboam ben Nebat's founding of Dan and Bethel as national cult centers. Therefore, it may come as a surprise to find that neither of the texts is treated in the following chapters. This omission is deliberate. In short, they have been left out not because they are irrelevant to the cultic history of Tel Dan but because they are not the most relevant for my study of Strata III–II at the site. In the introduction to this study, I discussed the comparative method and the integration of archaeological and textual data, and there I concluded that the most useful texts for comparison are those that are closest in time and space to the archaeological remains under examination.[1] According to this approach, the most valuable biblical texts for our study are those that have a northern provenance[2] and that date to the ninth-eighth centuries B.C.E.[3]

---

1. See above, p. 2.

2. Given the present work's focus on northern texts, it is tempting to use the term "Israelian" to refer the northern cultic and literary traditions under examination This term was coined by H. Ginsberg as a geosocial designation particular to the northern

In my opinion, Judg 17–18 and 1 Kgs 12:25–33 do not satisfy these two criteria. While one can make a case that both have a northern orientation, a northern origin is less certain. However, it would be even harder

---

kingdom and was intended as an alternative to "Israelite," which has tended to denote both kingdoms (*The Israelian Heritage of Judaism* [New York: Jewish Theological Seminary of America, 1982], 1–2). More recently, however, the term has been associated with attempts, especially by G. Rendsburg, to isolate a northern dialect of ancient Hebrew, which he calls "Israelian Hebrew," and to define its features (see G. Rendsburg, "Israelian Hebrew in the Song of Songs," in *Biblical Hebrew in its Northwest Semitic Setting* [ed. S. Fassberg and A. Hurvitz; Winona Lake, Ind.: Eisenbrauns, 2006], 315–23; idem, *Israelian Hebrew in the Book of Kings* [Bethesda, Md.: CDL, 2002]; idem, "Israelian Hebrew Features in Genesis 49," *Maarav* 8 [1993]: 161–70; idem, *Linguistic Evidence for the Northern Origin of Selected Psalms* [SBLMS 43; Atlanta: Scholars Press, 1990]; idem, "The Northern Origin of Nehemiah 9," *Bib* 72 [1991]: 348–66; idem, "The Northern Origin of 'The Last Words of David (2 Sam 23, 1–7),'" *Bib* 69 [1988]: 113–21).

On the one hand, there is no question that various dialects existed in ancient Israel (see Judg 12:6). W. Garr, for example, has concluded that "physical geography … explains the recognizable deviations in northern Hebrew from the pattern of the southern dialect" (*Dialect Geography of Syria-Palestine, 100–586 B.C.E.* [Winona Lake, Ind.: Eisenbrauns, 2004], 233), and P. K. McCarter has written that "the modest corpus of surviving inscriptions from the Northern Kingdom is sufficient to show that its dialect displayed features that were significantly different from that of Judah, as it is known from a more generous inscriptional corpus and, indeed, from the Hebrew Bible itself" ("Hebrew," in *The Cambridge Encyclopedia of the World's Ancient Languages* [ed. R. Woodard; New York: Cambridge University Press, 2004], 320).

On the other hand, many scholars have rightly questioned our ability to isolate them (see D. Fredericks, "A North Israelite Dialect in the Hebrew Bible? Questions of Methodology," *HS* 37 [1996]: 7–20; I. Young, "Evidence of Diversity in Pre-Exilic Judahite Hebrew," *HS* 38 [1997]: 7–20). For example, Rendsburg uses cognates from Phoenician, Aramaic, Ammonite, and Moabite to identify specific features of "Israelian Hebrew," but such comparisons are not themselves proof of a distinctive and unified dialect. Another problem is the prevalence of so-called Israelian features in biblical texts that cannot be considered northern. To take just one example, using the occurrence of 'ăkîlâ in 1 Kgs 19:8, Rendsburg remarks that the qĕtîlâ formation "appears disproportionately in northern contexts" (*Israelian Hebrew*, 56), but this formation is well-attested in non-northern texts (e.g., hălîkâ ["march"] in Nah 2:6; hălîpâ ["change"] in 1 Kgs 5:28).

3. These chronological parameters are based on the decision to focus our study of Tel Dan to Strata III–II, which date to the ninth–eighth centuries B.C.E. As discussed above (pp. 29–30), this decision was based on the relatively secure dating of these strata. In this case, the state of the archaeological data has dictated the temporal framework of our textual analysis.

to argue that the respective dates of Judg 17–18 and 1 Kgs 12:25–33 correspond to Strata III–II at Tel Dan. Such an argument is hampered by the composition history of each text, which makes it difficult to decide which parts of each passage are applicable to our study of Dan in the ninth and eighth centuries B.C.E. For example, even though 1 Kgs 12:25–33 is likely a polemical text written from the Jerusalemite viewpoint of the Deuteronomist, the passage is likely a genuine witness to northern cultic traditions. This point has been made effectively by G. Knoppers, who acknowledges the text's Deuteronomistic perspective but reasons that

> in indulging Jeroboam with this attention, the Deuteronomist concedes the antiquity and appeal of the sanctuaries at Bethel and Dan. If the tauromorphic iconography at Bethel and Dan was not popular and well-established, there would be no need to accommodate these shrines with such critical coverage.[4]

The question, then, is whether any part of 1 Kgs 12:25–33 can be correlated to Stratum III or II at Tel Dan, and this question cannot be answered affirmatively. For whatever early tradition is embedded in these verses is explicitly linked to Jeroboam, whose reign predates Stratum III, and although it is reasonable to assume that this cultic portrait remained valid during the ninth and eighth centuries B.C.E., we have no compelling reason to assign the text to a later reign, such as one of the Omride dynasty.[5] At the other end of this redaction history is the Deuteronomist's presentation of this early tradition, which dates after the end of Stratum II (i.e., 732 B.C.E.).[6]

---

4. G. Knoppers, *The Reign of Jeroboam, the Fall of Israel, and the Reign of Josiah* (vol. 2 of *Two Nations Under God: The Deuteronomistic History of Solomon and the Dual Monarchies*; HSM 53; Atlanta: Scholars Press, 1993), 41–42. See also Toews, *Monarchy and Religious Institution in Israel under Jeroboam I* (SBLMS 47; Atlanta: Scholars Press, 1993), 34–38; Z. Zevit, "Deuteronomistic Historiography in 1 Kings 12–2 Kings 17 and the Reinvestiture of the Israelian Cult," *JSOT* 32 (1985): 57–73.

5. Though see P. Ash, "Jeroboam I and the Deuteronomistic Historian's Ideology of the Founder," *CBQ* 60 (1998): 16–24.

6. G. Knoppers reasons that the polemic was probably written sometime after the fall of the northern kingdom but before the fall of Jerusalem in 586 B.C.E. He writes that "supporters of the temple could exalt the inviolability of Jerusalem in the aftermath of the Assyrian crisis (e.g., 2 Kgs 19:34; 20:6), but it would make little sense to lambaste Jeroboam's bull iconography, priesthood, sanctuaries, pilgrimage, and festival in the aftermath of Judah's humiliation in the Babylonian exile" ("Aaron's Calf and Jeroboam's Calves," in *Fortunate the Eyes That See: Essays in Honor of David Noel*

These same problems attend Judg 17–18. Many scholars recognize that this narrative conveys an early cultic tradition about Dan that originated in the north and was later edited in the south, but most reconstructions of this redactional history assign the earliest stages of the tradition to Jeroboam I (or earlier).[7] Thus we are again faced with a situation in which the earliest tradition should be dated before Stratum III and subsequent redactions seem to date after the end of Stratum II (see Judg 18:30–31).[8] Although Judg 17–18 and 1 Kgs 12:25–33 unquestionably shed light on cultic life at Tel Dan, neither text matches the chronological framework of the present study. If we were examining Stratum IVA, which has preliminarily been dated to the reign of Jeroboam I,[9] then these two texts would be indispensable. However, this dating is not yet certain, and until the Iron Age pottery and stratigraphy have been published, a full study of 1 Kgs 12:25–33 and Judg 17–18 vis-à-vis Area T at Tel Dan must be set aside for a future project.

From this discussion, it should be clear that the most relevant biblical texts for our study of Tel Dan are not necessarily the ones that explicitly mention Dan or even those that address some aspect of its cultic history. While all these references are significant, usually they inform more about southern attitudes toward Dan than about Dan itself. Because the goal of the next two chapters is to explore biblical texts that approximate

---

Freedman in Celebration of His Seventieth Birthday [ed. A. Beck et al.; Grand Rapids: Eerdmans, 1995], 104; see also idem, *Reign of Jeroboam*, 43).

7. See H. Niemann, *Die Daniten: Studien zur Geschichte eines altisraelitischen Stammes* (FRLANT 135; Göttingen: Vandenhoeck & Ruprecht, 1985), 129–37; M. Bartusch, *Understanding Dan: An Exegetical Study of a Biblical City, Tribe and Ancestor* (JSOTSup 379; Sheffield: Sheffield Academic Press, 2003), 170–202.; J. Bray, *Sacred Dan: Religious Tradition and Cultic Practice in Judges 17–18* (LHB/OTS 449; New York: T&T Clark, 2006), 23–28.

8. Niemann, for example, argues that the *Grunderzählung* of Judg 17–18 was first revised under Jeroboam I but not again until after 733 B.C.E. (*Die Daniten*, 131–34), and in one of his two hypotheses, Bartusch argues for a redactional stage during the reign of Jeroboam I followed by another redaction during the exile (*Understanding Dan*, 181–85). For a review and critique of these and other reconstructions, see Bray, *Sacred Dan*, 23–28. Finally, some, like Bray, argue that Judg 17–18 was composed in its entirety after the fall of the northern kingdom (ibid., 28; see also Y. Amit, "Hidden Polemic in the Conquest of Dan: Judges XVII–XVIII," *VT* 40 [1990]: 4–20; Toews, *Monarchy and Religious Institution*, 115–23).

9. See Biran, *Biblical Dan*, 165–83.

the archaeological strata under examination, the most relevant passages are those that can be correlated to Strata III–II at Tel Dan.

From this perspective and according to the twin criteria of spatial and temporal proximity, I contend that the most valuable texts for understanding the ninth and eighth centuries B.C.E. at Tel Dan are the Elijah narrative in 1 Kgs 18 and the book of Amos, respectively, and for this reason, they are the focus of the next two chapters. I will begin each chapter by demonstrating their relevance to my study of Tel Dan: first, I will try to establish the northern provenience of each; and second, I will argue that each text can be assigned a date that approximates the strata examined at Tel Dan. In particular, in chapter 4 I follow those scholars who argue for a Jehu redaction of the Elijah narrative, which would situate the text in the ninth century B.C.E., around the time of Stratum III. Then in chapter 5 I subscribe to arguments for dating the book of Amos to the eighth century B.C.E., which would correspond to Stratum II at Tel Dan. In both chapters, after establishing the texts' northern provenience and dates of composition, I will mine the texts for information they might yield about cultic traditions in the northern kingdom during the time of Strata III–II at Tel Dan. The Elijah narrative and the book of Amos are possibly our best witnesses to the religion that was practiced in northern sanctuaries during that time, and for this reason they will provide an important check on some of the interpretations developed in the preceding chapters, which dealt strictly with the archaeological remains of Tel Dan. The goal of these comparisons is to integrate archaeological and textual evidence for a more comprehensive perspective on Israelite religion. Now that I have completed my analysis of the archaeological data, I turn my attention to the textual witnesses of the Hebrew Bible.

4
NINTH-CENTURY B.C.E. TEXTUAL STRATUM: 1 KINGS 18

4.1 INTRODUCTION

In seeking out biblical texts to shed light on cultic attitudes in the northern kingdom during the Iron IIB, I turn now to the Elijah cycle (1 Kgs 17–19), especially chapter 18. Verses 20–40 of this chapter describe the contest on Mount Carmel between Elijah and the prophets of Baal in which both sides prepare a sacrifice without setting fire to it; then the prophets of Baal invoke the name of their god. When Baal fails to answer, Elijah calls upon YHWH, who immediately torches the sacrifice and its altar. YHWH's triumph is acknowledged by the people, who bow down and proclaim his divinity.[1] This scene provides information on several facets of Israelite cult, such as the preparation of sacrifices and the invocation of YHWH, but especially relevant to the present study is its description of sacred space: how it is constructed and how it is managed. Discussion of these issues will constitute the bulk of this chapter, but a few introductory remarks are in order. Since the analysis of this text is intended to shed light on the cultic situation at Tel Dan in the Iron IIB, I will need to establish 1 Kgs 18:20–40 (hereafter, simply 1 Kgs 18) as a text worthy of comparison.

First of all, the narrative is relevant to the present study because of its northern setting.[2] According to 1 Kgs 18:19 the contest takes place in northern Israel on Mount Carmel, a coastal promontory that heads a range

---

1. Not all of ch. 18 is devoted to the contest; in fact, the scene on Mount Carmel is framed by a famine story, which many regard as a separate tradition. Verses 1–19 recount the famine in Samaria and Elijah's encounter with the palace official Obadiah, and at the end of the chapter, vv. 41–46 show the resolution of the famine story.

2. In this respect I disagree strongly with scholars who find Mount Carmel an entirely arbitrary site for the contest (e.g., S. DeVries, *I Kings* [2nd ed.; WBC 12; Nashville: Thomas Nelson, 2003], 227).

of limestone hills running southeast toward Yoqne'am. The Carmel narrative's northern locale has led some scholars, beginning with C. Burney,[3]
to classify its linguistic anomalies as features of a northern dialect. In the
introduction to part 2, I noted some problems with the so-called Israelian
Hebrew dialect (see above, pp. 109–10 n. 2), and caution is further recommended by W. Schniedewind and D. Sivan, who have systematically
studied the linguistic anomalies in the Elijah and Elisha narratives and
concluded that decisive evidence of a northern dialect is lacking.[4] Thus the
distinctive vocabulary of the Carmel narrative, while noteworthy, cannot
be used to confirm its northern milieu,[5] but nonetheless its northern setting and its familiarity with the politics of the Omride dynasty suggest a
northern provenance.

Even if the contest's northern setting were the only relevant aspect
of the story, the episode would warrant careful examination, but as it is,
there are several similarities between Carmel and Dan, which make 1
Kgs 18 especially important for the present study. First, both sites seem
to have had a long-standing religious significance. Just as Biran proposed
that a Middle Bronze temple may lie beneath the Iron Age cultic precinct at Tel Dan,[6] the various names of Mount Carmel in Egyptian and
Assyrian sources suggest that it too was a cult site in the Bronze and Iron
Ages. In the records of three different pharaohs—Thutmose III (1479–
1425 B.C.E.), Ramses II (1279–1213 B.C.E.), and Ramses III (1184–1153
B.C.E.)—Mount Carmel is listed as *Rš qdš*, or "Holy Cape."[7] This tanta-

---

3. C. Burney, *Notes on the Hebrew Text of the Books of Kings* (Oxford: Clarendon,
1903), 207–9.

4. W. Schniedewind and D. Sivan, "The Elijah-Elisha Narratives: A Test Case for
the Northern Dialect of Hebrew," *JQR* 87 (1997): 303–37. They have shown that linguistic anomalies can often be explained by factors other than geography (e.g., genre,
literary stylizing).

5. A notable exception is the noun *kad* ("jar"), which occurs only in northern
(e.g., 1 Kgs 18:34) or foreign contexts and was also found inscribed on an eighth-cen-
tury-B.C.E. potsherd from the Galilee region (Schniedewind and Sivan, "Elijah-Elisha
Narratives," 327–28).

6. For evidence of Tel Dan's status as a cult center in the Bronze Age, see above,
pp. 26–28 n. 24.

7. The lists of Thutmose III and Ramses II are discussed by W. Helck in *Die Beziehungen Ägyptens zu Vorderasien im 3. und 2. Jahrtausend v. Chr.* (2nd ed.; ÄgAbh
5; Wiesbaden: Harrassowitz, 1971), 126 and 209, respectively. (Helck thinks that the
Thutmose III inscription refers to Mount Carmel but the Ramses II text does not.)

lizing name leaves little for us to examine, but it does show that in the centuries leading into the Iron Age the Egyptians recognized Mount Carmel as a sacred area. A few centuries later we find another reference to Mount Carmel in the annals of the Neo-Assyrian king Shalmaneser III (858–824 B.C.E.). His description of the Assyrian campaign against Hazael of Damascus in his eighteenth year (i.e., 841 B.C.E.) is recorded in at least three inscriptions, and each concludes with the following report: "I marched to the mountains of Ba'li-rasi, which is above the sea opposite Tyre. I erected a statue of my royalty there. I received the tribute of Ba'al-manzēr, the Tyrian, and of Jehu, the son of Ḥumrî."[8] The objections of

---

Ramses III also includes this toponym in his Medinet Habu list, but this list is likely stereotyped and lacks any historical value. The reference to *Rš qdš*, for example, appears in a section that has been copied (in reverse) from the Ramses II list (ibid., 237).

The identification of *Rš qdš* with Mount Carmel is made by S. Aḥituv, who notes that it appears in the Thutmose list between Acco and Carmel/Karmin, precisely where we expect the "head" of the Carmel ridge (*Canaanite Toponyms in Ancient Egyptian Documents* [Jerusalem: Magnes, 1984], 162); see also Y. Aharoni, "Mount Carmel as Border," in *Archäologie und altes Testament: Festschrift für Kurt Galling zum 8.Januar 1970* (ed. A. Kuschke and E. Kutsch; Tübingen: Mohr Siebeck, 1970), 2; A. Rainey and R. Notley, *The Sacred Bridge: Carta's Atlas of the Biblical World* [Jerusalem: Carta, 2006], 208; R. de Vaux, "The Prophets of Baal on Mount Carmel," in *The Bible and the Ancient Near East* (trans. D. McHugh; London: Darton, Longman & Todd, 1972), 238; S. Yeivin, "The Third District in Tuthmosis III's List of Palestino-Syrian Towns," *JEA* 36 (1950): 59.

8. Akk. *a-na* kur-*e* kur *ba-'a-li-ra-'a-si ša* sag *tam-di ša pu-ut* kur *ṣur-ri al-lik ṣa-lam man-ti-ia ina lìb-bi ú-še(*)-ziz ma-da-tu šá* ᵐ*ba-'a-li-ma-an*-numun ᵐ*ṣur-ra-a-a ša* ᵐ*ia-a-ú* dumu *ḫu-um-ri-i* (*RIMA* 3 A.0.102.10 iv 7–11). Except for a few minor differences and at least one major difference, this report is repeated in two other annalistic texts (*RIMA* 3 A.0.102.8:22"-27"; 102.12:28–30). The important difference is that only the marble slab (*RIMA* 3 A.0.102.10) includes the decisive phrase *ša pu-ut* kur *ṣur-ri* ("opposite the land of Tyre"). This addition is significant because it suggests that the logogram sag should be read as *pūtu* instead of *rēšu* (see E. Michel, "Die Assur-Texte Salmanassars III. (858-824)," *WO* 2 [1954]: 38–39; cf. J. Wilson, "The Kurba'il Statue of Shalmaneser III," *Iraq* 24 [1962]: 94). Although *rēšu* ("cape") is quite attractive as a parallel to *Rā'ši-qodšu* and Ba'li-rasi, the preposition *pūtu* results in better syntax. On the other hand, the translation of *pūtu* as "along" misses Shalmaneser's emphasis on height, which made the site suitable for his statue. For our translation, we have split the difference and translates the logogram sag as "above." Also noteworthy is the phrase ᵐ*ia-a-ú* dumu *ḫu-um-ri-i* (*RIMA* 3 A.0.102.10 iv 11; cf. 102.8:27"; 102.12:30). Although Grayson translates this name and patronymic as "Jehu (Iaua) of the house of Omri (Ḥumrî)" and K. Younger as "Jehu (*Ia-a-ú*), (man of) Bīt-Ḥumri (Omri)" (*COS* 2:113C–E), the text itself reads "son" (dumu), not "house" (*bītu*). Grayson and

E. Lipiński notwithstanding, scholars have identified $^{\text{KUR}}Ba$-'a-li-ra-'a-si in this text with Mount Carmel and with Rš qdš from Egyptian sources.[9] Again we are left with only a toponym from which to infer the cultic status of Mount Carmel, but the promontory's association with the god Baal, combined with its earlier identification as the "Holy Cape," are certainly enough to conclude that Mount Carmel, like Tel Dan, was regarded as a sacred mountain in the Bronze and Iron Ages.[10]

A second, and more controversial, aspect of the Carmel narrative that makes it relevant to my analysis of Tel Dan is its antiquity. So far in this chapter I have referred to 1 Kgs 18 as a ninth-century-B.C.E. text— its selection for study was based on this date—but this remains a matter of spirited debate. While an exhaustive review of this important issue is beyond the scope of the present work, I can nonetheless highlight certain trends and state the suppositions that will guide the present work. Basically, the field is divided between an early date and late date for the Elijah and Elisha cycles. On the one hand are those scholars like A. Campbell and M. O'Brien, B. Lehnart, O. Steck, and M. Sweeney who associate these narratives with Jehu and thus date them in the ninth-eighth-century-B.C.E. range.[11] On the other hand, scholars like G. Fohrer, S. McKenzie, E.

<hr />

Younger, like many scholars, have clearly interpreted the designation as an indication of succession rather than filiation and thus supply "house." Yet the precise language is worth preserving and may even have historical implications (see P. McCarter, "'Yaw, Son of 'Omri': A Philological Note on Israelite Chronology," *BASOR* 216 [1974]: 5–7).

9. For Ba'li-rasi as Mount Carmel, see A. Green, "Sua and Jehu: The Boundaries of Shalmaneser's Conquest," *PEQ* 111 (1979): 36; M. Astour, "841 B.C.: The First Assyrian Invasion of Israel," *JAOS* 91 (1971): 385–86; Y. Aharoni, "Mount Carmel as Border," 6–7. For the identification of Ba'li-rasi with Rā'ši-qodšu, see Ahituv, *Canaanite Toponyms*, 163; Y. Aharoni, "Mount Carmel as Border," 6–7. Only E. Lipiński still maintains that Ba'li-rasi should be identified with Ras en-Naqura; notably he also takes Ba'li-rasi and Rā'ši-qodšu as referring to the same toponym ("Ba'li-ra'ši et Ra'šu Qudšu," *RB* 78 [1971]: 84–92).

10. See R. Clifford, *The Cosmic Mountain in Canaan and the Old Testament* (HSM 4; Cambridge: Harvard University Press, 1972), 134.

11. (1) A. Campbell and M. O'Brien in their recent *Unfolding the Deuteronomistic History: Origins, Upgrades, Present Text* (Minneapolis: Fortress, 2000), and Campbell in his earlier *Of Prophets and Kings: A Late Ninth-Century Document (1 Samuel 1–2 Kings 10)* (CBQMS 17; Washington, D.C.: Catholic Biblical Association of America, 1986) argue for the existence of the so-called Prophetic Record, a northern text that was primarily concerned with the prophetic designation and rejection of kings and that was composed in the late ninth century B.C.E. by the disciples of Elisha in the

Würthwein, and S. Otto argue that the Elijah narratives are the product of Deuteronomistic efforts and belong to the exilic or even postexilic periods.[12] In my opinion, the weight of evidence falls on an earlier dating, not

---

aftermath of Jehu's reforms (*Of Prophets and Kings*, 103–10). At this time, certain earlier traditions that had been preserved by the disciples were enfolded in the Prophetic Record (ibid., 115). Thus the redacted text of the Carmel narrative can be dated to just a few decades after the period in which it is set. (2) B. Lehnart, *Prophet und König im Nordreich Israel: Studien zur sogenannten vorklassischen Prophetie im Nordreich Israel anhand der Samuel-, Elija- und Elischa-Überlieferungen* (VTSup 96; Leiden: Brill, 2003), 327–57, esp. 349–51. Like Campbell, Lehnart argues that the Elijah traditions are connected to the prophetic group that produced the Elisha tradition (349–50). As for dating the Elijah cycle, he more cautiously locates it after Jehu's revolt and before the end of the northern kingdom (345). Cf. see also M. Cogan, who accepts a common origin for the Elijah and Elisha cycles but is wary of connecting the stories to the reign of Jehu (*I Kings* [AB 10; New York: Doubleday, 2000], 93, 448 n. 4). (3) O. Steck, *Überlieferung und Zeitgeschichte in den Elia-Erzählungen* (WMANT 26; Neukirchen-Vlyun: Neukirchener, 1968). Steck argues that the Elijah narratives in 1 Kgs 17–19, 21 were composed in three stages. In his scheme the drought narrative and the Carmel narrative belong to the first stage, which dates to the reign of Ahab. After the addition of some Jezebel traditions, such as 19:1–3, the Horeb scene was the last to be added, sometimes during the wars of Hazael. Most important for our purposes is Steck's insistence that the Carmel narrative originated in the Omride period and was redacted during Jehu's reign (81–90). This reconstruction is more or less followed by DeVries (*1 Kings*, 208–9). (4) M. Sweeney, *I and II Kings: A Commentary* (OTL; Louisville: Westminster John Knox, 2007), 26–30. Sweeney modifies Campbell and O'Brien's Prophetic Record by arguing that this northern composition culminates not with Jehu but with his successor, Jeroboam II. Hence he calls it the Jehu Dynastic History and dates it to the eighth century B.C.E. but still thinks "the Elijah and Elisha cycles appear to have an independent composition history prior to being taken up and edited into the Jehu history" (29).

    12. (1) G. Fohrer, *Elia* (rev. ed.; ATANT 53; Zürich: Zwingli, 1968). Fohrer perceives Deuteronomistic influence in 1 Kgs 17–19 and offers examples of terminology that reflect this influence (53–55). (2) S. McKenzie, *The Trouble with Kings: The Composition of the Book of Kings in the Deuteronomistic History* (VTSup 42; Leiden: Brill, 1991). In a section on 1 Kgs 17–19 (pp. 81–87) McKenzie rejects Fohrer's case for a Deuteronomistic redaction of 1 Kgs 17–19 and argues instead that typical language and themes of the Deuteronomist are absent in these chapters. He concludes from this absence that the Elijah cycle is actually a post-Deuteronomistic addition to the account of Ahab's reign. (3) After initially acknowledging a pre-Deuteronomist stage of the 1 Kgs 18:21–39 in his 1984 commentary (*Die Bücher der Könige* [2 vols.; ATD 11; Göttingen: Vandenhoeck & Ruprecht, 1977–1984], 2:207–20, esp. 219), Würthwein reconsidered this dating in a subsequent article in which he concluded that the Carmel narrative *originated* in a late Deuteronomistic context ("Zur Opferprobe Elias

least because several who argue for the Carmel narrative's late inclusion in the Deuteronomistic History acknowledge that the tradition itself could be early.[13] Furthermore, the attribution of 1 Kgs 18 to the Deuteronomist raises as many questions as it supposedly answers. For example, if Deuteronomistic ideology is so prevalent in these chapters, then how did a non-Jerusalemite cult place like Carmel become the site of a Yahwistic altar (1 Kgs 18:32)?[14] Another issue unaddressed by the latter group of scholars is the verb *psḥ, which describes the "hopping" of the Israelites in 1 Kgs 18:21 and, later in verse 26, of the prophets of Baal. This verb is of course the root of the pesaḥ festival, about which Deuteronomic law gives specific and distinctive instruction (Deut 16:1–17).[15] The verb *psḥ, like the non-Jerusalemite cult place, is an important issue for the Deuteronomist, but 1 Kgs 18 displays no knowledge of these laws. If we are to accept 1 Kgs 18 as a Deuteronomistic composition, the text's silence on these two subjects must be addressed more convincingly.

I Reg 18,21–39," in *Studien zum Deuteronomistischen Geschichtswerk* [BZAW 227; Berlin: de Gruyter, 1994], 138; repr. from *Prophet und Prophetenbuch. Festschrift für Otto Kaiser zum 65. Geburtstag* [ed. V. Fritz et al.; Berlin: de Gruyter, 1989]). (4) S. Otto, "The Composition of the Elijah-Elisha Stories and the Deuteronomistic History," *JSOT* 27 (2003): 487–508. In this summary of her doctoral dissertation, Otto follows McKenzie in arguing that 1 Kgs 17–19 lacks many hallmarks of the Deuteronomistic ideology and therefore should be considered a post-Deuteronomist composition that was inserted in the late sixth century B.C.E. She regards 18:21–39, in particular, as an independent narrative from the late exilic period (504 n. 44).

13. Most recently, R. Albertz has argued that 1 Kgs 17–18 should be read as an exilic compilation, but he still grants "dass die Grunddaten der in 1. Kön 17-18 geschilderten Auseinandersetzung durchaus historische Plausibilität haben, auch wenn später stark überhöht und ins Grundsätzliche ausgezogen wurde" (*Elia: Ein feuriger Kämpfer für Gott* [Biblische Gestalten 13; Leipzig: Evangelische Verlagsanstalt, 2006], 27; see also 73–81). Similarly, McKenzie writes that "the stories themselves may be much earlier, but they were edited and added to the DH in the exile or afterwards," and then cites Šanda's arguments for a ninth-century-B.C.E. date (*Trouble with Kings*, 87 and n. 12). Cf. also Fohrer, *Elia*, 37–38, 50.

14. M. Noth's answer to this question is telling: "Here then Dtr. makes extraordinarily large concessions to the tradition, even if this is an exceptional case" (*The Deuteronomistic History* [trans. J. Doull et al.; JSOTSup 15; Sheffield: JSOT Press, 1981], 142 n. 6).

15. See B. Levinson, *Deuteronomy and the Hermeneutics of Legal Innovation* (New York: Oxford University Press, 1997), 53–97.

Moreover, Jehu's reign provides a compelling benchmark for the redaction history of 1 Kgs 17–19, because the anti-Ahab and pro-Jehu tendencies of 1 Kgs 17–22 and 2 Kgs 9–10, respectively, are unmistakable,[16] and those who advocate a later date have been unable to propose an equally compelling milieu. A few (post-)Deuteronomistic phrases do not themselves amount to a (post-)Deuteronomistic *Kreis* for the entire narrative but may simply be later insertions.[17] A. Campbell's fundamental criticism of W. Dietrich—the latter's overemphasis on selected additions but neglect of a pre-Deuteronomistic core text or *Vorlage*[18]—might well be directed at more recent redaction critics. Indeed, these scholars neglect the fact that for most of their parade of examples of (post-)Deuteronomistic theology in 1 Kgs 18, the LXX has variant readings, which together may constitute a textual stratum that pre-dates the MT.[19] For now it seems that arguments for a pre-Deuteronomistic Elijah narrative remain the most compelling, and a strong case can be made for the ninth century B.C.E. in particular. In seeking biblical texts that reflect cultic life in the northern kingdom during this period, we can do no better than the Carmel narrative.

---

16. Admittedly, 1 Kgs 19:15–18 presents a more ambiguous picture of Jehu, but this passage should be attributed to a different, probably later, source altogether (Campbell and O'Brien, *Unfolding the Deuteronomistic History*, 398–99). Its divergence from the rest of the Elijah tradition is especially apparent in Elijah's unfulfilled commission to anoint Hazael, Jehu, and Elisha.

17. For Würthwein three such phrases are enough ("Zur Opferprobe Elias," 138). Otto, however, needs none; for her, Elijah's success itself attests an author who was "full of hope for a new beginning after the national disaster of exile" ("Composition of the Elijah-Elisha Stories," 504).

18. Campbell, *Of Prophets and Kings*, 6–7. W. Dietrich, in his seminal work, *Prophetie und Geschichte: eine redaktionsgeschichtliche Untersuchung zum deteronomistischen Geschichtswerk* (FRLANT 108; Göttingen: Vandenhoeck & Ruprecht, 1972), argued that intervening the DtrH(istorie) and the DtrN(omist), posited by R. Smend, was a prophetic edition (DtrP). These three editions, all dated by Dietrich to the exilic period, became the foundation for the so-called Göttingen school.

19. See A. Schenker, *Älteste Textgeschichte der Königsbücher. Die hebräische Vorlage der ursprünglichen Septuaginta als älteste Textform der Königsbücher* [OBO 199; Fribourg-Göttingen: Academic Press, 2004], 14–33; idem, "Was bedeutet die Wendung 'einen Altar heilen' in 1 Könige 18:30? Ein übersehener religionsgeschichtlicher Vorgang," in *Studien zu Propheten und Religionsgeschichte* (SBAB 36; Stuttgart: Verlag Katholisches Bibelwerk, 2003), 99–115; P. Hugo, *Les deux visages d'Élie* (OBO 217; Fribourg-Göttingen: Academic Press, 2006), 213–49.

The following analysis of 1 Kgs 18 will focus on the story's depiction of sacred space and will again employ spatial categories taken from Lefebvre's conceptual triad. As in my examination of sacred space at Tel Dan in Strata III–II, I will look first at the spatial practice of the Carmel narrative, that is, the physical particularities of the space: its topography and dimensions, the architecture and objects that occupy the space, the rituals that take place in it, and the participants of those rituals. Next, I will consider the conceptual space of 1 Kgs 18, that is, the mental blueprint that underlies the narrative, asking what concerns, ideologies, and priorities have been mapped in the representation of sacred space that we find in this chapter. Last, I will compare the conceptual space of the Carmel narrative to the conceptual space of Area T in Stratum III to see if there is any overlap in these two witnesses of religious life in the northern kingdom in the ninth century B.C.E.

4.2. SPATIAL PRACTICE IN 1 KINGS 18

4.2.1. THE ALTARS

A good place to begin discussing the spatial practice in 1 Kgs 18 is the altars, which are the loci of the chapter's cultic activity. An important point to make from the beginning is that according to the MT there are two separate altars: one for the prophets of Baal and another for Elijah.[20] The first is described in verses 26–29, as the prophets of Baal arrange their sacrifice and try in various ways to elicit a response from Baal. Their efforts are summed up in verse 29, which states that "there was no sound, no one answering, and no notice" (wĕ'ên-qôl wĕ'ên-'ōneh wĕ'ên qāšeb). Besides underlining the prophets' failure, this phrase also turns the read-

---

20. Interpreters have been divided over the number of altars depicted in 1 Kgs 18. Some have assumed the existence of two altars (e.g., de Vaux, "Prophets of Baal on Mount Carmel," 238; G. von Rad, *Old Testament Theology* [trans. D. Stalker; New York: Harper & Row, 1965], 2:17; D. Ap-Thomas, "Elijah on Mt. Carmel," *PEQ* 92 [1960]: 150), while others have argued for a single cult site (e.g., A. Alt, "Das Gottesurteil auf dem Karmel," in vol. 2 of *Kleine Schriften zur Geschichte des Volkes Israel* [3 vols.; Munich: Beck, 1953], 138–39; M. Noth, *The History of Israel* [trans. P. Ackroyd; 2nd ed.; London: Black, 1960], 242 n. 6). More recently, R. Albertz seems to agree with Alt's interpretation that a single cult place is being described in 1 Kgs 18, but he rejects Alt's reconstruction of its history (*A History of Israelite Religion in the Old Testament Period* [trans. J. Bowden; 2 vols.; Louisville: Westminster John Knox, 1994], 1:153–54).

er's attention away from the prophets and toward the sacrifice of Elijah, which promptly begins in verse 30.[21] Yet in the MT the prophets of Baal do not stop their sacrifice when Elijah begins his own; rather, both sacrifices proceed at the same time. This simultaneity is clear from the MT's two references to the evening offering (*minḥâ*). On the one side are the prophets of Baal, who are said in verse 29 to prophesy from noon till the time of the offering; but importantly, the actual hour of the offering does not occur in the narrative until verse 36. This passage of time is made explicit by the phrase *ka'ăbōr haṣṣohŏrayim* in verse 29, which indicates that noon was just passing.[22] Thus according to the MT, the prophets of Baal are futilely prophesying right through verse 36. On the other side during this same span between verse 29 and verse 36, Elijah takes center stage, arranging his sacrifice on his own altar.[23] The prophets of Baal recede to the background, but according to the narrative sequence of the MT, they do not stop prophesying. The events described in the MT make sense only if one assumes that the two cult events were carried out on two separate altars: one for the prophets of Baal and one for Elijah.

As for the altars themselves, the one used by the prophets of Baal receives hardly any description. It is explicitly mentioned only in verse 26, and even this reference, in which the prophets are said to dance around "the altar which he made [*'āśâ*]," is obscure.[24] Because there is no obvious

---

21. Hugo, *Les deux visages d'Élie*, 227.

22. Waltke and O'Connor note that the preposition *kĕ-* with an infinitive construct denotes "the more immediately preceding of time" (*IBHS* 36.2.2b). This assessment has been confirmed by the analysis of D. Gropp, who has shown that the "*kĕ-* + infinitive construct [i.e., *ka'ăbōr*] nearly always implies contingent temporal succession with the following main verb [i.e., *wayyitnabbĕ'û*]" ("Progress and Cohesion in Biblical Hebrew Narrative: The Function of kĕ-/bĕ- + the Infinitive Construct," in *Discourse Analysis of Biblical Literature: What It Is and What It Offers* [ed. W. Bodine; Atlanta: Scholars Press, 1995], 209). Furthermore, Gropp's analysis allows us to classify *ka'ăbōr haṣṣohŏrayim* in v. 29 as an example of "backreference by lexical repetition," which refers to the phrase *mēhabbōqer wĕ'ad-haṣṣohŏrayim* in v. 26 and recapitulates its time designation (ibid., 187–89).

23. Interestingly, the LXX version of 1 Kgs 18 indicates only one altar that is shared by Elijah and the prophets of Baal (see Hugo, *Les deux visages d'Élie*, 227; Schenker, *Älteste Textgeschichte der Königsbücher*, 15). In a future article I will explore more fully the different religious traditions represented by the MT and LXX versions of 1 Kgs 18.

24. Some have gone so far as to call MT's *'āśâ* "inexplicable" (DeVries, *1 Kings*, 224) and "incontrovertibly faulty" (Cogan, *I Kings*, 86). Even W. Thiel, who rarely

masculine singular antecedent for *'āśâ*, some translators understand the verb as an impersonal, which should be read as a passive—"it was made."[25] The altar, it seems, just happened to be there, and we are left with no information regarding its origin or appearance.

Elijah's altar, by contrast, receives considerable attention, especially in verses 30–32a, which describe how "he healed the altar of YHWH that had been ruined" (*wayrappē' 'et-mizbaḥ yhwh hehārûs*).[26] The most salient details of Elijah's altar are the use of the verb **rp'*, the twelve stones that Elijah uses to repair the altar, and the reference to Jacob. The verb "to heal" involves "restoring a wrong, sick, broken, or deficient condition to its original and proper state" and most commonly refers to physical and figurative maladies.[27] Perhaps the closest parallel to *wayrappē'* in verse 30 is the verb's occurrence in 2 Kgs 2:21, where Elisha "heals" (*rippi'tî*) a spring, thus making it available for use again. Similarly, in Jer 19:11 the verb describes a smashed piece of pottery that cannot be "healed" (*lō'-yûkal lěhērāpēh*).[28] Perhaps, like these examples, Elijah's altar is a once-useful implement that has fallen into disrepair and disuse. Indeed, some have suggested that it is an older Israelite altar that was abandoned or destroyed when Baal worship spread through the area.[29] This possibility may also explain another aspect of **rp'*, which in the Hebrew Bible is often correlated to sin and impurity (see Hos 6:1; 7:1; 14:5; Ps 41:5; Isa

---

favors the LXX reading, regards *'āśâ* as "fehlerhaft" ("Beobachtungen am Text von 1 Könige 18," in *"Einen Altar von Erde mache mir..." Festschrift für Diethelm Conrad zu seinem 70. Geburtstag* [ed. J. Diehl et al.; KAANT 4/5; Waltrop: Hartmut Spenner, 2003], 287).

25. Joüon §155b. Thus the JPS translation, "that had been set up." Sweeney keeps the verb in the active ("which he had made") but leaves the pronominal subject unidentified (*I and II Kings*, 217). Alternatively, the LXX reads the plural *epoiēsan*.

26. This location of this phrase represents another important difference between the MT and the LXX. It occurs in the MT in v. 30 as Elijah's first cultic act, but in the LXX the healing takes place in v. 32a, just after Elijah has constructed the stones and before he digs the channel. For Schenker and Hugo, this discrepancy is an important example of the different narratives represented by the two versions (Schenker, *Älteste Textgeschichte der Königsbücher*, 14–33; idem, "Was bedeutet die Wendung," 99–115; Hugo, *Les deux visages d'Élie*, 234–36).

27. M. Brown, "רפא *rāpā*'," *TDOT* 13:596–97.

28. The borrowing of forms between final-*aleph* verbs and final-*heh* verbs is not uncommon (GKC §75nn–rr).

29. Sweeney, *I and II Kings*, 229; Cogan, *I Kings*, 442; de Vaux, "Prophets of Baal on Mount Carmel," 238 n. 3.

6:10; 2 Chr 7:13–14; 30:18–20). Given Mount Carmel's location at Israel's border with Phoenicia (see pp. 138–39 below), it is possible that the old altar's "healing" is a reference to some previous association with Baal worship and its resultant cultic "affliction."

Elijah's process for this renewal involves the erection of the twelve stones in verse 31, which correspond to the tribes of Israel (*kĕmispar šibṭê* [*bĕnê-]ya'ăqōb*). Many commentators have noted how this detail resonates with other stone representations of the twelve tribes at sacred sites, in particular Exod 24:4 and Josh 4:1–9. In the Joshua passage twelve stones memorialize the passage of the Ark of YHWH and the Israelites across the Jordan River,[30] while the twelve pillars (*maṣṣēbâ*[31]) in the Exodus passage represent the tribes of Israel at the ratification of the Sinai covenant.[32] In these texts the stones or pillars stand as witnesses of what the tribes themselves have witnessed and thus symbolize (see *'ôt* in Josh 4:6) Israel's collective presence at an event of national significance.[33]

---

30. Scholars since Wellhausen have recognized two recensions in Josh 4, which both recount the crossing of the Jordan River and which feature parallel traditions concerning the twelve stones. J. Soggin, in addition to reviewing various proposals for dividing the chapter, argues that one account consists of vv. 1–3, 6–8a, b, 20, and the other of vv. 4–5, 8a, 9, 15–19, 21–24; vv. 10–12 are a shared tradition (*Joshua: A Commentary* [OTL; Philadelphia: Westminster, 1972], 52–53, 64–65). The first recension culminates in the installation of the stones in Gilgal, where they will be a memorial (*wĕhāyû hā'ăbānîm hā'ēlleh lĕzikkārôn* [v. 7]) to the passage of the ark of the covenant. The second account locates the stones within the river itself, where they commemorate the standing place of the priests who carried the ark.

31. Propp recognizes a single author, whom he identifies as the Elohist, for Exod 24:1–15a (ibid., 147–48).

32. F. M. Cross has even argued that Exod 24:4 and Josh 4 are both linked to a cultic festival at Gilgal, which would have ritually reenacted Israel's entry into the promised land (*Canaanite Myth and Hebrew Epic: Essays in the History of the Religion of Israel* [Cambridge: Harvard University Press, 1973], 99–105; see also idem, *From Epic to Canon: History and Literature in Ancient Israel* [Baltimore: Johns Hopkins University Press, 1998], 44).

33. Cogan, *I Kings*, 442. Here "all Israel," which Cogan takes from Ahab's summons to *kol-bĕnê yiśrā'ēl* in 1 Kgs 18:20, can only refer to the ten northern tribes, which had seceded with Jeroboam (1 Kgs 11:31). Indeed, H.-J. Zobel has noted that after this division in the book of Kings, "Israel" refers only to the northern kingdom ("ישראל *yiśrā'ēl*," *TDOT* 6:405). Thus we are left with an apparent discrepancy between the number of stones and the number of tribes actually present, but G. Knoppers, citing 1 Kgs 18:36, has shown that even during the divided monarchy "certain locutions, such as 'YHWH, the God of Israel,' reflect the historical links … between Israel's

The question is how much of this meaning underlies the twelve stones used by Elijah. M. Cogan is certainly right that "Elijah's twelve-stone altar joins other symbolic constructions that mark the participation of 'all Israel' in the proceedings being commemorated."[34] But one important difference is that the stones in 1 Kgs 18 are not just "standing by" like the stones in Josh 4 and the pillars in Exod 24 but are literally integrated into the altar and thus into the event itself. This integration, together with the divine name, is nothing less than the instrument of the altar "healing." Thus the twelve stones in 1 Kgs 18 are not simply witnesses but play a new and transformative role in a cultic event. Furthermore, their integration mirrors the direct involvement of the assembly itself, whose participation in the sacrifice is foreshadowed by Elijah's employment of the twelve stones.

A third important detail given about Elijah's altar is the reference to Jacob/Israel in verse 31b, in which we are reminded that YHWH said to him: "Israel will be your name." Many commentators neglect this allusion, and those who do usually link it to Gen 35, in which Jacob fulfills his vow by returning to Bethel (see Gen 28:20–22) and building there an altar to YHWH; then in verse 10 YHWH changes his name from Jacob to Israel.[35] Certainly, comparison of these two texts reveals several similarities, most especially their shared focus on altar-building as a device for transforming a preexisting cultic space.[36] While these similarities may shed light

---

twelve tribes" (*The Reign of Solomon and the Rise of Jeroboam* [vol. 1 of *Two Nations Under God: The Deuteronomistic History of Solomon and the Dual Monarchies*; HSM 52; Atlanta: Scholars Press, 1993], 204). In this light the discrepancy does not lessen the significance of the number twelve but increases it, since the tradition of the twelve tribes remained so strong that the number twelve persisted, even when it did not correspond to the actual number of tribes. This same tradition occurs in Ezra where twelve goats (6:17) and twelve bulls (8:35) are sacrificed "for all Israel" (*'al-kol-yiśrā'ēl*) and "according to the number of tribes of Israel" (*lĕminyān šibṭê yiśrā'ēl*; see H. Williamson, *Ezra, Nehemiah* [WBC 16; Nashville: Thomas Nelson, 1985], 84).

34. See, for example, E. Würthwein, "Die Erzählung vom Gottesurteil auf dem Karmel," in *Studien zum Deuteronomistischen Geschichtswerk* (BZAW 227; Berlin: de Gruyter, 1994), 120; Hugo, *Les deux visages d'Élie*, 231, 236. Other scholars, such as J. Montgomery (*A Critical Commentary on the Books of Kings* [ed. H. Gehman; ICC; New York: Scribner's, 1951], 304) and H. Junker ("Der Graben un den Altar des Elias," *TTZ* 69 [1960]: 69–70), mention Gen 32:29 as well but only briefly.

35. Schenker, "Was bedeutet die Wendung,'" 102; see also Hugo, *Les deux visages d'Élie*, 236.

36. There is a strong consensus that Gen 35:1–15 consists of two separate sources, and although debate over the first source persists, nearly all commentators agree that

on the Mount Carmel contest, it may be just as illuminating, if not more so, to connect the allusion to Jacob's name change in verse 31b not to the relatively late Gen 35:10[37] but instead to Gen 32:23–33, which describes the wrestling match at Penuel between Jacob and an unidentified assailant who ultimately renames him "Israel."[38] In addition to the earlier date of the Penuel tradition, which belongs in the eighth century B.C.E. at the latest,[39] its linkage with 1 Kgs 18:31b is advantageous for the way it connects thematically with Elijah's "healing" of the altar. Although many aspects of the wrestling match remain obscure, nearly all scholars agree that Jacob's renaming as Israel represents his transformation from trickster to heir of the patriarchal promises.[40] By connecting Elijah's altar to Jacob's transformation at Penuel, the narrator links it to the very origins of "Israel." Just as Jacob emerges from the struggle with renewed honor and divine blessing, so also the altar on Mount Carmel is "healed" of its disrepair and reconstituted as a Yahwistic cult place. This architectural transformation of the

---

vv. 9–13 are the work of the Priestly (P) writer. See the summary of G. Wenham, *Genesis 16–50* (WBC 2; Nashville: Thomas Nelson, 1994), 323.

37. For this point, see also S. Timm, *Die Dynastie Omri: Quellen und Untersuchungen zur Geschichte Israels im 9. Jahrhundert vor Christus* (FRLANT 124; Göttingen: Vandenhoeck & Ruprecht, 1982), 78–79; and J. Trebolle Barrera, *Centena in libros Samuelis et Regum: variantes textuales y composición literaria en los libros de Samuel y Reyes* (Madrid: Consejo Superior de Investigaciones Científicas, 1989), 141. Initial comparison of Gen 32:29 and 35:10 would seem to favor the latter as a better parallel for 1 Kgs 18:31b, since they share the exact same phrase (*yiśrā'ēl yihyeh šěmekā*), while Gen 32:29 contains the less concise: *lō' ya'ăqōb yē'āmēr 'ôd šimkā kî 'im-yiśrā'ēl*. In the LXX, however, v. 28 (= MT v. 29) reads *kai eipen autō Ou klēthēsetai eti to onoma sou Iakōb, alla Israēl to onoma sou estai*, appearing under the obelus in the Hexaplaric manuscripts. Given this haplography, we should probably restore *yihyeh šimkā* to the Hebrew text, which would yield an apt parallel for 1 Kgs 18:31b. Significantly, this is not the only instance in which the LXX reading of Gen 32:28 (MT 29) has priority; see R. Hendel, *The Epic of the Patriarch: The Jacob Cycle and the Narrative Traditions of Canaan and Israel* (HSM 42; Atlanta: Scholars Press, 1987), 103.

38. This dating is based on the close relationship between Hos 12:4–5 and Gen 32:23–33 and the likelihood that the former is based on the latter (see W. Holladay, "Chiasmus, the Key to Hosea XII 3–6," *VT* 16 [1966]: 53–64; H. Wolff, *Hosea: A Commentary on the Book of the Prophet Hosea* [trans. G. Stansell; Philadelphia: Fortress, 1974], 212–13). A more cautious approach is taken by S. McKenzie, who acknowledges that the Hosea passage is closely related to the Gen 32:23–33 but is not necessarily dependent on it ("The Jacob Tradition in Hosea XII 4–5," *VT* 36 [1986]: 320).

39. Wenham, *Genesis 16–50*, 297.

40. Junker, "Der Graben um den Altar des Elias," 65–74.

altar has been underlined by the allusion to this transformative event in the history of "Israel."

All of these narrative details contribute to the depiction of the Elijah's altar and make the altar a distinctive part of 1 Kgs 18's spatial practice. The use of the verb *rp' and the allusion to Gen 32 emphasize the altar's transformation, and the reconstruction with twelve stones highlights the integration of the twelve tribes into the altar and their participation in the rituals that will follow. Less distinctive is the altar used by the prophets of Baal, which is given no description at all. In fact, it is only mentioned once, and that mention, with its impersonal verb, actually clouds rather than clarifies our picture of it. In a way, its vague origins and lack of description are precisely the point. Although the story depicts Elijah and the prophets of Baal as opponents, the obscurity of the prophets' altar foreshadows the ineffectiveness of their cultic equipment and practices.

4.2.2. THE SACRIFICES

Having studied the altars that serve as the loci of the sacrifices offered by the prophets of Baal and then by Elijah, the next step to understanding the spatial practice of 1 Kgs 18 is to examine the sacrifices themselves. Most of the attention devoted to the cultic practices of the Mount Carmel contest has concerned the more enigmatic aspects of the proceedings. In particular, the self-laceration of the prophets of Baal and the channel dug by Elijah and filled with water have captured the imagination of scholars and resulted in numerous suggestions. Regarding the channel, for example, its water has been interpreted as part of a purification rite[41] or else a rainmaking ceremony,[42] but others have suggested that the water was simply used to underscore the miracle of the fire.[43] Still another reading understands the liquid to be naphtha, which facilitated the miracle![44]

---

41. Ap-Thomas, "Elijah on Mount Carmel," 153; N. Tromp, "Water and Fire on Mount Carmel: A Conciliatory Suggestion," *Bib* 56 (1975): 495; J. Gray, *I and II Kings* (OTL; Philadelphia: Westminster, 1963), 356–57; Sweeney, *I and II Kings*, 229.

42. Cogan, *I Kings*, 443, citing the rabbinic exegete David Qimḥi.

43. R. Kennett cited in Montgomery, *Books of Kings*, 307; see also J. Collins, *Introduction to the Hebrew Bible* (Minneapolis: Fortress, 2004), 265.

44. Within the Hebrew Bible itself, we find instances where the root *gdd seems to involve some sort of mourning rite (e.g., Jer 16:6; Mic 4:14). The case for a mourning rite has been made (or assumed) by F. Fensham, "A Few Observations on I Kings 17–19," *ZAW* 92 (1980): 235. Few today seem to follow Ap-Thomas's interpretation,

Likewise, various proposals have been offered for the prophets' self-laceration, with most explanations taking the mutilation as a mourning practice[45] or a rite meant to induce an ecstatic state[46]—or both.[47]

Although I will return briefly to the self-laceration and water channel below, I think these two details, though intriguing, offer the least opportunity for fresh insights. A new textual or iconographic parallel notwithstanding, the possibility of resolving interpretive problems posed by these two cultic acts seems rather slim. In light of this situation, a more fruitful approach might be to look more carefully at some of the less obscure aspects of the Mount Carmel sacrifice. For while several of the terms found in 1 Kgs 18 are well known from other parts of the Hebrew Bible, their full significance in the Carmel narrative remains to be explored. This is certainly the case with ʿōlâ and minḥâ, the two offerings explicitly mentioned in the text. Indeed, a close reading of their respective contexts will show that their usage in this chapter is rather exceptional and instructive for understanding northern cult in the ninth century B.C.E.

The ʿōlâ sacrifice is mentioned by name in 1 Kgs 18:34, 38, and in these instances the term refers to the sectioned bull and wood that were amassed on Elijah's altar. From these references we can assume that Elijah's instruc-

---

despite his assurance: "It is also quite certain that the prophets' self-laceration until blood flowed could be a rain-bringing device, since Frazer lists several examples among primitive peoples" ("Elijah on Mount Carmel," 153).

45. Starting again with comparative biblical evidence, we turn to Zech 13:6, which shows that this practice was part of the prophetic repertoire. Moreover, an Akkadian text from Ugarit has linked the mourning rite to prophetic practice: "My brothers bathe in their [bl]ood like prophets (maḫḫê)" (Ugaritica V 162:11; see J. Roberts, "A New Parallel to 1 Kings 18:28–29," JBL 89 [1970]: 76–77; for a complete and more recent translation of this text, B. Foster, "A Sufferer's Salvation," COS 1:152; for lines 2–12, see M. Nissinen, Prophets and Prophecy in the Ancient Near East [SBLWAW 12; Atlanta: Society of Biblical Literature, 2003], 184–85). The term maḫḫê comes from the verb maḫû, meaning "to become frenzied; to go into a trance" (CAD M/1, 115), and its use here indicates that bloodshed was related to the ecstatic trances prophets experienced in their conveyance of divine messages.

46. Although scholars have tended to focus on the maḫḫê in Ugaritica V 162, T. Lewis has noted that the text itself describes a mourning ritual, such that the "frenzied prophets" may be connected in some way to the ritual (Cults of the Dead in Ancient Israel and Ugarit [HSM 39; Atlanta: Scholars Press, 1989], 100–101).

47. The key component here is the wood. As we will see below, Elijah's command not to set it afire was probably not the normal practice but is distinctive to the Carmel narrative.

tions to the prophets of Baal and his own cultic actions represent various components of the ʿōlâ sacrifice, as the narrator understood it. These actions and their order are described in verses 23, 33: after two bulls are given and the prophets of Baal have received theirs, each is to section their bull (*nṯḥ) and set it (*śym) on the wood. But then strangely, they are told to not set fire to it (ʾēš lōʾ tāśîmû).[48] The entire process is summed up by the verb *ʿśh ("to prepare"), which takes the bull as its object in verses 23, 26.

Remarkably, the cultic preparations are the same for each side; the prophets of Baal prepare their sacrifice just as Elijah does. This lack of differentiation has led G. Anderson to conclude that "*the distinctiveness of the Israelite cult is nothing other than the limitation of cultic activity to one particular patron deity.*"[49] Although I agree that the parallelism between the two sacrifices is significant (see pp. 139–40 below), there are several unique aspects of Elijah's sacrifice, which suggest that the distinctiveness of his offering lay in the cultic actions themselves and not merely in their limitation to YHWH. Although Elijah and the prophets of Baal *prepare* similar sacrifices and they both agree to "call on" (*qrʾ bĕ- [vv. 24–28[50]]) their respective gods, the cultic actions that accompany their invocations are quite different. The prophets of Baal begin by simply calling his name but soon resort to dancing and self-laceration, both of which have no counterpart in Elijah's invocation of YHWH. Additionally, Elijah's water rites are unique to his sacrifice. Moreover, the uniqueness of Elijah's sacrifice becomes even more apparent when we recognize that his ʿōlâ sacrifice differs not only from the opponents' sacrifice but also from other biblical representations of this sacrifice. Our best biblical evidence for the ʿōlâ comes from the Priestly writings in the Hebrew Bible, which provide details—not always consistent—about its cultic procedure.[51] One point on

---

48. The key component here is the wood. As we will see below, Elijah's command not to set it afire was probably not the normal practice but is distinctive to the Carmel narrative.

49. G. Anderson, *Sacrifices and Offerings in Ancient Israel: Studies in their Social and Political Importance* (HSM 41; Atlanta: Scholars Press, 1987), 3, emphasis original.

50. We should also include Gr. *aneboēsen* in v. 36, which probably has translated Heb. *wayyiqrāʾ* (cf. 1 Kgs 17:20).

51. Admittedly, the prescriptive and descriptive ritual texts that constitute the Priestly writings represent an altogether separate genre from the Carmel narrative, and this difference recommends great caution in comparing the two. The goal of this comparison is not to let one text fill in the gaps of another but to probe the similarities and differences that make the account in 1 Kgs 18 distinctive.

which all the writings agree is that ʿōlâ sacrifice is distinctive for its consumption of the entire animal by fire,[52] and overall the Priestly material presents a coherent picture of the sacrifice. According to Lev 1, the ʿōlâ sacrifice proceeded as follows: a layperson (ʾādām) brings an animal to the altar to be sacrificed (v. 3), lays his hands on the animal's head, and then slaughters it (vv. 4–5). At this point the priest sprinkles blood around the altar,[53] and the offerer flays and sections (wĕnittaḥ) the animal (vv. 5–6). Finally, while the offerer cleans the entrails, the priest sets the sections on the burning altar, which produce a "pleasing aroma" (rêaḥ-nîḥôaḥ) for YHWH (vv. 8–9). This delegation of cultic acts is affirmed by Lev 8:18–21,[54] though later in Lev 9:12–14 Aaron himself performs every aspect of the sacrifice.[55]

When we compare the Priestly ʿōlâ sacrifice with the cultic events described in 1 Kgs 18, we do find some similarities of course. For example, the cultic procedure in 1 Kgs 18 follows the same order described in Lev 1, sometimes with the same verbs (*nth, *ʿrk). Also the consumption of the entire bull by fire (1 Kgs 18:38) accords with the Priestly account. Yet the

---

52. For a discussion of how ʿōlâ came to replace kālîl as the cultic term for a "whole offering," see J. Milgrom, *Leviticus 1–16* (AB 3; New York: Doubleday, 1991), 172–73.

53. On the significance of blood in Israelite cult, see T. Lewis, "Covenant and Blood Rituals: Understanding Exodus 24:3–8 in Its Ancient Near Eastern Context," in *Confronting the Past: Archaeological and Historical Essays on Ancient Israel in Honor of William G. Dever* (ed. S. Gitin et al.; Winona Lake, Ind.: Eisenbrauns, 2006), 341–50.

54. Based it seems on Exod 29:15–18, D. Kellermann has supposed that Moses is the subject of the third-person singular verbs in Lev 8:19 ("עלה/עולה ʿōlâ/ʿôlâ," *TDOT* 11:99), but Milgrom has convincingly shown that these verbs have an impersonal subject and should be translated passively, thus conforming with the Lev 1 account, which he takes as the basis for Lev 8 (*Leviticus 1–16*, 526). In fact, Milgrom argues that "the writer of Lev 8 used Lev 1 as a corrective for his disagreements with his Exod 29 model" (ibid.; for more on the relationship between Lev 8 and Exod 29, see 513–15, 545).

55. For J. Milgrom this difference does not amount to contradiction, since "in the formal, public cult the slaughtering was performed by the professional staff, that is to say the priests … or the Levites" (Milgrom, *Leviticus 1–16*, 582). He and others have also drawn attention to the fact that prescriptive and descriptive texts will inevitably involve certain differences (ibid., 495; B. Levine, "The Descriptive Tabernacle Texts of the Pentateuch," *JAOS* 85 [1965]: 307–18; A. Rainey, "The Order of Sacrifices in Old Testament Ritual Texts," *Bib* 51 [1970]: 485–98).

differences between the Priestly ʿōlâ and Elijah's sacrifice are striking. For
example, Elijah's channel and water-pouring rite have no counterpart in
Lev 1,[56] and the hand-leaning and blood manipulation of Lev 1 are missing from Elijah's ʿōlâ sacrifice. But because these differences may simply
owe to the narrative setting of Elijah's sacrifice, the uniqueness of Elijah's
ʿōlâ sacrifice is best discerned by examining its function vis-à-vis other
ʿōlôt known from the Hebrew Bible. Of course, the question of function
can involve myriad answers. This plurality of meanings is captured well
in J. Milgrom's assessment of the ʿōlâ in the Priestly sacrificial system, in
which he concludes that "entreaty, then, is the manifest purpose of the
burnt offering. But entreaty covers a wide range of motives: homage,
thanksgiving, appeasement, expiation. … The burnt offering then is a
gift, with any number of goals in mind."[57] If these numerous motivations
can be discerned in the Hebrew Bible's best-attested cultic system, then
we should suppose at least as many underlying Elijah's sacrifice, whether
we can detect them or not. In the following analysis I will explore those
meanings that are discernible and remain mindful that others lie beyond
my view.

In terms of function, Elijah's ʿōlâ stands out from other examples of
the sacrifice, whose primary purpose seems to be entreaty, as Milgrom
describes, or attraction, as B. Levine has argued.[58] Indeed, in 1 Kgs 18 it is
not the sacrifice itself that attracts YHWH's attention and makes entreaty

---

56. As already suggested above, it is possible that the water rites in 1 Kgs 18
are purely for dramatic effect, which would account for their absence in the Priestly
corpus. On the other hand, water rites are elsewhere associated with altars (see Josh
9:27).

57. Milgrom, *Leviticus 1–16*, 175–76. Similarly, R. Hendel has written, "the primary locus of meaning is the system of religious concepts, not a single postulated
essence that guides a rite through history" ("Sacrifice as a Cultural System: The Ritual
Symbolism of Exodus 24, 3–8," *ZAW* 101 [1989]: 369). Finally, see also E. Evans-
Pritchard's study listing as many as fourteen possible motivations for sacrifice within
a single culture (*Nuer Religion* [Oxford; Clarendon, 1962], 282).

58. Levine writes: "The essential role of the ʿōlāh seems to have been that of
attraction. The ʿōlāh was offered up with the objective of evoking an initial response
from the deity prior to bringing the primary concerns of his worshippers to his attention" (*In the Presence of the Lord* [SJLA 5; Leiden: Brill, 1974], 22 [italics original]).
Moreover, he finds Elijah's sacrifice on Mount Carmel emblematic of the ʿōlâ sacrifice
because it "epitomizes the basic function of the ʿōlāh as a sort of signal directed at the
deity, residing in heaven, in an effort to get him to respond and to approach his worshippers, or to do their bidding from the distance of his heavenly abode" (ibid., 24).

but Elijah's prayer (vv. 36–37). The text itself is unambiguous on this point. After Elijah and his opponents have taken care not to light their respective sacrifices, the fire finally comes from YHWH at the conclusion of Elijah's prayer. The use of the *waw*-consecutive at the beginning of verse 38 clearly demonstrates that the two events are related.[59] These changes subvert traditional understandings of the *'ōlâ* sacrifice, in that the nexus of divine and human contact is not the "pleasing odor" of the burnt offering, but Elijah's speech.[60] Far from epitomizing the *'ōlâ* as a means of eliciting a divine response, the *'ōlâ* sacrifice in 1 Kgs 18 is itself the response, with YHWH (not a human priest) as the officiant.

This deviation from the traditional *'ōlâ* is further confirmed by the fact that no offering comes after Elijah's sacrifice. As many scholars have noted, the *'ōlâ* sacrifice occurs most frequently in the Hebrew Bible as the first in a series of offerings, namely, the *minḥâ*, *šĕlāmîm*, *ḥaṭṭā't*, and *'āšām*,[61] but in 1 Kgs 18 the *'ōlâ* occurs by itself. The biblical text is again unambiguous about this detail, since the divine fire consumes not only the sacrifice but the entire cultic apparatus (v. 38), thus precluding any further offerings.[62]

---

59. In the LXX this correlation is further stressed by the fact that Elijah begins his prayer with a cry to the sky (*eis ton ouranon*), after which the fire falls from the heavens (*ek tou ouranou*).

60. Cf. 1 Kgs 17:20–22, where the emphasis is also on Elijah's petition. After he prays on behalf of the (nearly) dead boy, "YHWH heard the voice of Elijah" and responded.

61. This is the order one finds in Lev 1–5. The same list appears elsewhere in the Hebrew Bible with a different order, such as *'ōlâ*, *minḥâ*, *ḥaṭṭā't*, *'āšām* and *šĕlāmîm* found in Lev 6–7. Rainey has argued that actual procedural order of offerings was *ḥaṭṭā't/'āšām*, *'ōlâ* (with *minḥâ*) and *šĕlāmîm* ("Order of Sacrifices," 494–98), though J. Watts maintains the priority of the *'ōlâ* ("*'ōlāh*: The Rhetoric of Burnt Offerings," *VT* 56 [2006]: 128–30).

It is noteworthy that at Ugarit the *šrp* sacrifice (< **šrp* "to burn"), which seems to be the functional equivalent of the Israelite *'ōlâ* sacrifice, also occurs in a sequence of offerings and frequently occurs in the composite expression *šrp . wšlmm* (see, e.g., KTU 1.39:4; 1.46:7; 1.109:15). For a cautious comparison of these terms and related bibliography, see G. del Olmo Lete, *Canaanite Religion according to the Liturgical Texts of Ugarit* (trans. W. Watson; Bethesda, Md.: CDL, 1999), 36–37; D. Pardee, *Ritual and Cult at Ugarit* [SBLWAW 10; Atlanta: Society of Biblical Literature, 2002], 233; see also, Milgrom, *Leviticus 1–16*, 172–73.

62. There is some disagreement in the versions as to what exactly is destroyed by the fire. According to the MT, the fire consumes the sacrifice, the wood, the stones, and the dust, while only "licking" (*liḥēkâ*) the water; while in the LXX the fire con-

In this way the Carmel narrative is far from conventional in its depiction of the ʿōlâ sacrifice. Although its formal procedure is recognizable, it has deviated from the functions that scholars have traditionally ascribed to it. Instead of a means of attracting YHWH, the ʿōlâ sacrifice in 1 Kgs 18 has become a mode of divine revelation, or to use Milgrom's definition, the entreaty is found not in the offering itself but Elijah's words.

This divergence does not negate these traditional functions but rather points up the exceptionality of Elijah's sacrifice. Given the northern orientation of the Carmel narrative, it is tempting to connect the distinctive aspects of this sacrifice with its northern setting, but such a connection is impossible to prove. Still it is worth mentioning that the best analogue to the Carmel sacrifice is Gideon's encounter with the angel of YHWH, which is also set in a northern context, namely, in the tribal territory of Manasseh. In both cases an offering is laid out, a liquid is poured over it, and miraculously the offering is consumed by a divine fire (Judg 6:11–24).[63] Although a full comparison of these two passages is beyond the scope of the present project, their similarities suggest that the distinctive aspects of Elijah's sacrifice were not idiosyncratic but may represent an alternative understanding of Israel's cultic system.

On the other hand, it seems that the other offering mentioned by name in 1 Kgs 18—the minḥâ cited in verses 29 and 36—is meant to connect the sacrifice on Mount Carmel to the cultic schedule of the Jerusalem temple. The minḥâ, which in its most basic sense means "gift,"[64] was part of the daily temple sacrifices offered once in the morning and again in the evening (Exod 29:38–42; 2 Kgs 3:20; 16:15).[65] Although the term eventually came to denote a cereal offering (see Lev 2), it can refer, as it does in 1 Kgs 18, to all the cultic activity associated with the morning and evening offerings, which included a burnt offering (ʿōlâ) and a libation (nesek).[66]

---

sumes the sacrifice, the wood, and the water, and only licks the stones and dust. In both versions the possibility for further cultic activity is eliminated.

63. In fact, this miracle is called a "sign" (ʾôt) in v. 17, which is reminiscent of the signs performed by YHWH in the book of Exodus. Those signs were given so that "you will know that I am YHWH" (Exod 10:2), which is precisely what Elijah calls YHWH to demonstrate in 1 Kgs 18:37.

64. See Anderson, Sacrifices and Offerings, 27–34; Levine, In the Presence, 16–17.

65. See M. Weinfeld, "מנחה minḥâ," TDOT 8:419–20. However, in the Hebrew Bible the minḥâ is not exclusively associated with the Jerusalem temple (cf. Amos 5:22, 25).

66. On this generic meaning, see Anderson, Sacrifices and Offerings, 29.

This generic usage is the most relevant to the Carmel narrative, because the *minḥâ* mentioned in 1 Kgs 18:29, 36 functions simply as a time designation. Elijah himself does not make any cereal offering, but the *minḥâ* is an event outside the narrative used to establish a time frame for events within the narrative. In this way, Elijah's sacrifice, for all its distinctiveness, finds its temporal frame in the cult of the Jerusalem temple.

Because of this effect some scholars regard the references to the *minḥâ* as evidence of a late composition. Besides the fact that the syntax in which the term is embedded is redolent of Late Biblical Hebrew,[67] many scholars regard the allusion to the Jerusalem temple cult as proof that the text has been composed in a Deuteronomistic or post-Deuteronomistic milieu.[68] But variant readings found in the LXX suggest that the references to the *minḥâ*, and the Jerusalemite perspective they represent, were later additions. In the LXX the *minḥâ* in verse 36 is missing altogether, and its occurrence in verse 29 is quite different; there the *minḥâ* coincides with Elijah's altar-building, not the sacrifice itself, as in the MT.[69] According to P. Hugo, these variants suggest that the MT represents a later attempt to synchronize Elijah's sacrifice with the evening *minḥâ* in Jerusalem.[70] Thus redaction critics are partly right that 1 Kgs 18:36 reflects Deuteronomistic theology, but this may only be true for the MT, in which Elijah's sacrifice has been made more amenable to the centralized cult. Nevertheless, as Hugo notes, the mere mention of the *minḥâ*, whatever its significance, interjects the Jerusalem cult into the Carmel narrative and creates a tension between those aspects of Elijah's sacrifice that are unique and those

---

67. See R. Polzin, *Late Biblical Hebrew: Toward an Historical Typology of Biblical Hebrew Prose* (HSM 12; Missoula, Mont.: Scholars Press, 1976), 60–61. On the use of *'ad ēl-* as characteristic of the Chronicler, see S. Japhet, *I and II Chronicles: A Commentary* (OTL; Louisville: Westminster John Knox, 1993), 928.

68. McKenzie, *Trouble with Kings*, 87; Timm, *Die Dynastie Omri*, 77; DeVries, *1 Kings*, 225.

69. In v. 29 of the LXX the time of the offering is simultaneous with the reference to the *minḥâ* (*kai egeneto hōs ho kairos tou anabēnai tēn thysian*), but in the MT the same hour is only anticipated (*'ad la'ălôt hamminḥâ*); the hour itself does not arrive until v. 36. This discrepancy establishes separate time frames for the two versions.

70. Hugo writes: "TM développe une perspective toute différente en totale harmonie avec la théologie deutéronomiste du Temple de Jérusalem. ... En effet, l'évocation de l'heure du sacrifice fait implicitement allusion au Temple. Elle manifeste que la prière d'Élie se fait au meme moment que la prière du sanctuaire de Jérusalem" (*Les deux visages d'Élie*, 241).

that correspond in some way to the Jerusalem temple. It is not unlike the tension between Elijah's 'ôlâ and the sacrifice prepared by the prophets of Baal. On the one hand, the two sacrifices are precisely paralleled, but on the other hand, there are elements of Elijah's cultic procedure that have no parallel in Phoenician cult, or for that matter in the Priestly writings from the Hebrew Bible.

4.2.3. RELIGIOUS PERSONNEL

This tension between the familiar and unique features of the spatial practice depicted in 1 Kgs 18 is also apparent with respect to religious personnel. Perhaps the most remarkable aspect of the sacrifice described in this narrative is the total absence of priests, a detail whose full weight has not been appreciated in scholarly literature, even though 1 Kgs 18 is hardly unique in this regard. In several biblical texts—for example, Exod 24:3–8; 1 Sam 2:11–26; 3:1–4:1a; 7:2–17—priestly mediation is absent from cultic activities, and nonpriests, like Elijah, assume cultic prerogatives, which other biblical traditions reserve for the institutional priesthood. In the Priestly literature, for example, such mediation is indispensable.[71] Even in offerings, like the 'ôlâ sacrifice in Lev 1 and 8, where the primary offerer is a layperson, priests play an integral role. Indeed, they are the only ones who manipulate the blood of the sacrifice, an act that "serves to distinguish between the realm of responsibility of the priesthood and that of the laity."[72] That is to say, even when nonpriests play a significant role, their access to the altar, which is the locus of divine presence and the holiest part of the cultic space, is restricted.[73] Moreover, J. Watts has demonstrated that the ritual priority of the 'ôlâ sacrifice in the Priestly texts correlates to the priests' own ritual primacy: "the 'ōlāh exemplifies the temple cult of the priests, apart from the lay people's participation in it. … The implication of its rhetorical prominence then is that the 'ōlāh represents the purist form of divine service," at least in the Priestly tradition.[74]

---

71. On the functions and elite status of the priesthood in P, see Milgrom, *Leviticus 1–16*, 52–57; I. Knohl, *The Sanctuary of Silence: The Priestly Torah and the Holiness School* (Minneapolis: Fortress, 1995), 152–57.

72. Gilders, *Blood Ritual in the Hebrew Bible*, 83.

73. Moses's manipulation of blood in Exod 24:6, 8 may be an exception to this remark.

74. Watts, "'ōlāh: The Rhetoric of Burnt Offerings," 132.

All this serves to underline the exceptionality of Elijah's 'ōlâ sacrifice, which features none of the mediation found in the Priestly texts. There is mediation, to be sure—just not priestly mediation. By performing cultic acts, which are usually the province of priests, Elijah establishes himself as the sole mediator between YHWH and the people of Israel; he alone is fit to perform the priestly sacrifice, and he alone is able to invoke YHWH's name with success. As observed above, Elijah's prayer in verses 36–37 effectively replaces the sacrifice as the mechanism of divine-human contact and thus shifts focus away from the ritual itself and onto the person of Elijah. The sacrifice has become an opportunity to demonstrate the efficacy of his prayer, according to the terms laid out at the beginning of the contest (v. 24). It is possible that Elijah's assumption of priestly duties is simply a way to elevate his status; after all, the groundwork for his unique mediation is laid early in the contest, when Elijah announces his singularity: "I alone (*'ănî … lĕbaddî*) am left as a prophet of YHWH" (1 Kgs 18:22).

This cultic role played by Elijah in 1 Kgs 18 in several ways resembles the cultic duties carried out by Samuel at the northern sites of Shiloh (1 Sam 2:11–26; 3:1–4:1a) and Mizpah (7:2–17).[75] These stories emphasize not only the prophet's role as intercessor but also how this role is established at the expense of the priesthood. In the Shiloh stories, for example, Samuel's faithful service and divine favor are contrasted with the wickedness of the sons of the priest Eli, whom the prophet supplants.[76] The cultic implications of this shift are on display in 1 Sam 7, in which Samuel makes a burnt offering (*'ôlâ*), then cries out (*wayyiz'aq*) to YHWH, who answers him (*wayya'ănēhû*) and intervenes in a storm theophany (vv. 9–10). The parallels with Elijah's sacrifice—its procedure and its efficacy—are obvious. Like Elijah, Samuel has assumed cultic prerogatives usually associated with priests,[77] and in light of the northern orientation of both accounts, it seems reasonable to ascribe these sacrificial duties to an institutional identity that was prevalent in northern Israel, as M. Sweeney has argued.

---

75. For the northern provenience of these texts, see McCarter, *I Samuel*, 18–26.

76. See also J. Willis, "An Anti-Elide Narrative Tradition from a Prophetic Circle at the Ramah Sanctuary," *JBL* 90 (1971): 288–308; A. Jenks, *The Elohist and North Israelite Traditions* (SBLMS 22; Missoula, Mont.: Scholars Press, 1977), 88.

77. Samuel's inclusion in a Levitical genealogy (1 Chr 6:1–13) seems to be an attempt to harmonize his nonpriestly status with his priestly actions. See I. Kalimi, *The Reshaping of Ancient Israelite History in Chronicles* (Winona Lake, Ind.: Eisenbrauns, 2005), 152–53.

Sweeney argues that priestly figures such as Samuel and Elijah represent a northern cultic tradition that was unfamiliar to the southern editors who produced the Deuteronomistic History.[78] Although these editors designated them "prophets" (*nābîʾ*), in fact they represent an early priestly office that was prevalent in the northern kingdom and distinct from the priesthood of the southern kingdom. While the figure of Samuel may only provide glimpses of this hypothetical priestly office, his cultic identity offers some insight into Elijah's role in 1 Kgs 18, and together their stories suggest that the religious personnel at northern sanctuaries may not belong to the same categories that are found in the Priestly writings but belong to a religious tradition that operated in the region.

4.3. CONCEPTUAL SPACE IN 1 KINGS 18

In assessing the conceptual space that underlies the Carmel narrative, I hope to show some of the organizing principles that have shaped its description of cultic space. Because it seeks out the values and concerns that guide the production of space, an examination of conceptual space in 1 Kgs 18 provides an opportunity to consider the religious sensibilities and ideologies that informed its depiction of cultic space. In this section, I will argue that border maintenance, accessibility, and uniqueness are three organizing principles that can be detected in the Carmel narrative, and though there are probably other principles that could be discussed, these three are especially noteworthy because of their correspondence with the conceptual space of Stratum III at Tel Dan.

4.3.1. BORDER MAINTENANCE

One feature of Mount Carmel that it shares with Tel Dan and that seems to be a defining characteristic of the sacred space described in 1 King 18 is its status as the border site. Geographically, Mount Carmel "forms a wedge-shaped barrier that divides the coastal plain,"[79] and from the time of the united monarchy this natural barrier served as the border between Israel

---

78. M. Sweeney, "Samuel's Institutional Identity in the Deuteronomistic History," in *Constructs of Prophecy in the Former and Latter Prophets and Other Texts* (ed. L. Grabbe and M. Nissinen; SBL Ancient Near East Monographs 4; Atlanta: Society of Biblical Literature, 2011), 165–74.

79. Rainey and Notley, *Sacred Bridge*, 37.

and Tyre.[80] (This location made Mount Carmel the ideal setting for Assyrian kings, like Shalmaneser III, to receive tribute from both kingdoms.[81]) In terms of the conceptual space of 1 Kgs 18, it is clear that Mount Carmel's position at the border between Israel and Tyre has significantly shaped the chapter's depiction of sacred space. Multiple examples of parallelism within the narrative serve to differentiate two cultic spaces, and Elijah's use of the twelve pillars further delineates the two spaces.

Mount Carmel's location made it a cultural transition zone, subject to alternating influence,[82] and yet the sacred space of 1 Kgs 18 is carefully delineated between the prophets of Baal, on the one hand, and Elijah, the prophet of YHWH, on the other. This demarcation is apparent in the parallel sacrifices that are prepared by the two sides at separate altars. At first, the nearly identical composition and preparation of two sacrifices suggests the cultural and religious overlap we might expect at a border site, but the similarities end when each side invokes their deity with distinctive rituals (the prophets' dancing and self-laceration and Elijah's water channel and prayer). Moreover, parallel structures in the narrative itself reinforce the opposition of the two sides. In verse 21 the choice between YHWH and Baal is presented by this repeated phrase: "If [DN] is god, follow him" (*'im* [DN] ... *lĕkû 'aḥărāyw*). Then in verse 24 Elijah tells the prophets of Baal to "call on the name of your god" (*ûqĕrā'tem bĕšēm hā'ĕlōhêkem*), and Elijah likewise will "call on the name of YHWH" (*'eqrā' bĕšēm-yhwh*). From this perspective, even the description of the people's vacillation—

---

80. See Alt, "Das Gottesurteil auf dem Karmel," 144–45; A. Lemaire, "Asher et le royaume de Tyr," in *Phoenicia and the Bible: Proceedings of the Conference Held at the University of Leuven on the 15th and 16th of March 1990* (ed. E. Lipiński; OLA 44; Leuven: Peeters, 1991), 152; H. Katzenstein, *The History of Tyre* (rev. ed.; Beer Sheva: Ben-Gurion University of the Negev Press, 1997), 105–7.

81. M. Astour writes: "It was there, at the promontory dedicated to Baal, which formed the boundary between Israel and Tyre and was equally sacred to the people of both kingdoms, that Shalmaneser set up an image of his royal self and received the tribute" ("841 B.C.: The First Assyrian Invasion of Israel," 386).

82. As E. Blake has noted, "border zones, as interstices, serve as laboratories for observing the conflicts between varying identities" ("Space, Spatiality, and Archaeology," in *A Companion to Social Archaeology* [ed. L. Meskell and R. Preucel; Malden, Mass.: Blackwell, 2007], 239; see also H. Donnan and T. Wilson, *Borders: Frontiers of Identity, Nation and State* [Oxford: Berg, 1999]).

"bouncing between two boughs" (v. 21)[83]—draws attention to the opposing spaces constructed by the narrative.

The two sacred spaces are also delineated by the twelve pillars that make up Elijah's altar. I argued above that the pillars represent tribal participation in the sacrifice, but it is likely that they also mark the boundary between Israel and Phoenicia and thus between the territories of YHWH and Baal. The use of pillars to mark boundaries is well attested in the Hebrew Bible.[84] In Exod 24, for example, the altar and twelve pillars that Moses erects at the foot of Mount Sinai are one way that he keeps Israel from approaching the mountain of YHWH, according to the divine command to "set bounds" (*gbl in Exod 19:12, 23). Similarly, in Josh 4:1–9 twelve stones are erected in the Jordan River to mark the entrance of the ark into the land of Israel and thus where YHWH's sovereignty begins.[85] Both of these texts are relevant to 1 Kgs 18, because all three texts describe twelve stones that divide space according to divine presence, that is, they cut a temenos. The Joshua passage is especially instructive because the stones in Josh 4:9, like those in 1 Kgs 18:31, mark a national boundary and the territorial authority of YHWH. Just as the stones in Exod 24 and Josh 4 mark a boundary of divine presence, in 1 Kgs 18 they draw attention to Mount Carmel's location on the border between Israel and Phoenicia and are a concrete representation of the division of sacred space between Elijah and the prophets of Baal.

This aspect of the conceptual space of 1 Kgs 18 invites comparison with Area T at Tel Dan, which constitutes another sacred space at a border site. Its setting on Israel's northern border has long been recognized, based largely on biblical evidence, such as the expression "from Dan to Beersheba" (Judg 20:1; 1 Sam 3:20; 2 Sam 3:10; 17:11; 24:2, 15; 1 Kgs 5:5) and also the phrase 'ad-dān, which denotes the land's northern limit (Gen

---

83. Heb. pōsĕḥîm 'al-šĕttê hassĕ'ippîm. The Heb. root *psḥ means "to limp" (cf. 2 Sam 4:4) or "to hop (over)" (cf. Exod 12:13, 23), and the root *s'p seems to indicate something that has been split in two (Judg 15:8, 11; Ps 119:113; Isa 2:21; 57:5); it is commonly used of twigs or branches (cf. Ezek 31:6, 8; Isa 10:33; 17:6; 27:10). Interestingly, the reordering of the alliterative consonants in the phrase (psḥ > s'p) mirrors Elijah's view of the people's shifting loyalties.

84. Besides the examples discussed here, see also the pillar erected by Jacob and Laban as part of their treaty (Gen 31:44–55).

85. On the significance of the stones in Josh 4:1–9, see E. LaRocca-Pitts, "Of Wood and Stone": The Significance of Israelite Cultic Items in the Bible and Its Early Interpreters (HSM 61; Winona Lake, Ind.: Eisenbrauns, 2001), 213.

14:14; Deut 34:1; 1 Kgs 12:30). Y. Aharoni took this recognition one step further and argued that Dan's location on the northern border, like Bethel's on the southern, is precisely what made the site attractive for a royal sanctuary.[86] As a border site, Tel Dan, like Mount Carmel, would have been subject to the similar external pressures, as Dan alternated between Israelite and Aramean hegemony. That it was under Aramean control for part of its Iron Age existence has been confirmed by the Tel Dan stela, which was written in Aramaic and which most scholars have interpreted as a victory stela of Hazael of Damascus.[87] The inscription also honors the Aramean god Hadad as the victor's patron deity. Moreover, certain architectural features, such as the column base from Area T and the area's overall layout, and other artifacts, such as a scepter-head from Area T and two bronze plaques from Area A, suggest Syro-Hittite influence.[88]

Yet "Aramean" material culture is notoriously difficult to assess at northern sites like Tel Dan and Hazor,[89] and it is hard to know how exactly Tel Dan's proximity to Damascus affected its sanctuary. Given this lack of evidence, we may find in the story of Elijah's sacrifice on Mount Carmel an instructive parallel for understanding how religious identities were main-

---

86. Aharoni writes: "The intention was to give divine and royal authority to the new borders" ("Arad: Its Inscriptions and Temple," *BA* 31 [1968]: 29). For Aharoni, other cult sites, such as Gilgal, Beersheba, and Arad, can also be interpreted as border shrines.

87. That Hazael is the author of the Tel Dan stela is not certain, but he remains the most likely candidate. This is the conclusion of W. Schniedewind ("Tel Dan Stela: New Light on Aramaic and Jehu's Revolt," *BASOR* 302 [1996]: 75–90) and P. McCarter (*Ancient Inscriptions: Voices from the Biblical World* [Washington, D.C.: Biblical Archaeological Society, 1996], 86–90). McCarter has discussed other possible authors (ibid.), and to these possibilities we should now add Hazael's son, known as Ben-Hadad II (or sometimes called Ben-Hadad III), whom G. Athas has recently proposed (*The Tel Dan Inscription: A Reappraisal and a New Interpretation* [New York: T&T Clark, 2003], 255–65).

88. E. Arie compares it to scepter heads recovered from Nimrud, which were inscribed with the names of Aramean kings and may have been the booty of Assyrian conquests in Syria and Phoenicia ("Reconsidering the Iron Age II Strata at Tel Dan: Archaeological and Historical Implications." *TA* 35 [2008]: 28–29). On the bronze plaques, see T. Ornan, "The Lady and the Bull: Remarks on the Bronze Plaque from Tel Dan," in *Essays on Ancient Israel in Its Near Eastern Context: A Tribute to Nadav Na'aman* (ed. Y. Amit et al.; Winona Lake, Ind.: Eisenbrauns, 2006), 297–312.

89. See A. Ben-Tor, "Hazor and the Chronology of Northern Israel: A Reply to Israel Finkelstein," *BASOR* 317 (2000): 11–12.

tained at border cult sites. Any analogies drawn between 1 Kgs 18 and Area T at Tel Dan are of course speculative, but if the former can shed any light on the latter, it may be in its depiction of religious and national boundaries. Although we might assume that a border site like Tel Dan would be especially likely to mix religious traditions, as the Syro-Hittite influence seems to suggest (and as we might expect from the Omride dynasty), 1 Kgs 18 offers a counterexample of a border site where religious boundaries are rigorously maintained. I am not arguing that its portrayal of dueling sacred spaces at the Carmel border should be superimposed on Area T's Stratum III, especially since 1 Kgs 18 may well represent an anomaly at Mount Carmel, a one-off exception to the religious syncretism that more commonly went on at the site. If anything, the story of Elijah's sacrifice on Mount Carmel suggests that religious identity at border sites, like Tel Dan, does not correspond neatly to political hegemony but may have fluctuated even within a particular period of Israelite or Aramean control. If Elijah can contest sacred space at Mount Carmel during a time of friendly political relations between Israel and Phoenicia, we should expect the politics of sacred space at Tel Dan to be no less complex.

4.3.2. ACCESSIBILITY

I have noted above the ways in which Elijah assumes cultic duties that are usually associated with the office of priesthood, but Elijah is not the only party in 1 Kgs 18 whose cultic status is substantially increased, for the assembled people also are featured in new ways. Far from detached bystanders, the people are depicted as genuine and indispensable participants in the events of 1 Kgs 18. First of all, throughout the chapter there is an emphasis on the physical closeness of all the cultic participants. This proximity is indicated by the repeated use of the word *ngš*: it first occurs in verse 21 to describe Elijah's approach to the people (*wayyiggaš 'ēlîyāhû 'el-kol-hā'ām*), and then in verse 30 just before Elijah rebuilds the altar, he instructs the people to come near (*gĕšû*) and they do so (*wayyiggĕšû*). This command brings the people close to the altar, and they even participate in the ritual when Elijah thrice instructs some of them to fill the jars with water and pour them over the *'ōlâ* sacrifice (vv. 33–34).[90]

---

90. A final example is *wayyiggaš* in v. 36, but the verb is missing in LXX and may be a secondary harmonization (see Hugo, *Les deux visages d'Élie*, 241).

The use of the people as the subject of this verb offers another contrast between the Carmel sacrifice and the Priestly cultic traditions. In the latter we can observe that the verb *ngš is used mostly of cultic personnel approaching the altar (e.g., Exod 28:43; 30:20; Lev 21:21, 23), so much so that J. Milgrom has concluded that in these cases the verb might well be translated "to have access."[91] Thus the verb *ngš underscores again the exceptional nonpriestly participation depicted in 1 Kgs 18.[92] This inclusion was already foreshadowed by the twelve altar stones, which represented the tribes of Israel and which Elijah integrated *within* the altar, and it is now clear that these stones do indeed represent "all the people." A final example of the people's heightened role in 1 Kgs 18 is their use as a structuring device for the entire narrative. P. Hugo has pointed out that the text may be divided according to Elijah's addresses to different interlocutors: "(all) the people" in verses 21,[93] 30, and 39; the prophets of Baal verse 25; and in verse 36 YHWH. In Hugo's analysis each of these references serves as the *ouverture* of its particular section by identifying the key players in the section.[94] The fact that in three of the five sections the people are fronted in this way demonstrates the importance of their presence.

The accessibility of the cultic space in 1 Kgs 18 is consistent with spatial arrangement of Area T at Tel Dan in Stratum III, which was also characterized by its openness. The portrait of worship that emerged from this stratum was one of communal feasts that took place around the central platform, the place that in the subsequent Stratum II will be surrounded by a temenos wall and effectively closed off to the public. The sacred precinct in Stratum III shows no such restrictions, at least not in its architecture, and I suggested in my discussion of this stratum that this openness was representative of the decentralized and egalitarian character of northern cultic traditions. This assessment finds an echo in the depiction of sacred space in 1 Kgs 18, which emphasizes the active participation of

---

91. J. Milgrom, *Studies in Levitical Terminology I: The Encroacher and the Levite, the Term 'Aboda* (Berkeley and Los Angeles: University of California Press, 1970), 35.

92. Admittedly, laypeople were allowed in the courtyard of the tabernacle, where they sometimes actively participate in sacrificial rites (see Milgrom, *Leviticus 1–16*, 147–48; M. George, *Israel's Tabernacle as Social Space* [SBLAIL 2; Atlanta: Society of Biblical Literature, 2009], 115).

93. LXX has only *pantas*, compared to MT's *kol-hā'ām*, but even if we regard MT's phrase as a harmonization to vv. 22, 30, Hugo's point remains valid.

94. Hugo, *Les deux visages d'Élie*, 219 n. 16.

the assembled people who are invited to come close to Elijah's altar. Without pressing their comparison too far, I think it is fair to suppose that Area T in Stratum III and the Carmel narrative in their own ways present sacred space where accessibility was valued. At Area T this value was expressed through the openness of the religious architecture, and in 1 Kgs 18 it was expressed by the prominent role of the assembly in the sacrifice and the narrative's emphasis on the people's closeness to the altar.

4.3.3. UNIQUENESS

However instructive it may be to compare 1 Kgs 18 and Area T at Tel Dan, their comparison is complicated by the uniqueness of Elijah's sacrifice on Mount Carmel. Already in the discussion of 1 Kgs 18's spatial practice I have mentioned several elements that seem to be unique or exceptional. For example, certain features of Elijah's sacrifice, such as the water channel and the pouring rites, lack strong parallels, and even though the ôlâ is a familiar sacrifice in Israelite cult, it is performed in isolation, without the offerings that usually accompany it. Moreover, the prominent roles assumed by the prophet Elijah and by the people suggest a distinctive cultic system that operates differently from other biblical traditions, such as the Priestly system. In fact, Elijah himself announces his own exceptionality, when he declares "I alone [lĕbaddî] am left as a prophet of YHWH" (1 Kgs 18:22), a claim that is reminiscent of Moses who was alone (lĕbbadô) permitted to approach YHWH (Exod 24:2) and whose priest-like role in Exod 24:3–8—another apparently northern text[95]—resembles Elijah's cultic role in 1 Kgs 18.[96] Furthermore, the uniqueness of the sacrifice and cultic personnel in 1 Kgs 18 has a reflex in its depiction of sacred space, especially in the description of Elijah's altar, whose existence as a cult place is coterminous with Elijah's sacrifice. Whatever the altar's origins may have been, the focus of the narrative is its disrepair; it is only serviceable after Elijah's "healing," and then only one offering is made at the altar—Elijah's ʿôlâ—before divine fire consumes the sacrifice and altar (1 Kgs 18:38), effectively canceling any further sacrifices. Like some elements of the sacrifice itself, the altar is depicted as a unique worship space.

---

95. Propp assigns the passage to the northern Elohist tradition (*Exodus 19–40*, 147–48).

96. The similarities between Moses and Elijah have long been noted; see S. McKenzie, *Trouble with Kings*, 83–84.

This uniqueness resonates with our understanding of Stratum III at Tel Dan. So far I have argued that 1 Kgs 18, because of its northern provenance and its ninth-century-B.C.E. date, offers a portrait of cultic space that may be instructive for reconstructing Area T in Stratum III, but the emphasis in the Carmel narrative on the singularity of Elijah and his altar suggests that its depiction of sacred space may be distinctive not only from southern cultic traditions but also from other northern traditions, Tel Dan included. In this way, 1 Kgs 18 is a reminder that even among northern cult sites there would have been significant differences.[97] As J. Hutton has shown, the common division of Israelite religion into a tripartite scheme of northern, southern, and eastern (Transjordanian) traditions is inadequate to account for the diversity of religious expressions within each region, and he argues for greater recognition of "micro-religions" that operated within these regional "macro-religions."[98]

If Elijah's altar in 1 Kgs 18 does represent a "micro-religion," then its relevance for Stratum III at Tel Dan is diminished, but in another way, the recognition of its uniqueness may provide us with just the right approach for interpreting features of Area T that lack analogues in archaeology and the Hebrew Bible. My discussion of Stratum III in chapter 2 showed that certain aspects of the temple complex, such as the construction of the podium and the use of pillars as devices for focusing attention, are familiar from archaeological and biblical sources, while other features, such as the spatial arrangement of Area T and its openness, lack strong parallels. The best analogues come from the open-air sanctuaries of the northern Levant, but even within this tradition Area T stands out. Perhaps then Area T, like Mount Carmel in 1 Kgs 18, represents a "micro-religion" that was similar enough to other northern sites to attest their regional commonalities but still maintained some cultic traditions that were unique to Tel Dan. If so, then 1 Kgs 18 would be instructive not so much as a strict parallel for understanding Area T in Stratum III but as a model of the tension between a site's regional cultic identity and its unique local traditions.

---

97. Cross, *Canaanite Myth and Hebrew Epic*, 195–215.

98. J. Hutton, "Southern, Northern and Transjordanian Perspectives," in *Religious Diversity in Ancient Israel and Judah* (ed. F. Stavrakopoulou and J. Barton; London: T&T Clark, 2010), 149–74.

5
EIGHTH-CENTURY B.C.E. TEXTUAL STRATUM: THE BOOK OF AMOS

5.1. INTRODUCTION

When we turn to the Hebrew Bible for textual data to complement our analysis of Stratum II at Tel Dan, the book of Amos presents itself as a useful source for comparison. In terms of geographical and temporal proximity, this book represents the best available textual stratum for exploring cultic practices in the northern kingdom during the eighth century B.C.E. First of all, although Amos himself was a Judahite, the book focuses on his prophetic activity in Israel. Its regional character is apparent not only in the frequent mention of northern toponyms but also in Amos's detailed description of life there.[1] Moreover, the passages of most interest to us— those that reflect cultic practices of the time—are directed almost exclusively at the northern kingdom, and all but one of them (5:21–27) associate those practices with particular sites, such as Bethel, Gilgal, Samaria, and Dan. Thus although Amos himself was a southerner, he displays sufficient familiarity with the kingdom of Israel that the book of Amos can be considered a northern text.

Establishing the temporal proximity of the book of Amos is a more complicated task. According to the superscription (1:1) and a short biographical passage (7:10–17), Amos prophesied in the northern kingdom during the reign of Jeroboam II (787–748 B.C.E.), and while these verses provide a reliable date for his life and prophetic activity, most scholars

---

1. See H. Wolff, *Joel and Amos: A Commentary on the Books of Joel and Amos* (trans. W. Janzen et al.; Hermeneia; Philadelphia: Fortress, 1977), 103–5; F. Andersen and D. Freedman, *Amos: A New Translation with Introduction and Commentary* (AB 24A; New York: Doubleday, 1989), 137–38.

doubt that the entire book can be attributed to Amos of Tekoa. Indeed, the fact that these two passages refer to him in the third person indicates some distance from the prophet himself, and many studies have attempted to discern the book's redactional layers. Most notable in this regard was H. Wolff's proposal of six independent layers—three from the time of Amos and his contemporary disciples and three from later centuries.[2] This "scissors-and-paste" method has been heavily criticized, especially by S. Paul, whose own commentary, published in the same series as Wolff's, argues that "the book in its entirety (with one or two minor exceptions) can be reclaimed for its rightful author, the prophet Amos."[3] Because our own interest concerns particular passages, there is no need here to debate the book's overall composition;[4] for each of the passages under examination I will briefly discuss its dating. My method for these passages will follow G. Tucker's advice to "trust but verify." In his recent essay on dating the book of Amos, he recommends that "if a prophetic text is presented as from a particular era, such as the eighth century for Amos, that needs to be the starting point."[5] While not every verse in the book of Amos dates to the time of Jeroboam II, it is nonetheless reasonable to regard selected passages as constitutive of an eighth-century-B.C.E. textual stratum. By examining the spatial practice and conceptual space that may be gleaned from the book of Amos, I hope to construct a picture of sacred space that can be compared with the picture found in Stratum II of Area T at Tel Dan.

5.2. Spatial Practice in the Book of Amos

5.2.1. Cultic Spaces

Certainly the fullest description of cultic space in the book of Amos is found in 7:10–17, a prose narrative that interrupts the five vision reports

---

2. Wolff, *Joel and Amos*, 106–13.

3. Paul, *Amos: A Commentary on the Book of Amos* (Hermeneia; Minneapolis: Fortress, 1991), 6.

4. An extensive bibliography on the subject may be found in M. D. Carroll R., *Amos—The Prophet and His Oracles: Research on the Book of Amos* (Louisville: Westminster John Knox, 2002), 114–18.

5. G. Tucker, "Amos the Prophet and Amos the Book: Historical Framework," in *Israel's Prophets and Israel's Past: Essays on the Relationship of Prophetic Texts and Israelite History in Honor of John H. Hayes* (ed. B. Kelle and M. Moore; LHB/OTS 446; New York: T&T Clark, 2006), 88.

that constitute much of Amos 7–9.[6] Most scholars agree that this report originated in the time of the prophet himself (or shortly afterward) and therefore offers a window to Amos's prophetic activity.[7] While most scholarly attention has focused on what the passage does or does not reveal about Amos's prophetic vocation, it is just as significant for its depiction of the state sanctuary at Bethel. Amos 7:10–17 recounts a confrontation between Amos and Amaziah the priest of Bethel in which the latter expels the former from the sanctuary "because it is the king's sanctuary and royal temple" (*kî miqdaš-melek hû' ûbêt mamlākâ hû'*). Both designations highlight royal authority as the defining characteristic of the Bethel sanctuary. Amaziah invokes none of the Bethel traditions that undergird the sanctuary; for him the king's patronage of the site is decisive for its identity. Indeed, the singularity of the king's authority over the sanctuary is further emphasized by the lack of any description of the sanctuary itself. In this passage there is no religious architecture, no cultic equipment, no performance of rituals; there is only the royal prerogative expressed through Amaziah.

In addition to this emphasis on royal control over cultic space, Amos 7:10–17 also offers some perspective on the kind of cultic personnel who operated in state sanctuaries. Of course, there is the priest Amaziah, who owes his appointment to the king (see 1 Kgs 13:33; 2 Kgs 17:32) and whose dutiful reports to the king (Amos 7:10–11) reflect his dependency on and his loyalty to his patron.[8] His office, like other intermediaries in the

---

6. The relationship between the prose narrative and the vision reports has been the subject of numerous studies, with many arguing that the former's insertion is related to the language it shares with 7:7–9, especially references to the "house of Jeroboam (II)" and his death by the sword (see Paul, *Amos*, 238–39 n. 3; J. Hayes, *Amos: The Eighth-Century Prophet: His Times and His Preaching* [Nashville: Abingdon, 1988], 231). Others, however, while acknowledging that vv. 10–17 are an interpolation, emphasize the thematic and rhetorical coherence of Amos 7–8 (see P. Noble, "Amos and Amaziah in Context: Synchronic and Diachronic Approaches to Amos 7–8," *CBQ* 60 (1998): 423–39; also A. Cooper, "The Meaning of Amos's Third Vision (Amos 7:7–9)," in *Tehillah le-Moshe: Biblical and Judaic Studies in Honor of Moshe Greenberg* (ed. M. Cogan et al.; Winona Lake, Ind.: Eisenbrauns, 1997), 13–21.

7. See L. Schmidt, "Die Amazja-Erzählung (Am 7,10–17) und der historische Amos," *ZAW* 119 (2007): 221–35; also Paul, *Amos*, 238; and Wolff, *Joel and Amos*, 309.

8. See I. Jaruzelska, "Amasyah—prêtre de Béthel—fonctionnaire royal (essai socio-économique préliminaire)," *FO* 31 (1995): 54–56. In this same article the author argues that *'admātĕkā* in Amos 7:17 refers to a fief received by Amaziah as payment

ancient Near East, relied on the king's patronage, and this dependency was true not just for priests but also for prophets, such as the court prophets known from the Hebrew Bible (see 1 Kgs 18:19; 22:6, 10).[9] Indeed, Amaziah seems to assume that Amos's prophetic office, like Amaziah's own priestly office, depends on royal patronage. Tellingly, he addresses Amos as a ḥōzeh, "seer," in 7:12, a term for prophets who "were officially attached to the court."[10] Amaziah may assume that he is speaking to Amos as one royal dependent to another, as if the prophet also owes his office to the king, but Amos's rejoinder in 7:14 exposes the assumption as false: he is not a professional prophet (nābî') at all—court prophet (ḥōzeh) or otherwise—but a herdsman and a harvester of sycamore figs.[11] The exchange is interesting for what it reveals about access to the cultic space at Bethel. On the one hand is the nonprofessional prophet Amos who, by his own account, does not operate at the Bethel sanctuary in any "official" capacity.[12] His presence does not depend on any institutional office but simply on his status as an individual worshiper. On the other hand is Amaziah the priest of Bethel, whose behavior reflects a strict adherence to the hierarchical organization that supports his office. It is precisely when Amos does not conform to that organization that he is expelled from Bethel. The description of cultic space in Amos 7:10–17 presumes that worshipers are

---

for his priestly duties (ibid., 56–57, 67–69; see also idem, *Amos and the Officialdom in the Kingdom of Israel: The Socio-Economic Position of the Officials in the Light of the Biblical, the Epigraphic and Archaeological Evidence* [Seria Socjologia 25; Poznań: Uniwersytetu im. Adama Mickiewicza w Poznaniu, 1998], 172–73).

9. See J. Couey, "Amos vii 10–17 and Royal Attitudes Toward Prophecy in the Ancient Near East," *VT* 58 (2008): 300–314.

10. Paul, "Prophets and Prophecy," *EncJud* 16:569; see also Z. Zevit, "A Misunderstanding at Bethel: Amos VII 12–17," *VT* 25 (1975): 787.

11. Though LXX reads *aipolos*, "goatherd," it is unnecessary to emend Heb. *bôqēr* to *nōqēd* (see 1:1). The occupations *nōqēd* and *bôqēr* are not mutually exclusive (see R. Steiner, *Stockmen from Tekoa, Sycamores from Sheba* [CBQMS 36; Washington, D.C.: Catholic Biblical Association of America, 2003], 73–80). As for the "harvester of sycamore figs" (Heb. *bôlēs šiqmîm*), see ibid., 5–31.

12. Some have argued that Amos's position as a *nōqēd* (1:1) has a religious connotation, based on its Ug. cognate *nqd*, which seems to have entailed religious duties. The term appears in several occupation lists, three of which list it alongside other cultic officials (KTU 4.68:71; 4.126:5; 4.416:5 [broken]). Also noteworthy is the colophon at the end of the Baal cycle, which describes the mentor of Ilimilku as the *rb khnm, rb nqdm* and *ṯ'y* (sacrificer?) of the king Niqmaddu (KTU 1.6 VI 55–56). Even with the religious connotations of *nōqēd*, it is clear that Amos has no cultic status at Bethel.

welcome at the sanctuary as long as they adhere to the hierarchy that governs the sanctuary and its personnel.

Finally, the passage also develops the theme of cultic exclusion, which will resurface in another description of cultic space at the end of the book. This theme is apparent in Amos 7:10–17 most obviously in Amos's expulsion from Bethel (vv. 12–13), but it is also apparent in the two prophetic declarations that bracket the passage. The prose narrative begins with the reported speech of Amos, who has declared that "Israel will be expelled from its land" (7:11), and it ends with this exact same phrase (7:17). In this way, the cultic space at Bethel becomes a microcosm (in reverse) of the expulsion that will take place kingdom-wide; Amos's exclusion from that space is thus a rehearsal of Israel's imminent estrangement from its land. This theme is picked up again in the last of the five vision reports, which describes YHWH standing by the altar (ʿal-hammizbēaḥ) and commanding that the capitals (hakkaptôr) be struck until the thresholds (hassippîm) shake (9:1). Although many commentators interpret the capital and the threshold as a merism for the destruction of the Bethel temple "from top to bottom,"[13] J. Jeremias has argued that capitals and thresholds more likely depict the entrance to the temple.[14] Its destruction would effectively prevent the Israelites from entering the sanctuary and would thus exclude them from the asylum it represented. This interpretation echoes—and reverses again—Amos's exclusion from the Bethel temple and provides another example of how cultic space functions in the book of Amos as the medium for expressing some of its key themes. In both Amos 7:10–17 and 9:1 the sacred space of the Bethel temple is contested space in which competing authority claims are negotiated around the politics of access and exclusion.

5.2.2. Cultic Rites

In addition to descriptions of cultic space, there are also several references in the book of Amos to cultic rituals that would have taken place in these cultic spaces. As spatial practice, these rituals contribute to our

---

13. Paul, *Amos*, 275; J. Mays, *Amos: A Commentary* (OTL; Philadelphia: Westminster, 1969), 153–54.

14. J. Jeremias, "Das unzugängliche Heiligtum. Zur letzten Vision des Amos," in *Hosea und Amos: Studien zu den Anfängen des Dodekapropheton* (FAT 13; Tübingen: Mohr, 1996), 244–56.

understanding of sacred space in Amos; by examining the kind of rituals that are mentioned and the context in which they tended to occur, we can, to a certain extent, reconstruct the cultic space in which they would likely have taken place. As the following two sections show, my own reconstruction categorizes the cultic rituals according to their public or private character. These categories are by no means the only system for organizing the references to cultic rituals, nor do I assume a hard division between them. (As we will see below, there are several instances of overlap.) Nonetheless, the categories of public and private worship will provide a helpful starting place for discussing how the book of Amos can inform our understanding of sacred space in eighth-century-B.C.E. Israel.

5.2.2.1. Public Worship

The clearest references to public worship come from Amos 5:21–27, which begins with an explicit reference to "festivals" (*ḥaggîm*) and "assemblies" (*ʿaṣṣĕrōt*). Both terms denote communal religious gatherings and in the Hebrew Bible refer to a variety of festivals, and *ḥaggîm* in particular involves pilgrimage to a sanctuary.[15] This picture of public cult continues in the passage with subsequent description of divine images in public procession (v. 26).[16] From the verb **nś'* we can surmise that sacred objects representing the gods Kaiwan and Sakkut were raised and carried in public,

---

15. The three best-known *ḥaggîm* are the annual pilgrimages—the Festivals of Unleavened Bread (*maṣṣôt*), Weeks (*šābuʿôt*), and Booths (*sukkôt*)—which are prescribed in the Covenant Code (Exod 23:14–17), the Yahwistic Decalogue (Exod 34:18–28), Deuteronomy (Deut 16:1–17), the Holiness Code (Lev 23:4–12, 34–44), and the Priestly Code (Num 28:16–31). Likewise, the term *ʿǎṣārâ* is variously associated with the Festival of Booths (Lev 23:36; Num 29:35) and the Festival of Unleavened Bread (Deut 16:8), but also with the dedication of Solomon's temple (2 Chr 7:9) and certain non-Yahwistic cultic events (e.g., 2 Kgs 10:20).

16. Several commentators have taken v. 26 as a later gloss, based on the correspondence between Sakkut in this verse and the reference in 2 Kgs 17:30 to *sukkôt běnôt*, a deity installed by the Babylonians who had been resettled in Samaria by the Assyrians (Wolff, *Joel and Amos*, 259–60, 264–66; M. Poley, *Amos and the Davidic Empire: A Socio-Historical Approach* [New York: Oxford University Press, 1989], 87, 154; O. Loretz, "Die babylonischen Gottesnamen Sukkut und Kajjamānu in Amos 5,26," *ZAW* 101 [1989]: 286–89; W. Schmidt, "Die deuteronomistische Redaktion des Amosbuches," *ZAW* 77 [1965]: 188–91). However, Sakkut has a long history in the ancient Near Eastern pantheon and likely arrived through Aramaic influence prior to the 722-B.C.E. resettlement (see M. Cogan, *Imperialism and Religion: Assyria, Judah and Israel in the Eighth and*

a ritual well attested in biblical and extrabiblical texts as well as in icono-graphical sources.[17] The transfer of the ark of the covenant in 2 Sam 6 rep-resents just such a procession, and also noteworthy are Jer 10:1–16 and Isa 46:1–7, which parody the procession of foreign gods with language similar to Amos 5:26. Such ritual processions are by nature public and inclusive; as soon as the cultic object is brought into common space, participation in the rite is virtually unrestricted.[18] Like the *ḥaggîm* and *'aṣṣērōt* in verse 21, the procession of divine images assumes a substantial religious assembly engaged in public worship.

The same can be said for the references in verse 22 to "your whole-burnt offerings and cereal-offerings" (*'ōlôt ûminḥōtêkem*) and "communion offering of your fatlings" (*šelem mĕrî'êkem*),[19] which most likely describe the kind of worship that would take place in these religious assemblies cited in verse 21.[20] Although the *'ōlâ* and the *minḥâ* are not exclusively offered at public festivals, as their occurrence in familial contexts makes clear (e.g., Judg 13:15–19; Num 15), they figure prominently in large reli-gious gatherings. Moreover, their parallelism between *'ōlôt ûminḥōtêkem* and *šelem mĕrî'êkem*, in which the latter certainly does refer to a commu-

---

Seventh Centuries B.C.E. [SBLMS 19; Missoula, Mont.: Scholars Press, 1974], 103–4; Andersen and Freedman, *Amos*, 536; Paul, *Amos*, 194–95).

17. See *ANEP*, figs. 305, 537. For a survey of iconographical depictions of ritual processions, see T. Lewis, "Syro-Palestinian Iconography and Divine Images," in *Cult Image and Divine Representation in the Ancient Near East* (ed. N. Walls; ASOR Books 10; Boston: American Schools of Oriental Research, 2005), 93–97.

18. Of the ritual procession during the *akītu* festival B. Pongratz-Leisten writes: "Während der Festzeit dagegen, bei der die Götterprozession den Höhepunkt bildet, wird die räumliche Distanz zum Kultbild aufgehoben, der Gott bewegt sich und begibt sich zu den Menschen; der Kontakt mit dem Göttlichen bleibt somit nicht nur auf ein spezialisiertes Kultpersonal beschränkt, sondern wird in der Festzeit auf ein Publikum ausgeweitet, dem der Zutritt in den Tempel im sakralen Alltag verwehrt ist" (Ina Šulmi Īrub: *Die kulttopographische und ideologische Programmatik der* akītu-*Prozession in Babylonien und Assyrien im I. Jahrtausend v. Chr.* [Baghdader Forschun-gen 16; Mainz am Rhein: Zabern, 1994], 14).

19. On this translation of *šelem/šĕlāmîm*, see M. Modéus, *Sacrifice and Symbol: Biblical* Šĕlāmîm *in a Ritual Perspective* (ConBOT 52; Stockholm: Almqvist & Wiksell International, 2005), 174.

20. Although some interpreters see in 5:22–25 a category-by-category indictment of Israelite cult rather than a continuation of the criticism began in v. 21 (Mays, *Amos*, 106; Paul, *Amos*, 188; Poley, *Amos and the Davidic Empire*, 100), I think these verses continue with the theme of public festivals.

nal sacrifice and celebration, suggests that the three offerings represent a single cultic context, namely public worship. Indeed, when the three occur together elsewhere in the Hebrew Bible, it is always in this public context. Examples of their combination include Aaron's inauguration (Lev 9), the dedication of the temple (1 Kgs 8:64), the Festival of Weeks (Lev 23:15–22), and the Festival of Booths (Num 29:12–39). Thus although the ʿōlâ and minḥâ occur in a variety of cultic contexts, when they are combined with "communion offerings" (šĕlāmîm), they seem to indicate a group of offerings that would be made at large religious assemblies.

Finally, a few remarks are in order regarding the šelem mĕrîʾêkem.[21] Like ʿōlâ and minḥâ, the šĕlāmîm offering is prevalent in private and public worship. For example, in the Priestly corpus it is combined with thanksgiving offerings (Lev 7:12–15), vow-fulfillment offerings (Lev 7:16; cf. Prov 7:14), freewill offerings (Lev 7:16), and ʾiššeh offerings (7:29–30). Elsewhere, however, it is connected with the Festival of Weeks (Lev 23:19) and môʿădîm (Num 10:10), and B. Levine and G. Anderson have both argued that the šĕlāmîm originated as a public cultic event, though they disagree on whether it began as a royal or tribal celebration.[22] Only later was the šĕlāmîm employed for more private cultic occasions, like thanksgiving offerings and the fulfillment of vows. That verse 22 refers to the older use of the cultic term, which involved a large religious assembly, is apparent from the mention of the "fatlings" (mĕrîʾêkem) that constituted the šelem. This word occurs only eight times in the Hebrew Bible, and most often it denotes a rather large animal for a large sacrificial feast. This is how mĕrîʾ is used in 2 Sam 6:13, where it is sacrificed along with a bull (Heb. šôr) as part of the ritual procession,[23] and it occurs again in 1 Kgs 1:9 as part of

21. There is no justification for emending šelem to the more common plural šĕlāmîm, as recommended by BHS and others. The uniqueness of the singular form is precisely why it should be retained as the lectio difficilior (see W. Rudolph, Joel, Amos, Obadja, Jona [KAT 13.2; Gütersloh: Mohn, 1971], 210).

22. B. Levine writes that it was "originally a sacrifice related to royal and/or national celebrations of a distinctive character, and which only subsequently became incorporated into the regular cult" (In the Presence of the Lord [SJLA 5; Leiden: Brill, 1974], 34), while G. Anderson argues that "the festive offering of šĕlāmîm is very important in the royal period, but not because the rite is uniquely associated with kingship. On the contrary, the rite is a major league institution which the royal interests seek to take over" (Sacrifices and Offerings in Ancient Israel: Studies in their Social and Political Importance [HSM 41; Atlanta: Scholars Press, 1987], 51).

23. Heb. šôr ûmĕrîʾ in this verse is possibly a case of hendiadys, i.e., "the fattened

the royal feast prepared by Adonijah for all the sons of the king and for all the men of Judah (see also vv. 19, 25). Moreover, the connection between *mĕrî'* and banquets finds support in the Ugaritic cognate *mr'u*, which primarily occurs in the context of large festive gatherings.[24]

Taken together the various offerings mentioned in Amos 5:21–27 depict spatial practice that is best characterized as public worship. These various cultic elements require the reader to create a cultic space that is large enough to accommodate religious festivals and their related sacrifices. It is a decidedly public space where worshipers gathered to celebrate in a communal setting.

5.2.2.2. Private Worship

However, the book of Amos elsewhere creates spaces for more private cultic celebrations. One of the best examples of this kind of cultic space is in Amos 4:4–5, in which the prophet facetiously invites the people to come to Bethel and Gilgal, where they should bring their "sacrifices" (*zibḥêkem*) and tithes (*ma'śĕrōtêkem*), "burn a thanks offering" (*qaṭṭēr ... tôdâ*) and proclaim "freewill offerings" (*nĕdābôt*).[25] Many commentators have assumed that the command to "come to Bethel and Gilgal" implies that these offerings are to be made in the context of a pilgrimage festival,[26] but when the verb *bō'û* occurs, as it does here, without a preposition, it usually

---

bull" (see P. K. McCarter, *II Samuel: A New Translation with Introduction, Notes and Commentary* [AB 9; Garden City, NY: Doubleday, 1984], 166).

24. Examples include Baal's banquet for the seventy sons of Athiratu (KTU 1.4 VI 41) and Kirta's instructions to slaughter the *mr'u* in advance of the seventy captains and eighty chiefs who are coming for a feast (KTU 1.15 IV 4–9).

25. J. Begrich was the first to identify this passage as a parody of "priestly Torah," whose original purpose was to "die verschiedenen Opferarten, ihre Anwendbarkeit und ihre Durchführung genau zu unterscheiden, die einzelnen Feste und die für sie gültigen Riten zu kennen und zu beachten" ("Die priesterliche Tora," in *Werden und Wesen des Alten Testament. Vorträge gehalten auf der Internationalen Tagung alttestamentlicher Forscher zu Göttingen von 4–10. September 1935* [ed. P. Volz et al.; BZAW 66; Berlin: Töpelmann, 1936], 71). Amos ironically recasts the Torah as an invitation to transgression rather than proper cult service.

26. J. Soggin asserts that 4:4–5 was spoken "in the presence of pilgrims in the course of a feast which we can no longer identify" (*The Prophet Amos: A Translation and Commentary* [trans. J. Bowden; London: SCM, 1987], 71–72), and Mays writes that the passage "must have been spoken during a festival assembly at Bethel" (*Amos*, 74).

means "to enter" a house, a temple, gates, and so on.[27] Thus the command
most likely means for worshipers to enter the sanctuary at Bethel and
Gilgal rather than "to go on pilgrimage."[28] Moreover, a close look at each
of the offerings mentioned in 4:4–5 shows that they represent examples
of private worship. Unlike 5:21–27, whose cultic vocabulary presupposes
a large public space for a religious assembly, the cultic space assumed in
4:4–5 is smaller and more family-oriented.

Evidence for this cultic context begins with *zibḥêkem*, or "your sacrifices." Although some automatically assume that this term stands for *zebaḥ
haššělāmîm*,[29] the absence of the latter word in 4:4 is significant. Indeed, R.
Rendtorff's study of *zebaḥ haššělāmîm* has shown that these terms originally denoted two separate sacrifices and furthermore that in numerous
attestations *zebaḥ* is depicted as a family sacrifice.[30] This meaning is exemplified by the *zebaḥ hayyāmîm*, or "yearly sacrifice," celebrated by Elkanah
and "his entire house" (*kol-bêtô*) in 1 Sam 1. These sacrifices, discussed
above, are occasioned by Elkanah's annual fulfillment of vows at Shiloh
(see v. 21) and are depicted as a family affair, especially when Elkanah and
Hannah, returning to dedicate Samuel as a Nazirite, slaughter the bull they
have brought (vv. 24–25).[31] The familial character of *zebaḥ hayyāmîm* is

---

27. See Judg 18:18; 1 Sam 1:24 (LXX); Ps 100:4; Jer 14:18; Hos 4:15; 9:4; Amos
5:19. By contrast, a preposition after *⋆bw'* usually indicates movement to a destination
(e.g., *'el* [Gen 14:7; Josh 24:11; Jer 39:1], *'al* [Judg 18:27; Jer 51:56] or *lě-* [Judg 20:10;
Isa 59:20]). This distinction is especially clear in 1 Sam 24:4, in which Saul first "came
to [*wayyābō' 'el*] the sheepfolds," then "entered [*wayyābō'*]" them.

28. Hayes, *Amos*, 142.

29. Ibid., 144; see also Mays, *Amos*, 75.

30. According to Rendtorff, the *šělāmîm* took place "sowohl im regelmäßigen
Festopferkult als auch bei besonderen Anlässen, insbesondere bei Altar- und Heilig-
tumsweihen und vielleicht deren regelmäßigen kultischen Nachvollzug" (*Studien zur
Geschichte des Opfers im Alten Israel* [WMANT 24; Neukirchen-Vluyn: Neukirchener,
1967], 126), while "der *zebach* niemals den Charakter eines öffentlichen Opfers hat.
Vielmehr ist es der Kreis der Familie oder der Sippe" (ibid., 143). He concludes by
arguing that the *zebaḥ šělāmîm* was a Priestly innovation that "deprivatized" the *zebaḥ*
by joining it to the *šělāmîm*, which was a blood rite already part of the priesthood's
cultic mandate (ibid., 166–67). This process of "deprivatization" had already begun in
the cultic reforms of Josiah, which brought the family-oriented *zebaḥ* to the temple in
Jerusalem (ibid., 144, 163–64).

31. The plural *wayyišḥāṭû* (MT, LXX[L]) is preferred over the singular (LXX[B],
4QSam[a]). See the discussion on p. 103 n. 87. M. Haran notes that "there is no allusion
to gathering of festal celebrants or to scenes of popular rejoicing, as the *ḥag*, being

further supported by 1 Sam 20:6, 9, where the phrase is synonymous with *zebaḥ mišpāḥâ* (20:6, 29). Similarly, 1 Sam 9:11–13, 22–25 offers a brief description of a *zebaḥ* that takes place on a *bāmâ* and is designated for the people (*lāʿām*). Again, there is no mention of cultic specialists on hand for the sacrifice, except for Samuel, who as seer (*rōʾeh*) must bless the sacrifice (v. 13). The lack of such specialists and Samuel's arrival after the slaughter of the animal suggests that one of the people was responsible for the *zebaḥ*. Of course, not every instance of *zebaḥ* in the Hebrew Bible supports its characterization as family religion—Absalom hosted a *zebaḥ* for two hundred people! (2 Sam 15:11)—but there are enough examples to suggest that its usage in Amos 4:4 represents a more family-oriented sacrifice that could be celebrated without the mediation of religious specialists.

The familial context of *zibḥêkem* is supported by its parallel *maʿśĕrōtêkem*, or "your tithes," an offering that is depicted in the Hebrew Bible as an individual or family offering.[32] The Deuteronomic commands on tithing provide valuable insight into its ritual context:

> bring your whole burnt-offerings [*ʿōlōtêkem*] and your sacrifices [*zibḥêkem*], your tithes and the gift of your hand [*tĕrûmat*[33] *yedkem*], your votive offerings, your freewill offerings,[34] and the firstlings of your herd and of your flock; and there you shall eat before YHWH your God, and you shall rejoice, you and your households, in all that you undertake, in which YHWH your God has blessed you. (12:6–7)

First, it is noteworthy that "households" (*bāttêkem*), namely sons, daughters, servants, and the Levite (v. 12), are primarily responsible for the offering; and second, the tithe is offered as part of a cultic family feast (cf. Deut 14:26–27). And it is not just the Deuteronomic Code that attests to this familial context for tithing, but 1 Sam 1:21 offers a similar picture. Having already discussed this verse's importance for understanding the familial character of *zebaḥ*, we should note that in the LXX[L] this verse concludes

---

public institution in its nature, is depicted in the Bible. It is clearly evident that reference is made here to a 'private,' personal pilgrimage pertaining to Elkanah and his household only ("Zebaḥ Hayyamîm," *VT* 19 [1969]: 12).

32. Interestingly, we find just the opposite in the Ugaritic corpus, where the village is the unit responsible for delivering the tithe (see M. Heltzer, "On Tithe Paid in Grain in Ugarit," *IEJ* 25 [1975]: 124–28).

33. See J. Milgrom, *Leviticus 1–16* (AB 3; New York: Doubleday, 1991), 473–81.

34. For a discussion of "freewill offerings" in Amos 4:5ab, see below, pp. 161–62.

with the payment of his vows *and* "the tithes of his land" (Gr. *apodounai ... pasas tas dekatas tēs gēs autou*). If we restore this phrase to the text, as P. K. McCarter proposes, then we have more evidence that tithes were paid in family units and were accompanied by a common meal.[35]

Of course, the biblical evidence also includes some depictions of tithing that differ from the Deuteronomic version. For example, unlike the Deuteronomic Code, which presents the tithe as an obligatory offering, Priestly references suggest that the tithe may have been a voluntary offering,[36] and examples of tithing in biblical narrative—as when Abram gives Melchizedek "a tenth of everything" (Gen 14:19–20) and when Jacob vows at Bethel to give back to God a tenth of all he receives (Gen 28:20–22)—support this understanding. Additionally, the tithe seems not to have been restricted to the cultic sphere (see 1 Sam 8:15–17). Even among these varied traditions, however, one detail remains consistent, namely that the tithe is given as either a private or family offering, and this consistency suggests that the tithe mentioned in Amos 4:4 likewise connotes an example of family religion.

Turning to Amos 4:5, we find in the first part of the verse three further cultic terms, which are indicative of private worship. The most significant of the three is *tôdâ*, or "thanks offering,"[37] which is probably a short form of the *zebah tôdâ*, mentioned in the Psalter (107:22; 116:17) and also in

---

35. P. K. McCarter, *I Samuel* (AB 8; Garden City, N.Y.: Doubleday, 1980), 55.

36. The evidence is admittedly uncertain. H. Jagersma ("The Tithes in the Old Testament," *OtSt* 21 [1981]: 118) and J. Milgrom (*Leviticus 23–27* [AB 3B; New York: Doubleday, 2001], 2426–31) maintain that the tithe was compulsory, but B. Levine has noted that the Leviticus reference "is not formulated in terms of priestly or levitical income. Although the formula *qôdeš l-YHWH* used in those priestly statements functionally connotes temple income, it does not specifically identify the Levites as recipients of tithes" (*Numbers 1–20* [AB 4A; New York: Doubleday, 1993], 450–51). The explicit assignment of tithes to the Levites is found only in the Numbers passage, but this text also lacks the language of obligation (see M. Haran, *Temples and Temple-Service in Ancient Israel: An Inquiry into the Character of Cultic Phenomena and the Historical Setting of the Priestly School*, 116–17 n. 8). Following Levine's point it seems that functionally the collection of tithes at the time of the annual harvest had the same effect as an obligation, but the Priestly source seems to avoid the language of obligation.

37. The fact that *tôdâ* occurs as the object of *qaṭṭēr* confirms that in this verse it refers to an offering and not an instance of praise or confession, both of which are common meanings for the word (see G. Mayer, "ידה *ydh*," *TDOT* 5:431–36).

the book of Leviticus (7:12–15; 22:29).[38] The former examples, both songs of individual thanksgiving, demonstrate a close association between sacrifice (*zbḥ) and thanksgiving (*ydh),[39] and in Ps 116 we also find *tôdâ* in parallel with the vow (vv. 17–18; cf. Pss 50:14; 56:13; Jonah 2:10), which is certainly an example of private worship.[40] This parallelism suggests that the thanks offering could serve as the fulfillment of a vow and, further, that the personal aspect of vows was also true for the thanks offering made for an answered petition.[41] Together these comparative examples of the *tôdâ* suggest that it was a private offering, albeit one that took place in a larger communal context. Indeed, the use of plural verbs throughout Ps 107 indicates the presence of a larger assembly, which is finally named in verse 32 as the *qěhāl-ʿām*; similarly, Ps 116 refers to the *kol-ʿammô* (vv. 14, 18).[42]

---

38. In Lev 7 the thanks offering appears, along with the *neder* and *nědābâ*, as one of the subcategories of the *šělāmîm* offering. Significantly, the instructions within which these offerings occur (vv. 11–21) are designated for the individual layman making the sacrifice (Milgrom, *Leviticus 1–16*, 413, 418). However, this reference in Lev 7 to the *zebaḥ tôdâ* is problematic because the Priestly writer has conflated it with the *šělāmîm*. The conflation, unique to the Priestly writer, is exemplified by the phrase *zebaḥ tôdat šělāmāyw* (v. 13), which Milgrom describes as "artificial and awkward" (*Leviticus 1–16*, 415). Further, he has argued that the *tôdâ* does not belong with the *neder* and *nědābâ*, as Lev 7:11–21 implies, since it "is based on a different motivation and is subject to a different procedure" (ibid., 219). One attempt to untangle these data is M. Modéus's recent study of the *šělāmîm* sacrifice, in which he proposes that *tôdâ* (and *neder* and *nědābâ*) should be understood as motivations for sacrifice rather than themselves sacrifices (*Sacrifice and Symbol*, 110).

39. For the identification of Ps 107:1–32 and Ps 116 as individual thanksgiving songs, see C. Westermann, *Praise and Lament in the Psalms* (trans. K. Crim and R. Soulen; Atlanta: John Knox, 1981), 102–12. This association is further demonstrated further by the "declarative praise" that concludes Ps 54, in which the psalmist's promise to sacrifice to YHWH (*ʾezběḥâ-lāk*) is paralleled with his promise to thank his name (*ʾôdeh šimkā*).

40. See T. Cartledge, *Vows in the Hebrew Bible and the Ancient Near East* (JSOT-Sup 147; Sheffield: JSOT Press, 1992), 26; and J. Berlinerblau, *The Vow and the "Popular Religious Groups" of Ancient Israel: A Philological and Sociological Inquiry* (JSOT-Sup 210; Sheffield: Sheffield Academic Press, 1996).

41. See Rendtorff, *Studien zur Geschichte*, 135–39.

42. M. Barré notes that "although paying one's vows is a private act, the proclamation of Yahweh's saving works that forms the context of such an act easily broadens into a communal chorus of praise" ("Psalm 116: Its Structure and Its Enigmas," *JBL* 109 [1990]: 74). On the dialectic between public and private worship in Pss 107 and 116, see also L. Allen, *Psalms 101–50* (rev. ed.; WBC 21; Nashville: Thomas Nelson,

On the one hand, the *zebaḥ tôdâ* was made by individuals in gratitude for deliverance from a particular circumstance, but on the other hand, it was sometimes celebrated in the presence of other worshipers. This tension between the private and public character of the thanks offering is instructive for Amos 4:4–5 because, as the plural imperatives indicate, the verses are addressed to a group. Like these psalms, then, Amos 4:5aα seems to be an instruction to a group for each person to make his or her individual thanks offering.

This analysis of *tôdâ* finds support in the adjacent verb *qaṭṭēr* and the prepositional phrase *mēḥāmēṣ*.[43] M. Haran has shown that the verb **qṭr* in the *piel* does not refer to incense but to some sort of burnt offering,[44] and D. Edelman has argued more specifically that **qṭr* in the *piel* means "to burn a food offering," sometimes as a complete rite and other times as part of a ritual sequence.[45] Although Edelman later claims that the *tôdâ* was performed only by priests, she herself admits that **qṭr* occurs with a nonpriestly subject at least thirty-six times.[46] Likewise, G. Mayer writes

---

2002), 154; and H.-J. Kraus, *Psalmen* [2nd rev. ed.; BKAT 15; Neukirchen-Vluyn: Neukirchener, 1961], 2:737).

43. I interpret the preposition *min-* attached to *ḥāmēṣ* as partitive (see Wolff, *Joel and Amos*, 220). Although the preposition seems to have privative meaning as well (cf. *IBHS* 11.2.11e), in fact both the partitive and privative derive from the basic meaning of separation (GKC §119w). It is worth noting that the only verse that explicitly links the *tôdâ* offering with *ḥāmēṣ* is Lev 7:13, which most interpreters read in light of Lev 2:11–12. These latter verses instruct that no leavened bread may be burned (*kol-śĕ'ōr ... lō'-taqṭîrû*) but only offered (*taqrîbû*). The mention of *ḥāmēṣ* in Lev 7:13 seems consistent with this directive and suggests that leaven was not part of burnt offerings (cf. Exod 23:18; 34:25), and it is this evidence that leads some to interpret the preposition *min-* before *ḥāmēṣ* in Amos 4:5 as privative. But it is just as likely that Amos is describing a cultic practice that was prevalent in the northern sanctuaries but that did not conform to the Priestly Code.

44. Outside of the Priestly writings, the root **qṭr* occurs most commonly in the *piel*, and in this stem it never refers to an incense offering. Within the Priestly writings, **qṭr* occurs only in the *hiphil* to refer to sacrificial portions of animals, meal offerings, and incense (see M. Haran, "The Uses of Incense in the Ancient Israelite Ritual," *VT* 10 [1960]: 116; see also R. Clements, "קטר, *qṭr*," *TDOT* 13:11).

45. Edelman, "The Meaning of *qiṭṭēr*," *VT* 35 (1985): 395–98.

46. She explains these examples away by suggesting that "references to leaders and common citizens performing a cultic act which was executed on the altar probably should not be taken literally. The actual burning would have been done on their behalf by priests, with the offering being 'credited' to the person who brought it" ("Meaning of *qiṭṭēr*," 396 n. 3).

of the *tôdâ* that "the individuals present their offerings but the priests are responsible for the technical details of the sacrifice."[47] However, even in the Priestly account of the *tôdâ* the accent is on the responsibility of the offerer to whom Lev 7 is addressed,[48] and this cultic immediacy is what we find in Amos 4:5 as well. Here the people are not instructed to give their offering to a priest who will offer it for them but are themselves the implied subject of the verb *qaṭṭēr*; they themselves are commanded to send up their *tôdâ* in smoke. According to this analysis, Amos 4:5 depicts the *tôdâ* as an offering performed by the individual worshipers at cult centers—Bethel and Gilgal—where they would have been surrounded by other worshipers and probably also religious specialists, whose intermediary role, at least in Amos 4:5, seems not to have been essential.

The last cultic element in Amos 4:4–5 to be addressed here is the *nĕdābâ*, or "freewill offering," which was not limited to a single cultic action but could be fulfilled by a variety of offerings. In the Priestly literature alone, we find it connected with the *'ōlâ* (Lev 22:18; Num 15:3; 29:39; Ezek 46:12), the *zebaḥ* (Lev 7:16; Num 15:3), the *zebaḥ šĕlāmîm* (Lev 22:21, 23), the *minḥâ*, and the *nesek* (Num 29:39). Elsewhere the term *nĕdābâ* denotes a gift given for the construction of a sanctuary, with no ritual accompanying the donation (Exod 35:29; 36:3). From this diversity, M. Modéus has argued that the *nĕdābâ* is best interpreted not as an offering per se but as the motivation for an offering, gift, or sacrifice. The defining characteristic of the *nĕdābâ* is not its sacrificial material or procedure but rather the voluntariness with which it is offered.[49]

Moreover, the private character of the *nĕdābâ* can first be observed from its close connection to the thanks offering and to the vow, with which it is sometimes a fixed pair (Lev 7:16; 22:18, 21; Num 15:3; 29:39; Deut 12:6, 17). Their association stems from the similar circumstances that motivate their offering: all three are demonstrations of gratitude for YHWH's divine help. Perhaps the closest parallel to *nĕdābâ* in Amos 4:5 is found in Ps 54, an individual lament that concludes with the psalmist

---

47. Mayer, "ידה *ydh*," *TDOT* 5:439.

48. Milgrom, *Leviticus 1–16*, 418–19. But he does not think priests were completely absent, supposing that the process "could be expeditiously supervised by the priests ... a brief inspection of the premises would quickly reveal potential violations."

49. Modéus, *Sacrifice and Symbol*, 91–93. This description is already implied by the root **ndb*, which means "to prove oneself freely willing" (see J. Conrad, "נדב *ndb*," *TDOT* 9:220).

thankfully promising to make a freewill sacrifice to YHWH (*bindābâ 'ezbĕḥâ-lāk* [v. 8]). His gratitude lies in his confidence that YHWH will deliver him from his particular crisis, but like the *nĕdābâ* in Amos 4:5, the private offering occurs in the assembly of other worshipers. In Ps 54 the *hinnēh* at the beginning of verse 6 is clearly addressed to his audience, and the reference in verse 9 to YHWH in the third person clearly implies that the psalmist is again addressing his audience; in both verses he proclaims to them his trust in YHWH. Likewise, the plural imperatives that govern *nĕdābâ* in Amos 4:5—*qir'û* and *hašmî'û*—presume a public setting for the freewill offering.[50] According to these examples, the *nĕdābâ*, like the *tôdâ*, may be understood as a private offering made by individuals according to particular circumstances, and the variety of offerings that could constitute a *nĕdābâ* is itself evidence that the occasion and content of the freewill offering involved personal preference. However, the *nĕdābâ*, again like the *tôdâ*, reveals a tension between its private occasion and its public setting. Both offerings commonly consist of a private, unmediated rite that takes place within the context of a public gathering, and the assessment holds true for the *tôdâ* and *nĕdābâ* mentioned in Amos 4:5.

Finally, before the conclusion of this section, there is one more passage in the book of Amos that deserves mention as an example of private worship. In 8:14 the prophet indicts

> Those who swear by the Guilt[51] of Samaria,
> And say, "(By) the life[52] of your god, O Dan ..."
> And, "(By) the life of the Way[53] of Beer-sheba ..."

---

50. The root *qr'* commonly denotes a proclamation to a crowd and sometimes refers to a religious convocation (Exod 32:5; Lev 23:2, 4, 21, 37); see F. Hossfeld and E.-M. Kindl, "קרא *qārā'*," *TDOT* 13:119–20. Likewise *šm'* in the *hiphil* regularly means to announce publicly a past or present action (e.g., Isa 48:20; 52:7; Jer 4:15; 31:7; 46:14; 50:2; Amos 3:9).

51. I agree with commentators who see the word not as an actual invocation but as a dysphemism, by which the prophet substitutes the name of the oath's divine guarantor with "guilt" (see Paul, *Amos*, 269 n. 15).

52. For this translation of Heb. *ḥê*, see B. Conklin, *Oath Formulas in Biblical Hebrew* (LSAWS 5; Winona Lake, Ind.: Eisenbrauns, 2011), 24–27.

53. MT's *derek* need not be emended, if the way or route to a shrine is understood as a hypostatic representation of the deity worshiped there, in the same way that the temple "Bethel" was personified and worshiped as a manifestation of YHWH (see

They will fall and not rise again.[54]

As the formulaic use of *šbʿ in the *niphal* with the preposition *bĕ*- and also the use of *hê* indicate, this verse depicts worshipers in the process of taking oaths.[55] Such oaths "consist of a *promise* that is strengthened by the addition of a *curse*, usually in conjunction with an appeal to the deity or king who could carry out the curse."[56] Unlike a vow, which requests divine action and is concluded by a human action, the oath promises a certain kind of human action that will forestall divine action. Whereas divine intervention after a vow is a blessing, divine action after an oath can only mean that a curse is being executed. In the Hebrew Bible, an oath was commonly used to guarantee the stipulations of a treaty or covenant (e.g., Gen 21:31–32; 26:28–31; 2 Kgs 11:4); to resolve legal disputes (e.g., Num 5:19–22); and to make a solemn promise (e.g., Gen 24:9; 47:29–31; Josh 2:12–14). One feature of these examples is the relative absence

---

P. K. McCarter, "Aspects of the Religion of the Israelite Monarchy," in *Ancient Israelite Religion: Essays in Honor of Frank Moore Cross* [Philadelphia: Fortress, 1987], 147; J. Burnett, *A Reassessment of Biblical Elohim* [SBLDS 183; Atlanta: Society of Biblical Literature, 2001], 110). Like *ʾašmat, derek* in Amos 8:14 can be interpreted as an aspect of a deity that has been personified and is regarded as a semi-deity.

54. Many regard this colon as a later addition, but the combination of falling and not rising is attested with the same verbs (*npl and *qwm) in Amos 5:2. They occur together again in Amos 9:11, where they are used positively.

55. I. Kottsieper, "שבע *šābaʿ*," *TDOT* 14:312–16. Such oaths are not the same as "confessions" (*pace* J. Jeremias, *The Book of Amos: A Commentary* [OTL; Louisville: Westminster John Knox, 1995], 152), nor "slogans" (*pace* M. Goulder, *The Psalms of the Sons of Korah* [JSOTSup 20; Sheffield: JSOT Press, 1982], 15, 29; and M. Bartusch, *Understanding Dan: An Exegetical Study of a Biblical City, Tribe and Ancestor* [JSOTSup 379; Sheffield: Sheffield Academic Press, 2003], 234, 241). Furthermore, it is significant that none of the toponyms are mentioned with a preposition to designate location; rather two occur in construct with the guarantor of the oath, and the third—Dan—occurs as a vocative. The first two seem to reflect the common practice of pairing a divine name with a place where that deity was worshiped (see McCarter, "Aspects of the Religion," 140–41). Such toponyms do not indicate where a blessing, vow, or oath was made but which manifestation of the deity was being invoked, and it is possible that the "guilt of Samaria" and the "way of Beer-sheba" in Amos 8:14 reflect a similar usage. By contrast, Dan is not used in a divine name-place name construct phrase but occurs in the vocative. This vocative form, together with the second-person suffix on *ʾĕlōheykā*, strongly suggests in this example that the prophet is depicting an oath sworn by the god of Dan in the city of Dan.

56. Cartledge, *Vows in the Hebrew Bible*, 15 (italics original).

of religious specialists; in all but one (Num 5:11–31), the oath is sworn between two individuals who choose which deities will act as its guarantor. For example, when Jacob and Laban make a covenant, each swears by his ancestral deity, or as Laban declares: "Let the God of Abraham and the God of Nahor judge between us." Accordingly, "Jacob swore by the Fear [*bĕpaḥad*] of his Father Isaac" (Gen 31:53).[57] With the majority of oaths found in the Hebrew Bible following a similar process, it seems probable that the formulae in Amos 8:14 should likewise be regarded as private rites performed by individuals on their own behalf without the religious specialists.

In looking at the spatial practice in the book of Amos, especially as it relates to sacred space, I have tried to show that the book's references to cult and cultic space collectively construct a worship space that is remarkably diverse, ranging from public festivals to various private celebrations. Perhaps this diversity is best captured in a verse not yet discussed, namely, Amos 3:14, in which YHWH declares that he will "punish the altars of Bethel, and the horns of the altar will be cut off and will fall to the ground." In light of the preceding discussion, it is interesting to note that here YHWH first condemns plural altars of Bethel (*mizbĕḥôt bêt-'el*), then focuses on the altar (*hammizbēaḥ*). Although some commentators have been troubled by the plural *mizbĕḥôt*, my analysis of cultic space in the book of Amos confirms S. Paul's point that there is "no convincing reason to deny the existence of multiple altars in Bethel, even if it had only one central sanctuary."[58] Indeed, it would be surprising if there were not mul-

---

57. Jacob's invocation of the "fear" of his father as guarantor of the covenant offers an instructive analogy for interpreting the "guilt" of Samaria and the "*derek*" of Beersheba. All three demonstrate the tendency to swear by divine representations of a deity rather than the deity itself, a preference that is apparent also in Amos 8:7, where YHWH himself derisively swears "by the pride of Jacob" (*nišbaʿ yhwh bigʾôn yaʿăqōb*). Jacob's pride has reached such heights that YHWH ironically acknowledges its awesomeness by invoking it in an oath. There are similar examples in Mesopotamian texts in which people commonly swear before the symbol of a deity rather than the deity's statue (see R. Harris, "The Journey of the Divine Weapon," in *Studies in Honor of Benno Landsberger on His Seventy-Fifth Birthday, April 21, 1963* (ed. Hans G. Güterbock and Thorkild Jacobsen; AS 16 [Chicago: University of Chicago Press, 1965], 217–24); J. Spaey, "Emblems in Rituals in the Old Babylonian Period," in *Ritual and Sacrifice in the Ancient Near East* [ed. J. Quaegebeur; OLA 55; Leuven: Peeters, 1993], 411–20).

58. Paul, *Amos*, 124.

tiple altars at Bethel. Moreover, I have tried to demonstrate that the book's cultic spaces were not just the target of prophetic invective, but they also encode important assumptions about religious authority, especially as it relates to access to sacred space and exclusion from it.

5.3. Conceptual Space in the Book of Amos

In this section I will discuss two aspects of the conceptual space that seems to have shaped the description of sacred space that we find in the book of Amos, namely, the interface of public and private worship and the centralization of worship space. While they certainly do not amount to an exhaustive treatment of conceptual space in Amos, these two aspects represent important organizing principles that reflect the values and concerns that have informed the book's depiction of cultic space. Moreover, these principles provide important links between the conceptual space detected in the book of Amos and the conceptual space that was identified in Stratum II at Tel Dan, and together they offer insight into the religious ideologies that were prevalent in the northern kingdom during the eighth century B.C.E.

5.3.1. Interface of Public and Private Worship

One aspect of sacred space that seems to be presumed in the book of Amos is the interface of public and private worship. Lefebvre addresses this overlap of public and private by proposing three levels of spatial organization—public, private, and mixed (transitional)—which are "bound together by relationships of reciprocal implication."[59] He shows that within each of these three levels of space there are micro-examples of the same three levels, so that a public space like a temple also contains private spaces (cellas, storerooms, chapels, etc.) and mixed spaces (thresholds, doorways, etc.).

A similar reciprocity can be observed in the spatial practice of the book of Amos. When cultic terms mentioned in the book are compared to their occurrences elsewhere in the Hebrew Bible, a portrait of diverse worship emerges. Far from homogenizing Israel's religious life,

---

59. Lefebvre, *The Production of Space* (trans. D. Nicholson-Smith; Cambridge: Blackwell, 1991), 153–55.

the prophet seems to target specific types of cultic practice, just as he commonly names particular cult centers, and one way to categorize these practices is according to their public or private character. For example, I have shown that Amos 5:21–27 is best interpreted not as a random sampling of sacrifices and offerings but as a depiction of a national festival. This cultic scenario is introduced by *ḥaggîm* in verse 21, and each element in the rest of the passage can be interpreted as cultic activities suited for a religious assembly. In these verses the prophet is targeting a particular kind of cultic occasion that involved a large public gathering. By contrast, the cultic events in Amos 4:4–5 and 8:13–14 seem to depict primarily private worship. Although many commentators take *bō'û* in 4:4 as a reference to a pilgrimage festival to Bethel, more likely it simply means to enter its sanctuary; moreover, each of the cultic elements that follows this command is a rite that seems to be individually motivated and celebrated and therefore may be regarded as private worship. Likewise, the oath formulae of Amos 8:13–14 were probably sworn by individuals according to a particular situation.

However, these categories of public and private worship are most instructive when cultic references do not fit neatly into one or the other. Several references produce a cultic space that includes characteristics of both public and private worship. This overlap is apparent, for example, in 4:4–5, which mentions several rites that are best classified as private cultic practices, but here they are explicitly identified with two cult centers—Bethel and Gilgal. Although *zĕbāḥîm*, tithes, *tôdôt*, and *nĕdābôt* represent occasions of private offerings, the book of Amos does not locate them in domestic settings or at local shrines, though these venues would have also been suitable; rather, they took place in the major sanctuaries of the northern kingdom. Likewise, the Dan oath (*ḥê 'ĕlōheykā dān*) cited in 8:14, which is probably the only one of the oaths that can be linked with the toponym it names,[60] demonstrates again the prevalence of private cult performed at a major religious center, which by coincidence happens to be the very site that has provided our archaeological portrait of Israelite religion in the eighth century B.C.E.

Another way the book of Amos sheds light on the spatial overlap of public and private worship is its depiction of the *tôdâ* and *nĕdābôt* in 4:5 as individual offerings that would have been made in the presence of the

---

60. See p. 163 n. 55 above.

larger religious community. An examination of these offerings in other biblical texts showed that they likely represent private worship, and yet they are the object of plural imperatives, one of which is the verb "to proclaim." This mixture of plural verbs with individual offerings as objects seems to demonstrate again the dialectic between private and public that would have existed at major cult sites. As we observed in the Psalter, the *tôdâ* and *nĕdābâ* are usually made by individuals before an assembly that serves as the witness of the offering. Such offerings should still be regarded as private worship, but their public setting suggests the presence of cultic assembly.

The interface of public and private worship in the book of Amos resonates deeply with the portrait of worship that emerged from Stratum II of Area T, which seems to display similarly overlapping cultic spheres. On the one hand were the monumental raised platform in T-North and the main altar in T-Center, which were designed to accommodate large religious assemblies. Although the rites associated with the raised platform remain obscure, its size alone would have made it a focal point for all visitors to Area T, and its staircase, rebuilt in the eighth century B.C.E., suggests that the superstructure was visited regularly. The other focal point of Area T was the altar in T-Center, which was expanded in this period. The large size of the altar can be inferred from its stone substructure, which suggests that it was used for large animal sacrifices. Both structures were associated with "official" religion based on the exceptional quality of their construction and their relative inaccessibility.

However, Area T also provided a venue for smaller-scale worship. In particular, I identified the Altar Room in T-West as an example of a cultic space where worshipers could make offerings on private occasions. The room itself could have housed considerably fewer participants than the T-Center courtyard, and this difference in scale and purpose is confirmed by the smaller size of the room's sacrificial altar (1 m^2) and its related faunal remains. Thus Area T in Stratum II, like the book of Amos, seems to have provided particular venues for particular kinds of offerings, but also like the book of Amos, Area T shows that these two types of worship were not isolated from each other. Indeed, they are literally interfaced at Area T in that T-West is directly adjacent to T-Center. Even though Dan was a national sanctuary, its religious purpose was not restricted to national festivals; worshipers at the site could make a private offering just as readily as they could participate in a public festival.

5.3.2. CENTRALIZATION

Another conceptual space shared by the book of Amos and Stratum II at
Area T is the political, religious, and spatial centralization that seems to
have been an organizing principle at state sanctuaries like Bethel and Dan.
In Amos this centralization is most apparent in the confrontation between
Amos and the priest Amaziah, which I discussed above. While this passage continues to be mined for insights into Amos's background and prophetic status, I have emphasized how the contentious exchange between
priest and prophet reflects a "conflict of perspectives" (to use P. Miller's
phrase) between professional cult officiants and peripheral intermediaries.[61]
The former is represented by Amaziah, who seems to have the authority
to regulate access to the royal sanctuary; this claim to authority is resisted
by Amos, who denies having any status that might be subject to the king's
prerogative. Although certain subtleties of this episode remain elusive, it
shows that by the eighth century B.C.E. access to the sacred precinct had
become closely regulated, and this shift may be attributed to the centralization achieved by Kings Joash (ca. 802–787 B.C.E.) and Jeroboam II (787–748
B.C.E.), whose reigns marked a period of unprecedented prosperity in the
northern kingdom.[62] As the western campaigns of the Assyrian king Adad-
nirari III (805–802 and 796) subdued Damascus and released Israel from
Aramean hegemony,[63] Joash was able to consolidate power and recover
lost territories (2 Kgs 13:25), as did his successor Jeroboam II (see 2 Kgs

61. P. Miller, "The Prophetic Critique of Kings," in *Israelite Religion and Biblical
Theology: Collected Essays* (JSOTSup 267; Sheffield: Sheffield Academic Press, 2000),
530. On Amos's status as a "peripheral prophet," see R. Wilson, *Prophecy and Society
in Ancient Israel* (Philadelphia: Fortress, 1980), 270.

62. Evidence of this prosperity and centralization is apparent in the Samaria
Ostraca, which date to the eighth century B.C.E. and most likely were written during
the reign of Jeroboam II (see I. Kaufman, "The Samaria Ostraca: An Early Witness to
Hebrew Writing," *BA* 45 [1982]: 229–39). Whether one reads the ostraca as records
of goods received *from* royal estates, or goods paid as taxes *to* the palace, they reveal
a well-structured economic system for the exchange of valuable commodities, like oil
and wine.

63. See above, p. 92; also W. Pitard, *Ancient Damascus: A Historical Study of the
Syrian City-State from the Earliest Times until Its Fall to the Assyrians in 732 B.C.E.*
(Winona Lake, Ind.: Eisenbrauns, 1987), 160–79.

14:25, 28).[64] This consolidation translated into a (re)new(ed) centralization of power in the northern kingdom, which likely had a reflex in the cultic life of the northern kingdom.[65] The royal authority promulgated by Amaziah in Amos 7:10–17 may be a textual witness of this process.

Significantly, a similar centralization seems to have occurred at Tel Dan's Area T in the eighth century B.C.E. Whereas in previous periods, the central altar platform was characterized by openness and accessibility on all its sides, in Stratum II there are clear efforts to regulate access to the altar. This shift is most apparent in the addition of a temenos wall around the altar. First, the wall reduced in size the paved area immediately around the altar, which had previously provided worship space for cultic participants, and it also effectively limited access to the sacrificial altar. Only two sides of the wall included passages through the temenos, and the boundary is all the more restrictive if we imagine a mud-brick superstructure atop the surviving stone foundation. This new temenos wall at Dan and Amaziah's efforts to expel Amos from Bethel likely belong to the same category of cultic transformation. Both seem to be consequences of a political centralization, which is indicated by both archaeological and textual sources and which came to be expressed in the cultic centers of the northern kingdom.

---

64. See G. Ahlström, *The History of Ancient Palestine from the Palaeolithic Period to Alexander's Conquest* (Sheffield: Sheffield Academic Press, 1993), 613–22.

65. See Miller, "Prophetic Critique of Kings," 526–34.

6
Summary of Conclusions

Regarding the interface of archaeological and textual data, Avraham Biran, the excavator of Tel Dan for over thirty years, offered this recommendation: "Let us study the archaeological evidence. If we can explain what we find through the biblical record, so much the better, but if we cannot, each discipline will have to stand on its own merits."[1] Indeed, both disciplines are indispensable for understanding the religion of ancient Israel, but each must be engaged independently before possible intersections can be explored. This approach has been a guiding principle of the preceding study, which began with an examination of two Iron Age strata from Tel Dan's sacred precinct (Area T) and continued with an analysis of certain biblical texts (1 Kgs 18:20–40; Amos 3:14; 4:4–5; 5:21–27; 7:10–17; 8:14; 9:1). These texts were selected because of their northern orientation and were studied in light of the religious traditions that seem to have been prevalent at Tel Dan. In this way, the present work has sought to put into dialogue two related disciplines—Syro-Palestinian archaeology and biblical studies—with the conviction that the reconstruction of ancient Israel's religious history requires both. According to Biran's recommendation, I have let the evidence from each discipline stand on its own merits but have also attempted to find instances where the archaeological and textual evidence are mutually informative.

In chapter 1, I set forth the methodological framework within which this study would proceed, focusing on the concept of "sacred space" and the spatial theory of Henri Lefebvre. The prevalence of the former in the

---

1. A. Biran, "To the God Who Is in Dan," in *Temples and High Places in Biblical Times: Proceedings of the Colloquium in Honor of the Centennial of Hebrew Union College–Jewish Institute of Religion, Jerusalem, 14–16 March 1977* (ed. A. Biran; Jerusalem: Nelson Glueck School of Biblical Archaeology of Hebrew Union College–Jewish Institute of Religion, 1981), 151.

study of ancient religion has made it necessary to define precisely what "sacred space" designates. While not totally rejecting Eliade's theory of the "autonomy of hierophanies," by which a space is endowed with sacred presence, I emphasized that the sacrality of a space cannot be separated from the social processes, especially ritual activity, that take place in that space. The social dimension of sacred space is crucial for exploring the multiple constituencies that would have worshiped at the Tel Dan temple—how they are represented in the material remains of Area T and how their various interests and priorities have shaped the area's cultic space. One way of exploring the formation of Tel Dan's cultic space is through Lefebvre's conceptual triad of spatial practice, conceptual space, and symbolic space. In particular, spatial practice, which refers to the material realities of space as it is perceived and experienced, and conceptual space, which refers to a mental blueprint of the values that have informed the organization of space, provided a framework for discussing the archaeological data from Area T as well as the biblical representations of sacred space.

Chapter 2 focused on the archaeological remains from Stratum III in Area T, which dates to the ninth century B.C.E. and most likely corresponds to the Omride dynasty. After a section-by-section description of this stratum's spatial practice, I identified three organizing principles that may be regarded as part of the area's conceptual space. First, the prominence of the ashlar podium in T-North, which Biran called the "bamah," and its location at the apex of the graded sacred precinct suggest that verticality is a defining characteristic of Area T's architecture. While we can only speculate about the podium's function, its elevation, monumentality, and fine construction indicate its importance and project the political and religious authority of the Omrides, who likely sponsored its construction. Second, I noted the prevalence of symmetry and duality in Area T's architecture, which are exemplified in the pair of columns that stood atop the T-Center platform, and I suggested that such symmetry may reinforce certain hierarchical oppositions that were part of the cultic life of Area T. The columns may have marked a transitional space that divided Area T, or they may have represented resident deities who were the focus of cultic activity. Finally, I argued that the sacred precinct in Stratum III was characterized by an openness that is unusual in the religious architecture of the ancient Near East. Many temples, including the biblical descriptions of the tabernacle and the temple, reflect in their architecture a sacral hierarchy that determines how worshipers could move through the sacred precinct, but such gradations are noticeably absent in the architecture of Stratum III.

Although we cannot know what sort of social barriers affected movement around the area, the openness of its architecture is nonetheless significant and may be related to the decentralized power structure of the northern kingdom, where political authority was not concentrated in a single city and religious authority was likewise divided between the two state sanctuaries of Dan and Bethel.

The accessibility of Stratum III is all the more noteworthy in light of the changes that took place in the subsequent Stratum II, which dates to the eighth century B.C.E. and was the focus of chapter 3. After examining the spatial practice of this stratum, I drew some conclusions about its conceptual space. First, I argued for centralization as an organizing principle of Area T in Stratum II. This concept is especially apparent in the altar complex in T-Center, which assumed greater prominence in Stratum II and surpassed the T-North podium as the primary focus of the area. Contemporaneous with the expansion of the altar was the construction of a temenos wall that enclosed it, effectively restricting access to it. The same kind of restriction can be observed, to a lesser degree, in the T-North podium, which in Stratum III could be mounted by as many as three staircases but in Stratum II featured only the staircase against its southern wall. The shift from the openness of Stratum III to the limited accessibility of Stratum II may be associated with the political consolidation achieved by Joash (802–787 B.C.E.) and Jeroboam II (787–748 B.C.E.). Whereas the openness of Stratum III was correlated with the tradition of decentralized political and religious power in the northern kingdom, the shift in Stratum II to a more hierarchical arrangement may mirror the centralization achieved by the northern kings of the eighth century B.C.E.

Second, I showed that the sacred precinct accommodated both "official" and family religion. The former is characterized at Tel Dan by the monumentality and prestige of the podium in T-North and the altar in T-Center, which display Area T's most expensive building materials and thus project the elite status of those who sponsored their construction and those who officiated cult there. Also T-Center's temenos wall restricted the availability of the main altar and suggests an effort by religious specialists to limit access to the sacrifices offered there. By contrast, the rooms of T-West show modest construction and no signs of limited access, even though the sacrificial altar of the Altar Room and its related faunal assemblage attest that T-West was also the site of ritual activity. The differences in size, building materials, and accessibility of its rooms suggest that the worship that took place there was on a smaller scale than at T-Center, and

I argued that T-West should be associated with family religion. We know from the Hebrew Bible that it was not uncommon for individuals to preside over a sacrifice on behalf of their kin group, and sometimes these sacrifices were offered at regional cult centers, such as Shiloh (see 1 Sam 1–2). The size and scale of the Altar Room are consistent with these biblical descriptions, and while it is unlikely that religious specialists were altogether absent from T-West, its modesty and accessibility may indicate that they were less directly involved in the offerings made there.

In chapter 4 I turned my attention to the analysis of biblical texts that could contribute to our understanding of the sacred precinct at Tel Dan. The focus of this chapter was the account of Elijah's sacrifice on Mount Carmel (1 Kgs 18:20–40), which was chosen because of its northern orientation and because it was most likely composed in the ninth century B.C.E. Thus, of the textual evidence available in the Hebrew Bible, the Carmel narrative most closely corresponds—geographically and temporally—to Stratum III at Tel Dan. Discussing first the spatial practice of the narrative, I focused on its description of the altars, the sacrifices, and the religious personnel before proposing three organizing principles of the conceptual space depicted in 1 Kgs 18, which may also shed light on our understanding of Area T. First, I argued that border maintenance is a defining characteristic of the sacred space constructed in the Carmel narrative. Mount Carmel's location in a cultural transition zone accounts for the narrative's careful delineation of Elijah and the prophets of Baal with parallel altars and dueling sacrifices. The reactionary intensity behind this delineation in 1 Kgs 18 may provide some measure of the cultural overlap that was prevalent at border sites, like Mount Carmel—and also like Tel Dan, whose location at Israel's border with Aram made it similarly susceptible to religious fluctuations, as it alternated between Israelite and Aramean hegemony. Second, I argued that the cultic space depicted in 1 Kgs 18 is notable for its accessibility, which is most apparent in the active participation of gathered assembly. Elijah's command for them to "come closer" (gĕšû ... wayyiggĕšû) differs from the Priestly ritual texts, in which only cultic personnel are allowed such access, but it is consistent with the openness that characterized the Stratum III sacred precinct at Tel Dan. Finally, I showed that the description of cultic space and ritual in the Carmel narrative draws attention to the uniqueness of both. For example, Elijah's sacrifice deviates from the procedure found elsewhere in the ritual texts of the Hebrew Bible, and his assumption of cultic duties is also exceptional. Likewise, the conflagration that consumes Elijah's sacrifice demolishes the entire altar, thus precluding any future use. This aspect of the sacred space depicted atop Mount Carmel resonates with Area T at Tel Dan in that several features of its architecture lack strong parallels. This study has argued that Tel Dan is best interpreted within a northern cultic milieu, but even within this northern tradition, Tel Dan represents some distinctive features.

In chapter 5 I examined selected passages from the book of Amos. Because the prophet Amos was active in the northern kingdom during the eighth century B.C.E., parts of the book correspond to Stratum II at Tel Dan. My discussion of spatial practice in the book of Amos focused first on passages in which cultic space is explicitly depicted (e.g., 3:14; 7:10–17; 9:1). Next I discussed those passages that address the cultic life at northern cultic sites, such as Bethel, Gilgal, and Dan, and argued that in its critique of northern cultic practices the book of Amos is far more precise than is often recognized. The prophet's censure is not a wholesale indictment of cult but is targeted at specific types of practices, which often assume a particular kind of cultic space. For example, some prophetic critiques, like Amos 5:21–27, are targeted at large religious festivals, such as the ḥaggîm, while others, like Amos 4:4–5 and 8:14, are directed at rites that would have been performed by smaller groups of worshipers or by individuals.

This analysis of spatial practice in the book of Amos led to the identification of two organizing principles, which make up the conceptual space depicted in the book. First, I argued that the book assumes the interface of public and private worship in a way that is consistent with the overlapping of "official" and family religion at Tel Dan. Significantly, the book's examples of private worship take place at major cult centers, like Bethel, Gilgal, and Dan, sanctuaries that are most often associated with major religious festivals but that also provided space for smaller cultic occasions. Both the archaeological evidence from Tel Dan and the textual evidence from the book of Amos indicate that such venues accommodated a range of cultic activity. Second, the centralization that took place in Stratum II of Area T is also apparent in the book of Amos, especially 7:10–17. This description of the confrontation between the prophet Amos and Amaziah the priest of Bethel indicates the degree to which royal interests had begun to exert influence in the religious sphere; indeed, Bethel is described as "the king's sanctuary and a royal temple" (Amos 7:13). Amaziah's attitude toward Amos suggests that by the eighth century B.C.E. cult centers like Bethel were reflecting the bureaucratic distinctions that resulted from the political consolidation and economic prosperity of that century. The priest's attempt to expel Amos from the sacred precinct indicates that sacred space had become a means of expressing status distinctions. In this way, the passage reiterates my interpretation of Area T, which argued that Stratum II reveals new efforts to restrict access to the certain areas of the sacred precinct. I suggested that these changes were related to the centralization achieved by Joash and Jeroboam, and it is significant that Amos 7:10–17 likewise connects the king's religious authority with access to cultic space.

In this way I have attempted to combine a detailed portrait of the Iron II levels of Area T at Tel Dan with analysis of biblical texts that correspond most closely to Tel Dan's northern location and to the time period represented by Strata III–II. By considering the evidence from archaeology and the Hebrew Bible first on their own respective merits and then, when possible, by putting them in dialogue, I have tried to integrate the two disciplines with the hope that their integration will make a contribution for the better.

BIBLIOGRAPHY

Abū 'Assāf, A. *Der Tempel von 'Ain Dārā.* Damaszener Forschungen 3. Mainz am Rhein: Zabern, 1990.

Ackerman, S. "Asherah, The West Semitic Goddess of Spinning and Weaving?" *JNES* 67 (2008): 1–29.

———. "Household Religion, Family Religion, and Women's Religion in Ancient Israel." Pages 127–58 in *Household and Family Religion in Antiquity.* Edited by J. Bodel and S. Olyan. Malden, Mass.: Blackwell, 2008.

———. "Who Is Sacrificing at Shiloh? The Priesthoods of Ancient Israel's Regional Sanctuaries." Pages 25–43 in *Levites and Priests in Biblical History and Tradition.* Edited by M. Leuchter and J. Hutton. SBLAIL 9. Atlanta: Society of Biblical Literature, 2011.

Aharoni, Y. "Arad: Its Inscriptions and Temple." *BA* 31 (1968): 1–32.

———. "Excavations at Tel Arad: Preliminary Report on the Second Season, 1963." *IEJ* 17 (1967): 233–49.

———. "The Horned Altar of Beer-sheba." *BA* 37 (1974): 2–6.

———. "Mount Carmel as Border." Pages 1–7 in *Archäologie und altes Testament: Festschrift für Kurt Galling zum 8.Januar 1970.* Edited by A. Kuschke and E. Kutsch. Tübingen: Mohr Siebeck, 1970.

Aḥituv, S. *Canaanite Toponyms in Ancient Egyptian Documents.* Jerusalem: Magnes, 1984.

Ahlström, G. *The History of Ancient Palestine from the Palaeolithic Period to Alexander's Conquest.* Sheffield: Sheffield Academic Press, 1993.

Akurgal, H. *The Art of the Hittites.* New York: Abrams, 1962.

Albertz, R. *Elia: Ein feuriger Kämpfer für Gott.* Biblische Gestalten 13. Leipzig: Evangelische Verlagsanstalt, 2006.

———. "Family Religion in Ancient Israel and its Surroundings." Pages 89–112 in *Household and Family Religion in Antiquity.* Edited by J. Bodel and S. Olyan. Malden, Mass.: Blackwell, 2008.

———. *A History of Israelite Religion in the Old Testament Period.* Translated by J. Bowden. 2 vols. Louisville: Westminster John Knox, 1994.

———. *Persönliche Frömmigkeit und offizielle Religion.* Calwer Theologische Monographien 9. Stuttgart: Calwer, 1978.

Albertz, R., and R. Schmitt. *Family and Household Religion in Ancient Israel and the Levant.* Winona Lake, Ind.: Eisenbrauns, 2012.

Albright, W. F. "The Jordan Valley in the Bronze Age." AASOR 6 (1924–25): 13–74.

———. "The Mouth of the Rivers." *AJSL* 35 (1919): 161–95.

Allen, L. *Psalms 101–50.* Rev. ed. WBC 21. Nashville: Thomas Nelson, 2002.

Alt, A. "Das Gottesurteil auf dem Karmel." Pages 135–49 in vol. 2 of *Kleine Schriften zur Geschichte des Volkes Israel.* 3 vols. Munich: Beck, 1953.

Amit, Y. "Hidden Polemic in the Conquest of Dan: Judges XVII–XVIII." *VT* 40 (1990): 4–20.

Andersen, F., and D. Freedman. *Amos: A New Translation with Introduction and Commentary.* AB 24A. New York: Doubleday, 1989.

Anderson, G. *Sacrifices and Offerings in Ancient Israel: Studies in their Social and Political Importance.* HSM 41. Atlanta: Scholars Press, 1987.

Ap-Thomas, D. "Elijah on Mt. Carmel." *PEQ* 92 (1960): 146–55.

Arie, E. "Reconsidering the Iron Age II Strata at Tel Dan: Archaeological and Historical Implications." *TA* 35 (2008): 6–64.

Ash, P. "Jeroboam I and the Deuteronomistic Historian's Ideology of the Founder." *CBQ* 60 (1998): 16–24.

Ashmore, W. "Social Archaeologies of Landscape." Pages 255–71 in *A Companion to Social Archaeology.* Edited by L. Meskell and R. Preucel. Malden, Mass.: Blackwell, 2007.

Astour, M. "841 B.C.: The First Assyrian Invasion of Israel." *JAOS* 91 (1971): 383–89.

———. *Hellenosemitica: An Ethnic and Cultural Study in the West Semitic Impact of Mycenaean Greece.* Leiden: Brill, 1965.

Athas, G. *The Tel Dan Inscription: A Reappraisal and a New Interpretation.* New York: T&T Clark, 2003.

Avigad, N. "The Priest of Dor." *IEJ* 25 (1975): 101–5.

Avigad, N., and B. Sass. *Corpus of West Semitic Stamp Seals.* Jerusalem: Israel Academy of Sciences and Humanities/Israel Exploration Society, 1997.

Bailey, L. "The Golden Calf." *HUCA* 42 (1971): 97–115.

Baines, J. "Palaces and Temples of Ancient Egypt." Pages 303–17 in vol.

1 of *Civilizations of the Ancient Near East*. 4 vols. Edited by J. Sasson. Peabody, Mass.: Hendrickson, 2004.

Barkay, G. "The Iron II–III." Pages 302–73 in *The Archaeology of Ancient Israel*. Edited by A. Ben-Tor. New Haven: Yale University Press, 1992.

Barré, M. "Psalm 116: Its Structure and Its Enigmas." *JBL* 109 (1990): 61–78.

Barrick, W. Review of M. Gleis, *Die Bamah. JBL* 118 (1999): 532–34.

———. "What Do We Really Know About 'High-Places'?" *Svensk Exegetisk Årsbok* 45 (1980): 50–57.

Bartusch, M. *Understanding Dan: An Exegetical Study of a Biblical City, Tribe and Ancestor*. JSOTSup 379. Sheffield: Sheffield Academic Press, 2003.

Begrich, J. "Die priesterliche Tora." Pages 63–88 in *Werden und Wesen des Alten Testament. Vorträge gehalten auf der Internationalen Tagung alttestamentlicher Forscher zu Göttingen von 4–10. September 1935.* BZAW 66. Edited by P. Volz et al. Berlin: Töpelmann, 1936. Reprinted in *Gesammelte Studien zum Alten Testament*. Theologische Bücherei 21. Munich: Kaiser, 1964.

Bell, L. "The New Kingdom 'Divine' Temple: The Example of Luxor." Pages 127–84 in *Temples of Ancient Egypt*. Edited by B. Shafer. Ithaca, N.Y.: Cornell University Press, 1997.

Ben-Dov, R. *Dan III: Avraham Biran Excavations 1966–1999. The Late Bronze Age*. Jerusalem: Nelson Glueck School of Biblical Archaeology, Hebrew Union College-Jewish Institute of Religion, 2011.

Ben-Tor, A. "Hazor and the Chronology of Northern Israel: A Reply to Israel Finkelstein." *BASOR* 317 (2000): 9–15.

Berlinerblau, J. *The Vow and the "Popular Religious Groups" of Ancient Israel: A Philological and Sociological Inquiry*. JSOTSup 210. Sheffield: Sheffield Academic Press, 1996.

Biran, A. *Biblical Dan*. Jerusalem: Israel Exploration Society/Hebrew Union College–Jewish Institute of Religion, 1994.

———. "The Dancer from Dan, the Empty Tomb and the Altar Room." *IEJ* 36 (1986): 168–87.

———. "An Israelite Horned Altar at Dan." *BA* 37 (1974): 106–7.

———. "A Mace-Head and the Office of Amadiyo at Dan." *Qadmoniot* 21 (1988): 11–17 (Hebrew).

———. "Sacred Spaces: Of Standing Stones, High Places and Cult Objects at Tel Dan." *BAR* 24.5 (1998): 38–45, 70.

———. "Tel Dan." *IEJ* 20 (1970): 118–19.

———. "Tel Dan." *BA* 37 (1974): 25–51.

———. "Tel Dan, 1975." *IEJ* 26 (1976): 54–55.

———. "Tel Dan, 1976." *IEJ* 26 (1976): 202–6.

———. "Tel Dan, 1977." *IEJ* 27 (1977): 242–46.

———. "Tel Dan, 1979, 1980." *IEJ* 31 (1981): 103–5.

———. "Tel Dan, 1984." *IEJ* 35 (1985): 186–89.

———. "Tel Dan—1989." *ESI* 9 (1989/1990): 86–88.

———. "The Temenos at Dan." *EI* 16 (1982): 15–43 (Hebrew).

———. "To the God Who Is in Dan." Pages 142–51 in *Temples and High Places in Biblical Times: Proceedings of the Colloquium in Honor of the Centennial of Hebrew Union College–Jewish Institute of Religion, Jerusalem, 14–16 March 1977*. Edited by A. Biran. Jerusalem: Nelson Glueck School of Biblical Archaeology of Hebrew Union College–Jewish Institute of Religion, 1981.

———. "Two Discoveries at Tel Dan." *IEJ* 30 (1980): 89–98.

Biran, A., D. Ilan, and R. Greenberg. *Dan I: A Chronicle of the Excavations, the Pottery Neolithic, the Early Bronze Age and the Middle Bronze Age Tombs*. Jerusalem: Nelson Glueck School of Biblical Archaeology, Hebrew Union College–Jewish Institute of Religion, 1996.

Biran, A., and R. Ben-Dov. *Dan II: A Chronicle of the Excavations and the Late Bronze Age "Mycenaean" Tomb*. Jerusalem: Hebrew Union College–Jewish Institute of Religion, 2002.

Blake, E. "Space, Spatiality, and Archaeology." Pages 230–54 in *A Companion to Social Archaeology*. Edited by L. Meskell and R. Preucel. Malden, Mass.: Blackwell, 2007.

Blenkinsopp, J. "The Family in First Temple Israel." Pages 48–103 in *Families in Ancient Israel*. Louisville: Westminster John Knox, 1997.

Bloch-Smith, E. "'Who Is the King of Glory?': Solomon's Temple and its Symbolism." Pages 18–31 in *Scripture and Other Artifacts: Essays on the Bible and Archaeology in Honor of Philip J. King*. Edited by M. Coogan et al. Louisville: Westminster John Knox, 1994.

———. "Will the Real *Massebot* Please Stand Up: Cases of Real and Mistakenly Identified Standing Stones in Ancient Israel." Pages 64–79 in *Text, Artifact, and Image: Revealing Ancient Israelite Religion*. Edited by G. Beckman and T. Lewis. BJS 346. Providence: Brown Judaic Studies, 2006.

Bokser, B. "Approaching Sacred Space." *HTR* 78 (1985): 279–99.

Borowski, O. "Hezekiah's Reforms and the Revolt against Assyria." *BA* 58 (1995): 148–55.

———. "A Note on the 'Iron Age Cult Installation' at Tel Dan," *IEJ* 32 [1982]: 58.

Brand, P. "Veils, Votives, and Marginalia: The Use of Sacred Space at Karnak and Luxor." Pages 51–83 in *Sacred Space and Sacred Function in Ancient Thebes*. Edited by P. Dorman and B. Bryan. SAOC 61. Chicago: Oriental Institute of the University of Chicago, 2007.

Branham, J. "Sacred Space in Ancient Jewish and Early Medieval Christian Architecture." Ph.D. diss., Emory University, 1993.

Bray, J. *Sacred Dan: Religious Tradition and Cultic Practice in Judges 17–18*. LHB/OTS 449. New York: T&T Clark, 2006.

Brown, R. "Eliade on Archaic Religions: Some Old and New Criticisms." *SR* 10 (1981): 429–49.

Brück, J. "Ritual and Rationality: Some Problems of Interpretation in European Archaeology." *European Journal of Archaeology* 2 (1999): 313–44.

Burnett, J. *A Reassessment of Biblical Elohim*. SBLDS 183. Atlanta: Society of Biblical Literature, 2001.

Burney, C. *Notes on the Hebrew Text of the Books of Kings*. Oxford: Clarendon, 1903.

Campbell, A. *Of Prophets and Kings: A Late Ninth-Century Document (1 Samuel 1–2 Kings 10)*. CBQMS 17. Washington, D.C.: Catholic Biblical Association of America, 1986.

Campbell, A., and M. O'Brien. *Unfolding the Deuteronomistic History: Origins, Upgrades, Present Text*. Minneapolis: Fortress, 2000.

Carroll R., M. *Amos—The Prophet and His Oracles: Research on the Book of Amos*. Louisville: Westminster John Knox, 2002.

Cartledge, T. *Vows in the Hebrew Bible and the Ancient Near East*. JSOTSup 147. Sheffield: JSOT Press, 1992.

Catling, H. *Cypriote Bronzework in the Mycenaean World*. Oxford: Clarendon, 1964.

Chidester, D. "The Poetics and Politics of Sacred Space: Towards a Critical Phenomenology of Religion." *Analecta Husserliana* 43 (1994): 211–31.

Chidester, D., and E. Linenthal. "Introduction." Pages 1–42 in *American Sacred Space*. Edited by D. Chidester and E. Linenthal. Bloomington: Indiana University Press, 1995.

Clerc, G., et al. *Fouilles de Kition II: Objets égyptiens et égyptisants*. Nicosia: The Department of Antiquities, Cyprus, 1976.

Clifford, R. *The Cosmic Mountain in Canaan and the Old Testament*. HSM 4. Cambridge: Harvard University Press, 1972.

Clines, D. "Sacred Space, Holy Places and Suchlike." Pages 542–54 in vol. 2 of *On the Way to the Postmodern: Old Testament Essays, 1967–1998*. 2 vols. JSOTSup 293. Sheffield: Sheffield Academic Press, 1998. Reprinted from *Trinity Occasional Papers* 12.2 (1993).

Cogan, M. *Imperialism and Religion: Assyria, Judah and Israel in the Eighth and Seventh Centuries B.C.E.* SBLMS 19. Missoula, Mont.: Scholars Press, 1974.

———. *I Kings: A New Translation with Introduction and Commentary.* AB 10. New York: Doubleday, 2000.

Cogan, M., and H. Tadmor. *II Kings: A New Translation with Introduction and Commentary.* AB 11. New York: Doubleday, 1988.

Cohn, R. *The Shape of Sacred Space: Four Biblical Studies.* SR 23. Chico, Calif.: Scholars Press, 1981.

Collins, J. *Introduction to the Hebrew Bible.* Minneapolis: Fortress, 2004.

Conklin, B. *Oath Formulas in Biblical Hebrew.* LSAWS 5. Winona Lake, Ind.: Eisenbrauns, 2011.

Cooper, A. "The Meaning of Amos's Third Vision (Amos 7:7–9)." Pages 13–21 in *Tehillah le-Moshe: Biblical and Judaic Studies in Honor of Moshe Greenberg.* Edited by M. Cogan et al. Winona Lake, Ind.: Eisenbrauns, 1997.

Couey, J. "Amos vii 10–17 and Royal Attitudes toward Prophecy in the Ancient Near East." *VT* 58 (2008): 300–314.

Cross, F. *Canaanite Myth and Hebrew Epic: Essays in the History of the Religion of Israel.* Cambridge: Harvard University Press, 1973.

———. *From Epic to Canon: History and Literature in Ancient Israel.* Baltimore: Johns Hopkins University Press, 1998.

Daviau, P. "Family Religion: Evidence for the Paraphernalia of the Domestic Cult." Pages 199–229 in vol. 2 of *The World of the Aramaeans.* Edited by P. Daviau et al. 3 vols. JSOTSup 324–26. Sheffield: Sheffield Academic Press, 2001.

———. "Stone Altars Large and Small: The Iron Age Altars from Ḥirbet el-Mudēyine (Jordan)." Pages 125–49 in *Bilder als Quellen = Images as Sources: Studies on Ancient Near Eastern Artefacts and the Bible Inspired by the Work of Othmar Keel.* Edited by S. Bickel et al. OBO. Fribourg: Academic Press; Göttingen: Vandenhoeck & Ruprecht, 2007.

Dever, W. "Archaeology and the Fall of the Northern Kingdom: What Really Happened?" Pages 78–92 in *"Up from the Gates of Ekron": Essays on the Archaeology and History of the Eastern Mediterranean on Honor of Seymour Gitin.* Edited by S. Crawford. Jerusalem: W. F.

Albright Institute for Archaeological Research; Israel Exploration Society, 2007.

——. *Did God Have a Wife? Archaeology and Folk Religion in Ancient Israel.* Grand Rapids: Eerdmans, 2005.

——. "Religion and Cult in the Levant: The Archaeological Data." Pages 383–90 in *Near Eastern Archaeology: A Reader.* Edited by S. Richard. Winona Lake, Ind.: Eisenbrauns, 2003.

——. Review of R. Albertz, *A History of Israelite Religion in the Old Testament Period. BASOR* 301 (1996): 83–90.

DeVries, S. *I Kings.* 2nd ed. WBC 12. Nashville: Thomas Nelson, 2003.

Dietrich, W. *Prophetie und Geschichte: eine redaktionsgeschichtliche Untersuchung zum deteronomistischen Geschichtswerk.* FRLANT 108. Göttingen: Vandenhoeck & Ruprecht, 1972.

Donnan, H., and T. Wilson. *Borders: Frontiers of Identity, Nation and State.* Oxford: Berg, 1999.

Dorman, P., and B. Bryan, eds. *Sacred Space and Sacred Function in Ancient Thebes.* SAOC 61. Chicago: Oriental Institute of the University of Chicago, 2007.

Dunand, M., and N. Saliby. *Le Temple d'Amrith dans la Pérée d'Aradus.* Bibliothèque Archéologique et Historique 121. Paris: Paul Geuthner, 1985.

Durkheim, É. *The Elementary Forms of the Religious Life.* Translated by J. Swain. Mineola, N.Y.: Dover, 2008.

Edelman, D. "The Meaning of *qiṭṭēr.*" *VT* 35 (1985): 395–404.

Eliade, M. *The Myth of the Eternal Return or, Cosmos and History.* Translated by W. Trask. Princeton: Princeton University Press, 1971.

——. *Patterns in Comparative Religion.* Translated by R. Sheed. London: Sheed & Ward, 1958.

——. *The Sacred and the Profane: The Nature of Religion.* Translated by W. Trask. San Diego: Harcourt, 1987.

Elitzur, Y. *Ancient Place Names in the Holy Land: Preservation and History.* Jerusalem: Magnes/Winona Lake, Ind.: Eisenbrauns, 2004.

Emerton, J. "Some Difficult Words in Genesis 49." Pages 81–94 in *Words and Meanings: Essays Presented to David Winston Thomas on His Retirement from the Regius Professorship of Hebrew in the University of Cambridge, 1968.* Edited by P. Ackroyd and B. Lindars. Cambridge: Cambridge University Press, 1968.

Evans, C. "Naram-Sin and Jeroboam: The Archetypal *Unheilsherrscher* in Mesopotamian and Biblical Historiography." Pages 114–25 in *Scrip-*

ture in Context II. Edited by W. Hallo et al. Winona Lake, Ind.: Eisenbrauns, 1983.

Evans-Pritchard, E. *Nuer Religion*. Oxford; Clarendon, 1962.

Faust, A. "Ethnic Complexity in Northern Israel during Iron Age II." *PEQ* 132 (2000): 2–27.

Fensham, F. "A Few Observations on I Kings 17–19," *ZAW* 92 (1980): 227–36.

Finkelstein, I. "City-States to States: Polity Dynamics in the 10th–9th Centuries B.C.E." Pages 75–83 in *Symbiosis, Symbolism, and the Power of the Past: Canaan, Ancient Israel, and Their Neighbors from the Late Bronze Age through Roman Palaestina, Proceedings of the Centennial Symposium, W.F. Albright Institute of Archaeological Research and American Schools of Oriental Research, Jerusalem, May 29–31, 2000*. Edited by W. Dever and S. Gitin. Winona Lake, Ind.: Eisenbrauns, 2003.

———. "Omride Architecture." *ZDPV* 116 (2000): 114–38.

Fitzmyer, J. *The Aramaic Inscriptions of Sefîre*. BibOr 19. Rome: Pontifical Biblical Institute, 1967.

Flanagan, J. "Ancient Perceptions of Space/Perceptions of Ancient Space." *Semeia* 87 (1999): 15–43.

Fohrer, G. *Elia*. Rev. ed. ATANT 53. Zürich: Zwingli, 1968.

Franklin, N. "Samaria: From the Bedrock to the Omride Palace." *Levant* 36 (2004): 189–202.

Fredericks, D. "A North Israelite Dialect in the Hebrew Bible? Questions of Methodology." *HS* 37 (1996): 7–20.

Fried, L. "The High Places (*bāmôt*) and the Reforms of Hezekiah and Josiah: An Archaeological Investigation." *JAOS* 122 (2002): 437–65.

Friedland, R., and R. Hecht. "The Politics of Sacred Place: Jerusalem's Temple Mount/*al-haram al-sharif*." Pages 21–61 in *Sacred Places and Profane Spaces: Essays in the Geographics of Judaism, Christianity, and Islam*. Edited by J. Scott and P. Simpson-Housley. CSR 30. New York: Greenwood, 1991.

Garr, W. *Dialect Geography of Syria-Palestine, 100–586 B.C.E.* Winona Lake, Ind.: Eisenbrauns, 2004.

George, M. *Israel's Tabernacle as Social Space*. SBLAIL 2. Atlanta: Society of Biblical Literature, 2009.

Gerstenberger, E. *Theologies in the Old Testament*. Translated by J. Bowden. Minneapolis: Fortress, 2002.

Gil'ad, D., and J. Bonne. "The Snowmelt of Mt. Hermon and Its Contribution to the Sources of the Jordan River." *Journal of Hydrology* 114 (1990): 1–15.

Gilders, W. *Blood Ritual in the Hebrew Bible: Meaning and Power*. Baltimore, Md.: Johns Hopkins University Press, 2004.

Ginsberg, H. *The Israelian Heritage of Judaism*. New York: Jewish Theological Seminary of America, 1982.

Gitin, S. "Incense Altars from Ekron, Israel and Judah: Context and Typology." *EI* 20 (1989): 52*–67*.

———. "New Incense Altars from Ekron: Context, Typology and Function." *EI* 23 (1992): 43*–49*.

Glassner, J.-J. *Mesopotamian Chronicles*. SBLWAW 19. Atlanta: Society of Biblical Literature, 2004.

Gleis, M. *Die Bamah*. BZAW 251. Berlin: de Gruyter, 1997.

Gorman, F. *The Ideology of Ritual: Space, Time and Status in the Priestly Theology*. JSOTSup 91. Sheffield: JSOT Press, 1990.

Goulder, M. *The Psalms of the Sons of Korah*. JSOTSup 20. Sheffield: JSOT Press, 1982.

Graesser, C. "Standing Stones in Ancient Palestine." *BA* 35 (1974): 34–63.

———. "Studies in *maṣṣēbôt*." Ph.D. diss., Harvard University, 1969.

Grant, E. *Beth Shemesh: Progress of the Haverford Archaeological Expedition*. Haverford, Pa.: Biblical and Kindred Studies, 1929.

Grant, E., and G. E. Wright. *Ain Shems Excavations (Palestine)*. Part 5. Haverford, Pa.: Biblical and Kindred Studies, 1939.

Gray, J. *I and II Kings*. OTL. Philadelphia: Westminster, 1963.

Green, A. "Sua and Jehu: The Boundaries of Shalmaneser's Conquest." *PEQ* 111 (1979): 35–39.

Greer, J. "Dinner at Dan: A Biblical and Archaeological Exploration of Sacred Feasting at Iron II Tel Dan." Ph.D. diss., Pennsylvania State University, 2011.

———. "An Israelite *mizrāq* at Tel Dan?" *BASOR* 358 (2010): 27–45.

Gropp, D. "Progress and Cohesion in Biblical Hebrew Narrative: The Function of kĕ-/ bĕ- + the Infinitive Construct." Pages 183–212 in *Discourse Analysis of Biblical Literature: What It Is and What It Offers*. Edited by W. Bodine. Atlanta: Scholars Press, 1995.

Gruber, M. "Breast-Feeding Practices in Biblical Israel." Pages 69–107 in *Motherhood of God and Other Studies*. Atlanta: Scholars Press, 1992. Reprinted from *JANESCU* 19 (1989).

Haines, R. *Excavations in the Plain of Antioch II: The Structural Remains of the Later Phases*. OIP 95. Chicago: University of Chicago Press, 1971.

Halpern, B. "Levitic Participation in the Reform Cult of Jeroboam I." *JBL* 95 (1976): 31–42.

———. "The Taking of Nothing: 2 Kings 14.25, Amos 6.14 and the Geography of the Deuteronomistic History." Pages 186–204 in vol. 1 of *The World of the Aramaeans*. Edited by P. Daviau et al. 3 vols. JSOTSup 324–26. Sheffield: Sheffield Academic Press, 2001.

Haran, M. *Temples and Temple-Service in Ancient Israel: An Inquiry into the Character of Cult Phenomena and the Historical Setting of the Priestly School*. Oxford: Clarendon, 1978.

———. "The Uses of Incense in the Ancient Israelite Ritual." *VT* 10 (1960): 113–29.

———. "Zebaḥ Hayyamîm." *VT* 19 (1969): 11–22.

Harris, R. "The Journey of the Divine Weapon." Pages 217–24 in *Studies in Honor of Benno Landsberger on His Seventy-fifth Birthday, April 21, 1963*. Edited by Hans G. Güterbock and Thorkild Jacobsen. AS 16. Chicago: University of Chicago Press, 1965.

Harrison, T., and J. Osborne. "Building XVI and the Neo-Assyrian Sacred Precinct at Tell Tayinat." *JCS* 64 (2012): 125–43.

Hawkins, R. *The Iron Age I Structure on Mt. Ebal: Excavation and Interpretation*. BBRSup 6. Winona Lake, Ind.: Eisenbrauns, 2012.

Hayes, J. *Amos: The Eighth-Century Prophet: His Times and His Preaching*. Nashville: Abingdon, 1988.

Heimann, A., and E. Sass. "Travertines in the Northern Hula Valley, Israel." *Sedimentology* 36 (1989): 95–108.

Helck, W. *Die Beziehungen Ägytpens zu Vorderasien im 3. und 2. Jahrtausend v. Chr.* 2nd ed. ÄgAbh 5. Wiesbaden: Harrassowitz, 1971.

Heltzer, M. "On Tithe Paid in Grain in Ugarit." *IEJ* 25 (1975): 124–28.

Hendel, R. *The Epic of the Patriarch: The Jacob Cycle and the Narrative Traditions of Canaan and Israel*. HSM 42. Atlanta: Scholars Press, 1987.

———. "Sacrifice as a Cultural System: The Ritual Symbolism of Exodus 24, 3–8." *ZAW* 101 (1989): 366–90.

Herzog, Z. *Archaeology of the City: Urban Planning in Ancient Israel and Its Social Implications*. Tel Aviv: Emery and Claire Yass Archaeology Press, 1997.

———. "Settlement and Fortification Planning in the Iron Age." Pages 231–74 in *The Architecture of Ancient Israel from the Prehistoric to the Persian Periods*. Edited by A. Kempinski and R. Reich. Jerusalem: Israel Exploration Society, 1992.

Herzog, Z., and L. Singer-Avitz. "Sub-Dividing the Iron Age IIA in Northern Israel: A Suggested Solution to the Chronological Debate." *TA* 33 (2006): 163–95.

Hoftijzer, J. "Das sogenannte Feueropfer." Pages 114–34 in *Hebräische Wortforschung. Festschrift zum 80. Geburtstag von Walter Baumgartner*. VTSup 16. Leiden: Brill, 1967.

Holladay, W. "Chiasmus, the Key to Hosea XII 3–6." *VT* 16 (1966): 53–64.

Hoop, R. de. *Genesis 49 in Its Literary and Historical Context*. OtSt 39. Leiden: Brill, 1999.

Hugo, P. *Les deux visages d'Élie*. OBO 217. Fribourg-Göttingen: Academic Press, 2006.

Hurowitz, V. *I Have Built You an Exalted House: Temple Building in the Bible in Light of Mesopotamian and Northwest Semitic Writings*. JSOTSup 115. Sheffield: Sheffield Academic Press, 1992.

Hutton, J. "Southern, Northern and Transjordanian Perspectives." Pages 149–74 in *Religious Diversity in Ancient Israel and Judah*. Edited by F. Stavrakopoulou and J. Barton. London: T&T Clark, 2010.

Ilan, D. "Northeastern Israel in the Iron Age I: Cultural, Socioeconomic and Political Perspectives." 2 vols. Ph.D. diss., Tel Aviv University, 1999.

Insoll, T. *Archaeology, Ritual, Religion*. London: Routledge, 2004.

Jacobsen, T. "The Mesopotamian Temple Plan and the Kitîtum Temple." *EI* 20 (1989): 79*–91*.

Jacoby, G. "Das Gebäude K." Pages 290–301 in *Ausgrabungen in Sendschirli IV*. Mittheilungen aus den orientalischen Sammlungen 14. Berlin: Reimer, 1911.

Jagersma, H. "The Tithes in the Old Testament." *OtSt* 21 (1981): 116–28.

Japhet, S. *I and II Chronicles: A Commentary*. OTL. Louisville: Westminster John Knox, 1993.

———. "Some Biblical Concepts of Sacred Space." Pages 55–72 in *Sacred Space: Shrine, City, Land: Proceedings of the International Conference in Memory of Joshua Prawer*. Edited by B. Kedar and R. Werblowsky. Jerusalem: Israel Academy of Sciences and Humanities, 1998.

Jaruzelska, I. "'Amasyah—prêtre de Béthel—fonctionnaire royal (essai socio-économique préliminaire)." *FO* 31 (1995): 53–69.

———. *Amos and the Officialdom in the Kingdom of Israel: The Socio-Economic Position of the Officials in the Light of the Biblical, the Epigraphic and Archaeological Evidence*. Seria Socjologia 25. Poznań: Uniwersytetu im. Adama Mickiewicza w Poznaniu, 1998.

Jenks, A. *The Elohist and North Israelite Traditions*. SBLMS 22. Missoula, Mont.: Scholars Press, 1977.

Jenson, P. *Graded Holiness: A Key to the Priestly Conception of the World.* JSOTSup 106. Sheffield: Sheffield Academic Press, 1992.

Jeremias, J. *The Book of Amos: A Commentary.* OTL. Louisville: Westminster John Knox, 1995.

———. "Das unzugängliche Heiligtum. Zur letzten Vision des Amos." Pages 244–56 in *Hosea und Amos: Studien zu den Anfängen des Dodekapropheton.* FAT 13. Tübingen: Mohr, 1996.

Junker, H. "Der Graben un den Altar des Elias." *TTZ* 69 (1960): 65–74.

Kalimi, I. *The Reshaping of Ancient Israelite History in Chronicles.* Winona Lake, Ind.: Eisenbrauns, 2005.

Kang, S. "Creation, Eden, Temple and Mountain: Textual Presentations of Sacred Space in the Hebrew Bible." Ph.D. diss., Johns Hopkins University, 2008.

Karageorghis, V. "Chronique des fouilles et découvertes archéologiques à Chypre en 1966." *Bulletin de Correspondance Hellénique* 91 (1967): 275–370.

———. *Kition: Mycenaean and Phoenician Discoveries in Cyprus.* London: Thames & Hudson, 1976.

———. "A Late Cypriote Hoard of Bronzes from Sinda." *RDAC* (1973): 73–82.

Katzenstein, H. *The History of Tyre.* Rev. ed. Beer Sheva: Ben-Gurion University of the Negev Press, 1997.

Kaufman, I. "The Samaria Ostraca: An Early Witness to Hebrew Writing." *BA* 45 (1982): 229–39.

Kempinski, A. *Megiddo: A City-State and Royal Centre in North Israel.* Materialen zur Allgemeinen und Vergleichenden Archäologie 40. Munich: Beck, 1989.

King, P., and L. Stager. *Life in Biblical Israel.* Louisville: Westminster John Knox, 2001.

Kitchen, K. "Two Notes on the Subsidiary Rooms of Solomon's Temple." *EI* 20 (1989): 107*–12*.

Kletter, R., and I. Ziffer. "Incense-Burning Rituals: From Philistine Fire Pans to the Improper Fire of Korah." *IEJ* 60 (2010): 166–87.

Knapp, A., and W. Ashmore. "Archaeological Landscapes: Constructed, Conceptualized, Ideational." Pages 1–30 in *Archaeologies of Landscape: Contemporary Perspectives.* Edited by W. Ashmore and A. Knapp. Malden, Mass.: Blackwell, 1999.

Knohl, I. *The Sanctuary of Silence: The Priestly Torah and the Holiness School.* Minneapolis: Fortress, 1995.

Knoppers, G. "Aaron's Calf and Jeroboam's Calves." Pages 92–104 in *Fortunate the Eyes That See: Essays in Honor of David Noel Freedman in Celebration of His Seventieth Birthday*. Edited by A. Beck et al. Grand Rapids: Eerdmans, 1995.

———. *The Reign of Solomon and the Rise of Jeroboam*. Vol. 1 of *Two Nations Under God: The Deuteronomistic History of Solomon and the Dual Monarchies*. HSM 52. Atlanta: Scholars Press, 1993.

———. *The Reign of Jeroboam, the Fall of Israel, and the Reign of Josiah*. Vol. 2 of *Two Nations Under God: The Deuteronomistic History of Solomon and the Dual Monarchies*. HSM 53. Atlanta: Scholars Press, 1993.

Knott, K. *The Location of Religion: A Spatial Analysis*. London: Equinox, 2005.

Kort, W. "Sacred/Profane and Adequate Theory of Human Place-Relations." Pages 32–50 in *Constructions of Space I: Theory, Geography, and Narrative*. Edited by J. Berquist and C. Camp. New York: T&T Clark, 2007.

Kottsieper, I. "The Tel Dan Inscription [*KAI* 310] and the Political Relations between Aram-Damascus and Israel in the First Half of the First Millennium BCE." Pages 104–34 in *Ahab Agonistes: The Rise and Fall of the Omri Dynasty*. Edited by L. Grabbe. LHB/OTS 421. London: T&T Clark, 2007.

Kraus, H.-J. *Psalmen*. 2nd rev. ed. BKAT 15. Neukirchen-Vluyn: Neukirchener, 1961.

Kunin, S. *God's Place in the World: Sacred Space and Sacred Place in Judaism*. London: Cassell, 1998.

Lamon, R., and G. Shipton. *Megiddo I: Seasons of 1925–34, Strata I–V*. OIP 42. Chicago: University of Chicago Press, 1939.

LaRocca-Pitts, E. *"Of Wood and Stone": The Significance of Israelite Cultic Items in the Bible and Its Early Interpreters*. HSM 61. Winona Lake, Ind.: Eisenbrauns, 2001.

Lefebvre, H. *The Production of Space*. Translated by D. Nicholson-Smith. Cambridge: Blackwell, 1991.

Lehmann, G., and A. Killebrew. "Palace 6000 at Megiddo in Context: Iron Age Central Hall Tetra-Partite Residencies and the *Bīt-Ḥilāni* Building Tradition in the Levant." *BASOR* 359 (2010): 13–33.

Leeuw, G. van der. *Religion in Essence and Manifestation: A Study in Phenomenology*. Translated by J. Turner. London: George Allen & Unwin, 1938.

Lehnart, B. *Prophet und König im Nordreich Israel: Studien zur sogenannten vorklassischen Prophetie im Nordreich Israel anhand der Samuel-, Elija- und Elischa-Überlieferungen.* VTSup 96. Leiden: Brill, 2003.

Lemaire, A. "Asher et le royaume de Tyr." Pages 135–52 in *Phoenicia and the Bible: Proceedings of the Conference Held at the University of Leuven on the 15th and 16th of March 1990.* OLA 44. Edited by E. Lipiński. Leuven: Peeters, 1991.

Levenson, J. *Sinai and Zion: An Entry into the Jewish Bible.* San Francisco: Harper & Row, 1985.

Levine, B. "The Descriptive Tabernacle Texts of the Pentateuch." *JAOS* 85 (1965): 307–18.

———. *In the Presence of the Lord: A Study of Cult and Some Cultic Terms in Ancient Israel.* SJLA 5. Leiden: Brill, 1974.

———. "Mythic and Ritual Projections of Sacred Space in Biblical Literature." *Journal of Jewish Thought and Philosophy* 6 (1997): 59–70.

———. *Numbers: A New Translation with Introduction and Commentary.* 2 vols. AB 4–4A. New York: Doubleday, 1993–2000.

Levinson, B. *Deuteronomy and the Hermeneutics of Legal Innovation.* New York: Oxford University Press, 1997.

Lewis, T. "Covenant and Blood Rituals: Understanding Exodus 24:3–8 in Its Ancient Near Eastern Context." Pages 341–50 in *Confronting the Past: Archaeological and Historical Essays on Ancient Israel in Honor of William G. Dever.* Edited by S. Gitin et al. Winona Lake, Ind.: Eisenbrauns, 2006.

———. *Cults of the Dead in Ancient Israel and Ugarit.* HSM 39. Atlanta: Scholars Press, 1989.

———. "Divine Images and Aniconism in Ancient Israel" (review of Tryggve N. D. Mettinger, *No Graven Image? Israelite Aniconism in Its Ancient Near Eastern Context*). *JAOS* 118 (1998): 36–53.

———. "Family, Household, and Local Religion at Late Bronze Age Ugarit." Pages 60–88 in *Household and Family Religion in Antiquity.* Edited by J. Bodel and S. Olyan. Malden, Mass.: Blackwell, 2008.

———. "How Far Can Texts Take Us? Evaluating Textual Sources for Reconstructing Ancient Israelite Beliefs about the Dead." Pages 169–217 in *Sacred Time, Sacred Place: Archaeology and the Religion of Israel.* Edited by B. Gittlen. Winona Lake, Ind.: Eisenbrauns, 2002.

———. "The Identity and Function of El/Baal Berith." *JBL* 115 (1996): 401–23.

———. Review of R. Albertz, *A History of Israelite Religion in the Old Testament Period. Int* 51 (1997): 73–77.

———. "Syro-Palestinian Iconography and Divine Images." Pages 69–107 in *Cult Image and Divine Representation in the Ancient Near East.* ASOR Books 10. Edited by N. Walls. Boston: American Schools of Oriental Research, 2005.

Lipiński, E. "Baʿli-raʾši et Raʾšu Qudšu." *RB* 78 (1971): 84–92.

———. "El's Abode: Mythological Traditions Related to Mount Hermon and to the Mountains of Armenia." *OLP* 2 (1971): 13–69.

Loretz, O. "Die babylonischen Gottesnamen Sukkut und Kajjamānu in Amos 5,26." *ZAW* 101 (1989): 286–89.

Loud, G. *Megiddo II, Seasons of 1935–39.* Vol. 2. OIP 62. Chicago: University of Chicago Press, 1948.

Loud, G., and C. Altman. *Khorsabad, Part II: The Citadel and the Town.* OIP 40. Chicago: University of Chicago Press, 1938.

Mack, A. "One Landscape, Many Experiences: Differing Perspectives of the Temple Districts of Vijayanagara." *Journal of Archaeological Method and Theory* 11 (2004): 59–81.

Mallowan, M. *Nimrud and its Remains.* 3 vols. New York: Dodd, Mead & Co., 1966.

Maʿoz, Z. *Dan Is Bāniyās, Teldan Is Abel-Beth-Maʿacha.* Aechaeostyle Scientific Research Series 2. Qazrin: Archaestyle, 2006.

Margueron, J.-C. "Prolégomènes a une étude portant sur l'organisation de l'espace sacré en Orient." Pages 23–36 in *Temples et sanctuaires: séminaire de recherche 1981–1983.* Edited by G. Roux. Travaux de la Maison de l'Orient 7. Lyon: GIS/Maison de l'Orient; Paris: Diffusion de Boccard, 1984.

Markoe, G. *Phoenicians.* Berkeley and Los Angeles: University of California Press, 2000.

Mays, J. *Amos: A Commentary.* OTL. Philadelphia: Westminster, 1969.

Mazar, A. "The 'Bull-Site': An Iron Age I Open Cult Place." *BASOR* 247 (1982): 27–42.

———. "The Spade and the Text: The Interaction between Archaeology and Israelite History Relating to the Tenth-Ninth Centuries BCE." *Proceedings of the British Academy* 143 (2007): 143–71.

———. "Temples of the Middle and Late Bronze Ages and the Iron Age." Pages 161–87 in *The Architecture of Ancient Israel from the Prehistoric to the Persian Periods.* Edited by A. Kempinski and R. Reich. Jerusalem: Israel Exploration Society, 1992.

Mazzoni, S. "Syrian-Hittite Temples and the Traditional *in antis* Plan." Pages 359–76 in *Kulturlandschaft Syrien: Zentrum und Peripherie; Festschrift für Jan-Waalke Meyer*. Edited by J. Becker et al. Münster: Ugarit-Verlag, 2010.

McCarter, P. K. *Ancient Inscriptions: Voices from the Biblical World*. Washington, D.C.: Biblical Archaeological Society, 1996.

———. "Aspects of the Religion of the Israelite Monarchy: Biblical and Epigraphic Data." Pages 137–55 in *Ancient Israelite Religion: Essays in Honor of Frank Moore Cross*. Philadelphia: Fortress, 1987.

———. "The Garden of Eden: Geographical and Etymological Ruminations on the Garden of God in the Bible and the Ancient Near East." Paper presented at the Colloquium for Biblical Research, Duke University, August 19, 2001.

———. "Hebrew." Pages 319–64 in *The Cambridge Encyclopedia of the World's Ancient Languages*. Edited by R. Woodard. New York: Cambridge University Press, 2004.

———. *I Samuel: A New Translation with Introduction, Notes and Commentary*. AB 8. Garden City, N.Y.: Doubleday, 1980.

———. *II Samuel: A New Translation with Introduction, Notes and Commentary*. AB 9. Garden City, NY: Doubleday, 1984.

———. "'Yaw, Son of 'Omri': A Philological Note on Israelite Chronology." *BASOR* 216 (1974): 5–7.

McEwan, C. "The Syrian Expedition of the Oriental Institute of the University of Chicago." *AJA* 41 (1937): 8–16.

McKenzie, S. "The Jacob Tradition in Hosea XII 4–5." *VT* 36 (1986): 311–22.

———. *The Trouble with Kings: The Composition of the Book of Kings in the Deuteronomistic History*. VTSup 42. Leiden: Brill, 1991.

Metzger, M. "Arbeiten im Bereich des 'spätbronzezeitlichen' Heiligtums." Pages 17–29 in *Bericht über die Ergebnisse der Ausgrabungen in Kāmid el-Lōz in den Jahren 1971 bid 1974*. Edited by R. Hachmann. Saarbrücker Beiträge zur Altertumskunde 32. Bonn: Habelt, 1982.

Meyers, C. "From Field Crops to Food: Attributing Gender and Meaning to Bread Production in Iron Age Israel." Pages 67–84 in *The Archaeology of Difference: Gender, Ethnicity, Class and the "Other" in Antiquity, Studies in Honor of Eric M. Meyers*. Edited by D. Edwards and C. McCollough. AASOR 60/61. Boston: American Schools of Oriental Research, 2007.

———. "Household Religion." Pages 118–34 in *Religious Diversity in Ancient Israel and Judah*. Edited by F. Stavrakopoulou and J. Barton. London: T&T Clark, 2010.

———. "Material Remains and Social Relations: Women's Culture in Agrarian Households of the Iron Age." Pages 425–44 in *Symbiosis, Symbolism, and the Power of the Past: Canaan, Ancient Israel, and Their Neighbors from the Late Bronze Age through Roman Palaestina, Proceedings of the Centennial Symposium, W. F. Albright Institute of Archaeological Research and American Schools of Oriental Research, Jerusalem, May 29–31, 2000*. Edited by W. Dever and S. Gitin. Winona Lake, Ind.: Eisenbrauns, 2003.

Michel, E. "Die Assur-Texte Salmanassars III. (858–824)." *WO* 2 (1954): 27–45.

Mierse, W. *Temples and Sanctuaries from the Early Iron Age Levant: Recovery after Collapse*. History, Archaeology, and Culture of the Levant 4. Winona Lake, Ind.: Eisenbrauns, 2012.

Milgrom, J. *Leviticus: A New Translation with Introduction and Commentary*. 3 vols. AB 3A–C. New York: Doubleday, 1991–2001.

———. *Studies in Levitical Terminology I: The Encroacher and the Levite, the Term 'Aboda*. Near Eastern Studies 14. Berkeley and Los Angeles: University of California Press, 1970.

Miller, P. "The Prophetic Critique of Kings." Pages 527–47 in *Israelite Religion and Biblical Theology: Collected Essays*. JSOTSup 267. Sheffield: Sheffield Academic Press, 2000. Reprinted from *ExAud* 2 (1986).

———. *The Religion of Ancient Israel*. Library of Ancient Israel. Louisville: Westminster John Knox, 2000.

Modéus, M. *Sacrifice and Symbol: Biblical Šĕlāmîm in a Ritual Perspective*. ConBOT 52. Stockholm: Almqvist & Wiksell International, 2005.

Montgomery, J. *A Critical Commentary on the Books of Kings*. Edited by H. Gehman. ICC. New York: Scribner's, 1951.

Monson, J. "The 'Ain Dara Temple and the Jerusalem Temple." Pages 273–99 in *Text, Artifact, and Image: Revealing Ancient Israelite Religion*. Edited by G. Beckman and T. Lewis. BJS 346. Providence: Brown Judaic Studies, 2006.

———. "The New 'Ain Dara Temple: Closest Solomonic Parallel." *BAR* 26.3 (2000): 20–35, 67.

Moore, J. "The Social Basis of Sacred Spaces in the Prehispanic Andes: Ritual Landscapes of the Dead in Chimú and Inka Societies." *Journal of Archaeological Method and Theory* 11 (2004): 83–124.

Moorey, P., and S. Fleming. "Problems in the Study of the Anthropomorphic Metal Statuary from Syro-Palestine before 330 B.C." *Levant* 16 (1984): 67–90.

Murray, A. *Excavations in Cyprus*. London: Trustees of the British Museum, 1900.

Naʾaman, N. "No Anthropomorphic Graven Image: Notes on the Assumed Anthropomorphic Cult Statues in the Temples of YHWH in the Pre-exilic Period." Pages 311–38 in *Ancient Israel's History and Historiography: The First Temple Period*. Vol. 3 of *Ancient Israel and Its Neighbors: Interaction and Counteraction*. 3 vols. Winona Lake, Ind.: Eisenbrauns, 2006. Reprinted from *UF* 31 (1999).

———. "The Northern Kingdom in the Late Tenth-Ninth Centuries BCE." *Proceedings of the British Academy* 143 (2007): 399–418.

Nakhai, B. *Archaeology and the Religions of Canaan and Israel*. ASOR Books 7. Boston: American Schools of Oriental Research, 2001.

———. "What's a 'Bamah'? How Sacred Space Functioned in Ancient Israel." *BAR* 20.3 (1994): 18–29, 77–79.

Negbi, O. "A Canaanite Bronze Figurine from Tel Dan." *IEJ* 14 (1964): 270–71.

———. *Canaanite Gods in Metal: An Archaeological Study of Ancient Syro-Palestinian Figurines*. Tel Aviv: Tel Aviv University, Institute of Archaeology, 1976.

———. "Israelite Cult Elements in Secular Contexts of the 10th Century B.C.E." Page 221–30 in *Biblical Archaeology Today, 1990: Proceedings of the Second International Congress on Biblical Archaeology, Jerusalem, June–July 1990*. Edited by A. Biran and J. Aviram. Jerusalem: Israel Exploration Society, 1993.

———. "Levantine Elements in the Sacred Architecture of the Aegean at the Close of the Bronze Age." *ABSA* 83 (1988): 339–57.

Niemann, H. *Die Daniten: Studien zur Geschichte eines altisraelitischen Stammes*. FRLANT 135. Göttingen: Vandenhoeck & Ruprecht, 1985.

———. "Royal Samaria—Capital or Residence? or: The Foundation of the City of Samaria by Sargon II." Pages 184–207 in *Ahab Agonistes: The Rise and Fall of the Omri Dynasty*. Edited by L. Grabbe. LHB/OTS 421. London: T&T Clark, 2007.

Nissinen, M. *Prophets and Prophecy in the Ancient Near East*. SBLWAW 12. Atlanta: Society of Biblical Literature, 2003.

Noble, P. "Amos and Amaziah in Context: Synchronic and Diachronic Approaches to Amos 7–8." *CBQ* 60 (1998): 423–39.

Noth, M. *The Deuteronomistic History*. Translated by J. Doull et al. JSOT-Sup 15. Sheffield: JSOT Press, 1981.

———. *The History of Israel*. Translated by P. Ackroyd. 2nd ed. London: Black, 1960.

Olivier, J. "In Search of a Capital for the Northern Kingdom." *JNSL* 11 (1983): 117–32.

Olmo Lete, G. del. *Canaanite Religion according to the Liturgical Texts of Ugarit*. Translated by W. Watson. Bethesda, Md.: CDL, 1999.

Olyan, S. *Rites and Rank: Hierarchy in Biblical Representations of Cult*. Princeton: Princeton University Press, 2000.

Ornan, T. "The Lady and the Bull: Remarks on the Bronze Plaque from Tel Dan." Pages 297–312 in *Essays on Ancient Israel in its Near Eastern Context: A Tribute to Nadav Na'aman*. Edited by Y. Amit et al. Winona Lake, Ind.: Eisenbrauns, 2006.

Orser, C., Jr. *A Historical Archaeology of the Modern World*. New York: Plenum, 1996.

Otto, R. *The Idea of the Holy: An Inquiry into the Non-Rational Factor in the Idea of the Divine and Its Relation to the Rational*. Translated by J. Harvey. London: Oxford University Press, 1958.

Otto, S. "The Composition of the Elijah-Elisha Stories and the Deuteronomistic History." *JSOT* 27 (2003): 487–508.

Ottosson, M. *Temples and Cult Places in Palestine*. Uppsala: Universitet, 1980.

Pakman, D. "Late Iron Age Pottery Vessels at Tel Dan." *EI* 23 (1992): 230–40 (Hebrew).

———. " 'Mask-like' Face Reliefs on a Painted Stand from the Sacred Precinct at Tel Dan." *EI* 27 (2003): 196–203 (Hebrew).

Pals, D. *Eight Theories of Religion*. 2nd ed. New York: Oxford University Press, 2006.

Pardee, D. *Ritual and Cult at Ugarit*. SBLWAW 10. Atlanta: Society of Biblical Literature, 2002.

Parker Pearson, M., and C. Richards. "Ordering the World: Perceptions of Architecture, Space and Time." Pages 1–37 in *Architecture and Order: Approaches to Social Space*. London: Routledge, 1996.

Paul, S. *Amos: A Commentary on the Book of Amos*. Hermeneia. Minneapolis: Fortress, 1991.

Pitard, W. *Ancient Damascus: A Historical Study of the Syrian City-State from the Earliest Times until Its Fall to the Assyrians in 732 B.C.E.* Winona Lake, Ind.: Eisenbrauns, 1987.

Poley, M. *Amos and the Davidic Empire: A Socio-historical Approach.* New York: Oxford University Press, 1989.

Polzin, R. *Late Biblical Hebrew: Toward an Historical Typology of Biblical Hebrew Prose.* HSM 12. Missoula, Mont.: Scholars Press, 1976.

Pongratz-Leisten, B. *Ina Šulmi Īrub: Die kulttopographische und ideologische Programmatik der* akītu-*Prozession in Babylonien und Assyrien im I. Jahrtausend v. Chr.* Baghdader Forschungen 16. Mainz am Rhein: Zabern, 1994.

Por, F., et al. "River Dan, Headwater of the Jordan, an Aquatic Oasis of the Middle East." *Hydrobiologia* 134 (1986): 121–40.

Porter, B. *Images, Power, and Politics: Figurative Aspects of Esarhaddon's Babylonian Policy.* Philadelphia: American Philosophical Society, 1993.

Preucel, R., and L. Meskell. "Places." Pages 215–29 in *A Companion to Social Archaeology.* Edited by L. Meskell and R. Preucel. Malden, Mass.: Blackwell, 2007.

Propp, W. *Exodus 19–40.* AB 2A. New York: Doubleday, 2006.

Rad, G. von. *Old Testament Theology.* Translated by D. Stalker. New York: Harper & Row, 1965.

Rainey, A. "The Order of Sacrifices in Old Testament Ritual Texts." *Bib* 51 (1970): 485–98.

Rainey, A., and R. Notley. *The Sacred Bridge: Carta's Atlas of the Biblical World.* Jerusalem: Carta, 2006.

Reich, R. "Palaces and Residencies in the Iron Age." Pages 202–22 in *The Architecture of Ancient Israel from the Prehistoric to the Persian Periods.* Edited by A. Kempinski and R. Reich. Jerusalem: Israel Exploration Society, 1992.

Rendsburg, G. "Israelian Hebrew Features in Genesis 49." *Maarav* 8 (1993): 161–70.

———. *Israelian Hebrew in the Book of Kings.* Bethesda, Md.: CDL, 2002.

———. "Israelian Hebrew in the Song of Songs." Pages 315–23 in *Biblical Hebrew in Its Northwest Semitic Setting.* Edited by S. Fassberg and A. Hurvitz. Winona Lake, Ind.: Eisenbrauns, 2006.

———. *Linguistic Evidence for the Northern Origin of Selected Psalms.* SBLMS 43. Atlanta: Scholars Press, 1990.

———. "The Northern Origin of Nehemiah 9." *Bib* 72 (1991): 348–66.

———. "The Northern Origin of 'The Last Words of David (2 Sam 23, 1–7).'" *Bib* 69 (1988): 113–21.

Rendtorff, R. *Studien zur Geschichte des Opfers im Alten Israel.* WMANT 24. Neukirchen-Vluyn: Neukirchener, 1967.

Renfrew, C., and P. Bahn. *Archaeology: Theories, Methods and Practice.* 5th ed. London: Thames & Hudson, 2008.

Richards, J. *Society and Death in Ancient Egypt: Mortuary Landscapes of the Middle Kingdom.* Cambridge: Cambridge University Press, 2005.

Roaf, M. "Palaces and Temples of Ancient Mesopotamia." Pages 423–41 in vol. 1 of *Civilizations of the Ancient Near East.* 4 vols. Edited by J. Sasson. Peabody, Mass.: Hendrickson, 2004.

Roberts, J. "A New Parallel to 1 Kings 18:28–29." *JBL* 89 (1970): 76–77.

Robinson, E. *Biblical Researches in Palestine, Mount Sinai and Arabia Petræa: A Journal of Travels in the Year 1838.* 3 vols. Boston: Crocker & Brewster, 1841.

Robinson. E., et al. *Later Biblical Researches in Palestine, and in the Adjacent Regions: A Journal of Travels in the Year 1852.* Boston: Crocker & Brewster, 1856.

Routledge, C. "Parallelism in Popular and Official Religion in Ancient Egypt." Pages 223–38 in *Text, Artifact, and Image: Revealing Ancient Israelite Religion.* Edited by G. Beckman and T. Lewis. BJS 346. Providence: Brown Judaic Studies, 2006.

Rudolph, W. *Joel, Amos, Obadja, Jona.* KAT 13.2. Gütersloh: Mohn, 1971.

Sasson, V. "The Old Aramaic Inscription from Tell Dan: Philological, Literary and Historical Aspects." *JSS* 40 (1995): 11–30.

Schaeffer, C. *Enkomi-Alasia: Nouvelles Missions en Chypre 1946–1950.* Vol. 1. Paris: Librairie C. Klincksieck, 1952.

Schenker, A. *Älteste Textgeschichte der Königsbücher. Die hebräische Vorlage der ursprünglichen Septuaginta als älteste Textform der Königsbücher.* OBO 199. Fribourg-Göttingen: Academic Press, 2004.

———. "Was bedeutet die Wendung 'einen Altar heilen' in 1 Könige 18:30? Ein übersehener religionsgeschichtlicher Vorgang." Pages 99–115 in *Studien zu Propheten und Religionsgeschichte.* SBAB 36. Stuttgart: Verlag Katholisches Bibelwerk, 2003.

Schloen, J. *The House of the Father as Fast and Symbol: Patrimonialism in Ugarit and the Ancient Near East.* Winona Lake, Ind.: Eisenbrauns, 2001.

Schmidt, L. "Die Amazja-Erzählung (Am 7,10–17) und der historische Amos." *ZAW* 119 (2007): 221–35.

Schmidt, W. "Die deuteronomistische Redaktion des Amosbuches." *ZAW* 77 (1965): 168–93.

Schniedewind, W. "Tel Dan Stela: New Light on Aramaic and Jehu's Revolt." *BASOR* 302 (1996): 75–90.

Schniedewind, W., and D. Sivan. "The Elijah-Elisha Narratives: A Test Case for the Northern Dialect of Hebrew." *JQR* 87 (1997): 303–37.

Schroer, S. *In Israel gab es Bilder: Nachrichten von darstellender Kunst im Alten Testament*. OBO 74. Fribourg: Universitätsverlag; Göttingen: Vandenhoeck & Ruprecht, 1987.

Schulman, A. "An Enigmatic Egyptian Presence at Tel Dan." Pages 235–44 in *Festschrift Jürgen von Beckrath zum 70. Geburtstag am 19. Februar 1990*. Hildesheimer Ägyptologische Beiträge 30. Hildesheim: Gerstenberg, 1990.

Seeden, H. *The Standing Armed Figurines in the Levant*. Munich: Beck, 1980.

Shanks, H. "Avraham Biran—Twenty Years of Digging at Tel Dan." *BAR* 13.4 (1987): 12–25.

Sharon, I., and A. Zarzecki-Peleg. "Podium Structures with Lateral Access: Authority Ploys in Royal Architecture in the Iron Age Levant." Pages 145–67 in *Confronting the Past: Archaeological and Historical Essays on Ancient Israel in Honor of William G. Dever*. Edited by S. Gitin et al. Winona Lake, Ind.: Eisenbrauns, 2006.

Shaw, I. "Balustrades, Stairs and Altars in the Cult of Aten at el-Amarna." *JEA* 80 (1994): 109–27.

Shields, R. *Lefebvre, Love and Struggle: Spatial Dialectics*. London: Routledge, 1999.

Simpson, W. *The Terrace of the Great God at Abydos: The Offering Chapels of Dynasties 12 and 13*. Publications of the Pennsylvania-Yale Expeditions to Egypt 5. New Haven: Peabody Museum of Natural History of Yale University; Philadelphia: University Museum of the University of Pennsylvania, 1974.

Smick, E. "The Jordan of Jericho." Pages 177–79 in *Orient and Occident: Essays Presented to Cyrus H. Gordon on the Occasion of his Sixty-Fifth Birthday*. AOAT 22. Edited by H. Hoffner. Kevelaer: Butzon & Bercker; Neukirchen-Vluyn: Neukirchener, 1973.

Smith, A. *The Political Landscape: Constellations of Authority in Early Complex Polities*. Berkeley and Los Angeles: University of California Press, 2003.

Smith, J. Z. *Map Is Not Territory: Studies in the History of Religions*. Chicago: University of Chicago Press, 1993.

———. *To Take Place: Toward Theory in Ritual.* Chicago: University of Chicago Press, 1987.

Smith, M. *Introduction with Text, Translation and Commentary of KTU 1.1–1.2.* Vol. 1 of *The Ugaritic Baal Narrative.* VTSup 55. Leiden: Brill, 1994.

Soggin, J. *Introduction to the Old Testament from Its Origins to the Closing of the Alexandrian Canon.* Rev. ed. Philadelphia: Westminster, 1980.

———. *Joshua: A Commentary.* OTL. Philadelphia: Westminster, 1972.

———. *The Prophet Amos: A Translation and Commentary.* Translated by J. Bowden. London: SCM, 1987.

Spaey, J. "Emblems in Rituals in the Old Babylonian Period." Pages 411–20 in *Ritual and Sacrifice in the Ancient Near East.* OLA 55. Edited by J. Quaegebeur. Leuven: Peeters, 1993.

Stager, L. "The Archaeology of the Family in Ancient Israel." *BASOR* 260 (1985): 1–35.

———. "The Fortress-Temple at Shechem and the 'House of El, Lord of the Covenant.'" Pages 228–49 in *Realia Dei: Essays in Archaeology and Biblical Interpretation in Honor of Edward F. Campbell, Jr. at His Retirement.* Edited by P. Williams and T. Hiebert. Atlanta: Scholars Press, 1999.

Stager, L., and S. Wolff. "Production and Commerce in Temple Courtyards: An Olive Press in the Sacred Precinct at Tel Dan." *BASOR* 243 (1981): 95–102.

Steadman, S. "Reliquaries on the Landscape: Mounds as Matrices of Human Cognition." Pages 286–307 in *Archaeologies of the Middle East: Critical Perspectives.* Edited by S. Pollock and R. Bernbeck. Malden, Mass.: Blackwell, 2005.

Steck, O. *Überlieferung und Zeitgeschichte in den Elia-Erzählungen.* WMANT 26. Neukirchen-Vlyun: Neukirchener, 1968.

Steiner, R. *Stockmen from Tekoa, Sycamores from Sheba.* CBQMS 36. Washington, D.C.: Catholic Biblical Association of America, 2003.

Stowers, S. "Theorizing the Religion of Ancient Households and Families." Pages 5–19 in *Household and Family Religion in Antiquity.* Edited by J. Bodel and S. Olyan. Malden, Mass.: Blackwell, 2008.

Sweeney, M. *I and II Kings: A Commentary.* OTL. Louisville: Westminster John Knox, 2007.

———. "Samuel's Institutional Identity in the Deuteronomistic History." Pages 165–74 in *Constructs of Prophecy in the Former and Latter Prophets and Other Texts.* SBL Ancient Near East Monographs 4.

Edited by L. Grabbe and M. Nissinen. Atlanta: Society of Biblical Literature, 2011.

Taçon, P. "Identifying Ancient Sacred Landscapes in Australia: From Physical to Social." Pages 33–57 in *Archaeologies of Landscape: Contemporary Perspectives*. Edited by W. Ashmore and A. Knapp. Malden, Mass.: Blackwell, 1999.

Thiel, W. "Beobachtungen am Text von 1 Könige 18." Pages 283–91 in *"Einen Altar von Erde mache mir …" Festschrift für Diethelm Conrad zu seinem 70. Geburtstag*. Edited by J. Diehl et al. KAANT 4/5. Waltrop: Hartmut Spenner, 2003.

Timm, S. *Die Dynastie Omri: Quellen und Untersuchungen zur Geschichte Israels im 9. Jahrhundert vor Christus*. FRLANT 124. Göttingen: Vandenhoeck & Ruprecht, 1982.

Toews, W. *Monarchy and Religious Institution in Israel under Jeroboam I*. SBLMS 47. Atlanta: Scholars Press, 1993.

Toorn, K. van der. *Family Religion in Babylonia, Syria, and Israel: Continuity and Changes in the Forms of Religious Life*. Studies in the History and Culture of the Ancient Near East 7. Leiden: Brill, 1996.

Trebolle Barrera, J. *Centena in libros Samuelis et Regum: variantes textuales y composición literaria en los libros de Samuel y Reyes*. Madrid: Consejo Superior de Investigaciones Científicas, 1989.

Tromp, N. "Water and Fire on Mount Carmel: A Conciliatory Suggestion," *Bib* 56 (1975): 480–502.

Tuan, Y. *Space and Place: The Perspective of Experience*. Minneapolis: University of Minnesota Press, 1977.

Tucker, G. "Amos the Prophet and Amos the Book: Historical Framework." Pages 85–102 in *Israel's Prophets and Israel's Past: Essays on the Relationship of Prophetic Texts and Israelite History in Honor of John H. Hayes*. Edited by B. Kelle and M. Moore. LHB/OTS 446. New York: T&T Clark, 2006.

Tufnell, O. *Lachish III: The Iron Age*. London: Oxford University Press, 1953.

Twain, M. *The Innocents Abroad, or The New Pilgrims' Progress*. 2 vols. New York: Harper & Row, 1869.

Uehlinger, C. "Anthropomorphic Cult Statuary in Iron Age Palestine and the Search for Yahweh's Cult Images." Pages 97–155 in *The Image and the Book: Iconic Cults, Aniconism, and the Rise of Book Religion in Israel and the Ancient Near East*. Edited by K. van der Toorn. Leuven: Peeters, 1997.

———. "Eine anthropomorphe Kultstatue des Gottes von Dan?" *BN* 72 (1994): 85–100.

Ussishkin, D. "Excavations at Tel Lachish—1973–1977." *TA* 5 (1978): 1–97.

———. "King Solomon's Palace and Building 1723 in Megiddo." *IEJ* 16 (1966): 174–86.

———. "King Solomon's Palaces." *BA* 36 (1973): 78–105.

———. *The Renewed Archaeological Excavations at Lachish (1973–1994) I.* 5 vols. Tel Aviv: Emery and Claire Yass Publications in Archaeology, 2004.

———. "Schumacher's Shrine in Building 338 at Megiddo." *IEJ* 39 (1989): 149–72.

Vandier, J. *Les Grandes Époques, La Statuaire.* Vol. 3 of *Manuel d'Archéologie Égyptienne.* 6 vols. Paris: Picard, 1958.

Vaughan, P. *The Meaning of "bāmâ" in the Old Testament: A Study of Etymological, Textual and Archaeological Evidence.* SOTSMS 3. London: Cambridge University Press, 1974.

Walters, S. "Hannah and Anna: The Greek and Hebrew Texts of 1 Samuel 1." *JBL* 107 (1988): 385–412.

Wapnish, P., and B. Hesse. "Faunal Remains from Tel Dan: Perspectives on Animals Production at a Village, Urban and Ritual Center." *Archaeozoologica* 4.2 (1991): 9–86.

Watts, J. "'ōlāh: The Rhetoric of Burnt Offerings." *VT* 56 (2006): 125–37.

Weinfeld, M. *Deuteronomy and the Deuteronomic School.* Winona Lake, Ind.: Eisenbrauns, 1992.

Weippert, H. *Palästina in vorhellenistischer Zeit.* Handbuch der Archäologie: Vorderasien 2/1. Munich: Beck, 1988.

Wenham, G. *Genesis 16–50.* WBC 2. Nashville: Thomas Nelson, 1994.

Westermann, C. *Genesis 37–50: A Commentary.* Translated by J. Scullion. Minneapolis: Augsburg, 1986.

———. *Praise and Lament in the Psalms.* Translated by K. Crim and R. Soulen. Atlanta: John Knox, 1981.

Wetzel, F., and F. Weissbach. *Das Hauptheiligtum des Marduk in Babylon, Esagila und Etemenanki.* WVDOG 59. Leipzig: Hinrichs, 1938.

Wightman, G. *Sacred Spaces: Religious Architecture in the Ancient World.* ANESS 22. Leuven: Peeters, 2007.

Willett, E. "Women and Household Shrines in Ancient Israel." Ph.D. diss., University of Arizona, 1999.

Williamson, H. *Ezra, Nehemiah.* WBC 16. Nashville: Thomas Nelson, 1985.

———. "Tel Jezreel and the Dynasty of Omri." *PEQ* 128 (1996): 41–51.

Willis, J. "An Anti-Elide Narrative Tradition from a Prophetic Circle at the Ramah Sanctuary." *JBL* 90 (1971): 288–308.

Wilson, J. "The Kurba'il Statue of Shalmaneser III." *Iraq* 24 (1962): 90–115.

Wilson, R. *Prophecy and Society in Ancient Israel.* Philadelphia: Fortress, 1980.

Wolff, H. *Hosea: A Commentary on the Book of the Prophet Hosea.* Translated by G. Stansell. Hermeneia. Philadelphia: Fortress, 1974.

———. *Joel and Amos: A Commentary on the Books of Joel and Amos.* Translated by W. Janzen et al. Hermeneia. Philadelphia: Fortress, 1977.

Wright, G. E. "Solomon's Temple Resurrected." *BA* 4 (1941): 17–31.

———. "The Fluted Columns in the Bronze Age Temple of Baal-Berith at Shechem." *PEQ* 97 (1965): 66–84.

Wright, G. R. H. *Ancient Building in Cyprus.* 2 vols. Leiden: Brill, 1992.

———. *Ancient Building in South Syria and Palestine.* 2 vols. Leiden: Brill, 1985.

Würthwein, E. "Die Erzählung vom Gottesurteil auf dem Karmel." Pages 118–31 in *Studien zum Deuteronomistischen Geschichtswerk.* BZAW 227. Berlin: de Gruyter, 1994.

———. "Zur Opferprobe Elias I Reg 18,21–39." Pages 132–39 in *Studien zum Deuteronomistischen Geschichtswerk.* BZAW 227. Berlin: de Gruyter, 1994. Reprinted from *Prophet und Prophetenbuch. Festschrift für Otto Kaiser zum 65. Geburtstag.* Edited by V. Fritz et al. Berlin: de Gruyter, 1989.

Yadin, Y. "'And Dan, Why Did He Remain in Ships' (Judges, V, 17)." *AJBA* 1 (1968): 9–23.

———. "Beer-sheba: The High Place Destroyed by King Josiah." *BASOR* 222 (1976): 5–17.

———. *Hazor: The Head of All Those Nations with a Chapter on Israelite Megiddo.* London: Oxford University Press, 1972.

Yadin, Y., et al. *Hazor I: An Account of the First Season of Excavations, 1955.* Jerusalem: Magnes, 1958.

———. *Hazor III–IV: An Account of the Third and Fourth Seasons of Excavation, 1957–1958.* Jerusalem: Israel Exploration Society/Hebrew University of Jerusalem, 1989.

Vaux, R. de. "The Prophets of Baal on Mount Carmel." Pages 238–50 in *The Bible and the Ancient Near East.* Translated by D. McHugh. London: Darton, Longman & Todd, 1972.

Yeivin, S. "The Third District in Tuthmosis III's List of Palestino-Syrian Towns." *JEA* 36 (1950): 51–62.

Yon, M. *Salamine de Chypre V: Un depôt de sculptures archaïques.* Paris: E. de Boccard, 1974.

Young, I. "Evidence of Diversity in Pre-Exilic Judahite Hebrew." *HS* 38 (1997): 7–20.

Zevit, Z. "Deuteronomistic Historiography in 1 Kings 12–2 Kings 17 and the Reinvestiture of the Israelian Cult." *JSOT* 32 (1985): 57–73.

———. "False Dichotomies in Descriptions of Israelite Religion: A Problem, Its Origin, and a Proposed Solution." Pages 223–35 in *Symbiosis, Symbolism, and the Power of the Past: Canaan, Ancient Israel, and Their Neighbors from the Late Bronze Age through Roman Palaestina, Proceedings of the Centennial Symposium, W. F. Albright Institute of Archaeological Research and American Schools of Oriental Research, Jerusalem, May 29–31, 2000.* Edited by W. Dever and S. Gitin. Winona Lake, Ind.: Eisenbrauns, 2003.

———. "A Misunderstanding at Bethel: Amos VII 12–17." *VT* 25 (1975): 783–90.

———. *The Religions of Ancient Israel: A Synthesis of Parallactic Approaches.* London: Continuum, 2001.

Zwickel, W. Der *Tempelkult in Kanaan und Israel: Studien zur Kultgeschichte Palästinas von der Mittelbronzezeit bis zum Untergang Judas.* FAT 10. Tübingen: Mohr Siebeck, 1994.

Scripture Index

CPSIA information can be obtained at www.ICGtesting.com
Printed in the USA
LVOW06s1216061113

360129LV00002B/14/P